Trotsky's Sink

Ninety-Eight Short Essays About Literature

Peter Nash and George Ovitt

Fomite
Burlington, VT

Copyright © 2021 Peter Nash and George Ovitt
Cover photograph "Trotsky's Sink" © Annie Nash, 2018

All rights reserved. No part of this book may be reproduced in any form or by any means without the prior written consent of the publisher, except in the case of brief quotations used in reviews and certain other noncommercial uses permitted by copyright law.

ISBN-13: 978-1-947917-96-5
Library of Congress Control Number: 2020949774
Fomite
58 Peru Street
Burlington, VT 05401
www.fomitepress.com

Ocean Vuong, "Aubade with Burning City" and and "Prayer for the Newly Damned" from *Night Sky with Exit Wounds*. Copyright © 2016 by Ocean Vuong. Reprinted with the permission of The Permissions Company, LLC on behalf of Copper Canyon Press, www.coppercanyonpress.org.

In Memory of Joan Monaghan Hart
(G.O.)

For Annie, Ezra, and Isaiah

When it was announced that the Library contained all books, the first reaction was unbounded joy. All people felt themselves the possessors of an intact and secret treasure... The universe was justified; the universe suddenly became congruent with the unlimited width and breath of humankind's hope.

Jorge Luis Borges, *The Library of Babel*

Contents

Where the Light Enters You (*Clarice Lispector*) 1

Only Submit (*Michel Houellebecq*) 4

The Dark Terminus of All We Know (*Stig Sæterbakken*) 13

Dysfunctional (*Arnon Grunberg*) 16

Cerote (*Horacio Castellanos Moya*) 21

False Dichotomy (*Tom McCarthy, Joseph O'Neill*) 24

Why Literary Fiction Matters: (*S. Y. Agnon*) 29

The Gate (*Natsume Sōseki*) 32

This Snarl of a Life (*James Wright*) 36

The Golden Age (*Richard Hugo, Stanley Moss*) 40

Paris, 1944: How Shall We Live? (*Simone de Beauvoir*) 46

Small Bombs (*Karan Mahajan*) 49

Wandering Soul (*François Cheng*) 54

The Blues (*Diann Blakely*) 57

Kill Your Television or Titian's Initials (T.V.) (*Jean-Philippe Toussaint*) 63

Idiots and Imbeciles (*Adam Cohen, Don Carpenter*) 68

Not All of the Ravages (*Paul Bowles*) 74

The Mirror of the World (*Mirza Asadullah Baig Khan*) 78

An Algerian Doll's House (*Ali Ghalem*) 82

Vampires, Lumps, and Curlicues (*Karen Russell, Jan Frederik Grönloh*) 85

Haitian Alphabet: One Soul's Rising (*Jean-Euphèle Milcé*) 89

Hell (*Jonathan Littell*) 92
The Troubles (*Elizabeth Bowen, William Trevor*) 79
The Man With the Golden Pencil (*Nelson Algren*) 100
Death In (Not Venice But) Rome (*Wolfgang Koeppen*) 103
Distant Fathers (*Antonio Skarmeta*) 112
Marriage (*Zeruya Shalev*) 117
Seasons and Writers (*Walt Whitman, Rebecca Solnit*) 119
The Open Mind of Lafcadio Hearn 125
For Tony (*Dumitru Tsepeneag*) 131
The Uses of History (*Fernando Del Paso*) 136
Beautiful Cortázar (*Julio Cortázar*) 141
Trotsky's Sink (*Leon Trotsky*) 146
Her Last Day on Earth (*Carole Maso*) 150
The Joys of Duty (*Siegfried Lenz*) 155
Hard Streets (*Luc Sante, Lawrence Block*) 160
Dictatorship of Flies (*Miguel Ángel Asturias*) 165
The Falling of the Dusk (*Sadegh Hedayat*) 168
Palestinians at Sea (*Jabra Ibrahim Jabra*) 173
Worship (*Martin Buber, Volker Weidermann*) 176
Into Africa (*Nadine Gordimer*) 187
Bildungsroman (*Elena Ferrante*) 192
What Happens (*Ann Petry*) 197
Eros, Philos, Agape (*Peter Stamm*) 200
Le Mot Juste *or* To Goad the Ox (*Gustave Flaubert*) 204

Is This the End? (*Richard Ford*) 211

Love and the Abyss (*Caesare Pavese*) 219

Spite (*Stig Sæterbakken, Han Kang*) 223

Madness Immortal (*Christina Stead*) 227

Ghost Writers and New Lives (*Dante, Leonid Tsypkin*) 230

Where the Stones Come From (*Oz Shelach*) 236

Falling Into, and Out of, Love (*Alain de Botton*) 241

China Blues (*Qian Zhongshu*) 248

Destruction (*Nihad Sirees*) 250

The Persistence of Suffering (*George Konrad*) 254

That Lost World (*Aharon Appelfeld*) 258

The Defense of the Human, The Defense of the Mind (*Clive James*) 263

Animals (*Diane Lefer, Ibrahim al-Koni*) 267

Machete (*Scholastique Mukasonga*) 274

Celine and Antunes on Hallucination (*Celine, Antonio Lobo Antunes*) 277

The Wonder That is India (*E.M. Forster*) 281

Mystical Work (*Mario Benedetti*) 285

Soul Swallower (*David Albahari*) 290

Does Great Literature Make Us Better? (*William Gass*) 293

Lebenslüge or Life-Lies (*Ward Just*) 298

Wanna Get Away? (*Ottessa Moshfegh*) 301

To She Who Loves So Sadly (*Dulce María Loynaz*) 307

Seeing! (*William Benton, Heather Rose*) 311

Under My Skin (*Javier Marías*) 316

Hiding Out In Lisbon (*Antonio Munoz Molina*) 320
To Build a Road (*Alberto Moravia*) 323
Life Alone (*Marlen Haushofer*) 328
The Eye of Ra (*Nawal el-Saadawi*) 331
Rural Beauty (*David Rhodes*) 334
Him (*George Steiner*) 338
The Five-Mile Wall (*Viet Thanh Nguyen, Ocean Vuong*) 342
Dutch Tao (*Maria Dermoût*) 349
A Bad Year for Men (*Anna Burns, Lucy Ellmann*) 352
Orientation 359
Papa! (*Leonardo Padura Fuentes*) 369
The Bewilderers (*Tsitsi Dangarembga*) 375
Lawrence (*Geoff Dyer*) 379
Mughal Dreams (*Anita Desai, William Dalrymple*) 387
Coming of Age (*Lily King*) 390
Minha Terra: Ivo's Brazil (*Lêdo Ivo*) 397
Balkan Ghosts (*Sara Nović*) 401
The Art of Nostalgia: (*Guiseppe di Lampedusa, Junichiro Tanizaki*) 405
Obscure for Sure (*Maurice Blanchot*) 411
After Babel: Foreigners and the English Language 415
The Workshop of Potential Literature (*Marcel Bénabou*) 419
A Lack Somewhere (*Nella Larsen*) 424
Neither Fish nor Fowl (*Marguerite Duras, David Grossman*) 427
Critics Be Damned (*Aharon Megged*) 432

The Second Circle (*Clare Messud, Leonardo Sciascia*) 435

The Natural Prayer of the Soul (*Patrick White*) 439

Apathetic and Not (*Katie Kitamura, Ta-Nehisi Coates*) 443

Unicuique suum (*Leonardo Sciascia*) 450

Death in the Afternoon (*A.L. Kennedy*) 453

Hope and Humility 457

Preface

We learn each day that a goodly percentage of what we hear and what we read is nonsense—untrue, driven by motives other than the conveying of information or truth. It is the great virtue of the vast majority of writers discussed in the following pages that they have pledged themselves to truth telling, to the uncovering of lies.

Human beings love stories—but more than stories, we agree that stories are secondary to literature's two greatest achievements: to create a commentary on human existence and to make transparent what is otherwise unknowable—the contents of human minds.

Literature enriches because great writers strip away the pretenses that shroud human behavior in a fog of deception. The writer, alone in her room, surrounded by the universe of language and a rich imagination, can shrug off her inhibitions, step outside of normal time and space, take a more expansive view of the world, and then set about telling us things we would otherwise never know.

These ninety-eight short essays—tiny missives from two life-long readers—are designed to share with you our conviction that important books can provide much more than distraction in a time of crisis—they might, if we let them, save our lives from lies.

Where the Light Enters You

There are times, when one has dropped one's guard, that the world slips in through the cracks. Staggered suddenly, we are overwhelmed by the pain and suffering around us. We see it as if for the first time—flagrant, gaudy, profane. It incriminates us, it makes us feel angry and helpless, it fills us with longing and dread. The triggers vary—a song, an illness, a blind man chewing gum. Sometimes everyday exhaustion does the trick. Yet for many such occasions, such flashes of insight, are woefully rare. By the time we're adults we've become so adept at keeping the world and its agonies at bay that we're hardly aware we're doing it—and with such vigilance, such energy, reflexively numbing (with video, with drugs and alcohol, with the daily violence of routine), if not blocking altogether, those precious sensors in our brains that allow us to sympathize, even to empathize, with the people around us, to see and feel this life truly.

W. H. Auden, in his famous poem, "Musée des Beaux Arts," writes,

> *About human suffering they were never wrong,*
> *The Old Masters; how well, they understood*

> *Its human position; how it takes place*
> *While someone else is eating or opening a window or*
> > *just walking*
> *dully along…*

These lines might very well have been the prompt, the inspiration, for Brazilian author Clarice Lispector's astonishingly trenchant short story, "Love". While not an Old Master, she was certainly a Modern One, a writer with an exquisitely refined sense of the pain and anguish of others. The premise of the story is simple: a relatively happy, self-satisfied housewife is on her way home from buying groceries one day when she spots a blind man from the window of the tram, a grim, if normally prosaic detail that somehow penetrates her defenses and shakes her to her core. Suddenly the safe, cozy bubble she has made of her life is burst. She puzzles:

> *But what else was there about him that made Anna sit up in distrust? Something disquieting was happening. Then she discovered what it was: the blind man was chewing gum…a blind man chewing gum. Anna still had time to reflect for a second that her brothers were coming to dinner—her heart pounding at regular intervals. Leaning forward, she studied the blind man intently, as one observes something incapable of returning our gaze. Relaxed, and with open eyes, he was chewing gum in the failing light. The facial movements of his chewing made him appear to smile then suddenly stop smiling, to smile and stop smiling. Anna stared at him as if he had insulted her. And anyone watching would*

have received the impression of a woman filled with hatred... A second signal from the conductor and the tram moved off with another jerk... The tram was rattling on the rails and the blind man chewing gum had remained behind forever. But the damage had been done.

The story itself is like the blind man chewing gum; it is a perfect example of what art does best, interrupting the usual narrative of our lives, giving us pause, even stopping us dead in our tracks. Rumi once said that "The wound is the place where the Light enters you." Of course, the "wound" he speaks of here is what great literature is all about—making us vulnerable to others, keeping us susceptible to the world in which we live.

P.N.

Only Submit

Michel Houellebecq, *Submission*

> " . . . *The sixth age shifts*
> *Into the lean and slippered pantaloon,*
> *With spectacles on nose and pouch on side,*
> *His youthful hose, well saved, a world too wide*
> *For his shrunk shank, and his big manly voice,*
> *Turning again toward childish treble, pipes*
> *And whistles in his sound. Last scene of all,*
> *That ends this strange eventful history,*
> *Is second childishness and mere oblivion,*
> *Sans teeth, sans eyes, sans taste, sans everything.*"

The melancholy and misanthropic Jacques possesses the gift of truth-telling that might be the only succor of old age; why delude yourself when you stand on the edge of a vast chasm into which you are about to tumble? Dylan Thomas's "Grave men, near death, who see with blinding sight/ Blind eyes could blaze like meteors and be gay, /Rage, rage against the dying of the light" captures the rage of the person whose life is receding into memory, but provides at least the comfort of defiance. Aging is frightful, death is terrifying, but how much more terrifying and horrible when one's dying coincides with the passing away of the order of the world, with civilization itself? The misreaders of Houellebecq miss this nuance in his work—easy enough to do with a writer who sets out to offend, and does.

Cultural pessimism has a long and distinguished history, beginning with Thucydides and traveling a great arc through the rise and fall of nations and empires—even in the midst of the Enlightenment, the age of optimism and belief in continuous liberal progress, there was Vico to remind us that the glorious age of humanity had passed with Rome, and that sour-puss Joseph de Maistre, whose reactionary attachment to absolute authority—in an age that embraced personal liberty as the only gospel—anticipated Oswald Spengler and the fascist movements of the twentieth century. (Fascism is the only possible resolution of cultural decadence this side of suicide). But pessimism about the products of rationality unchecked by religious belief and political hierarchy was routed by the material and cultural products of enlightened cosmopolitanism. Capitalism appeared to supply proof that reason deployed in the service of material progress would make a paradise of this world; the romantics offered the hope that a purely personal spiritual vision could transcend any use people might have for a providential God; and liberalism—the struggle to extend the promise of democratic empowerment—seemed to fulfill the Western dream of individual autonomy sketched out by Locke, Montesquieu, Jefferson, and Kant.

The pillars of modern cultural pessimism—Nietzsche and Thomas Mann and T. S. Eliot—understood that the shucking off of the Old Order, however desirable, has a cost. In *Beyond Good and Evil* and *Twilight of the Idols*, Nietzsche's scathing indictment of bourgeois Christian (and, perforce, hypocritical) morality is so entertaining that the careless reader, inclined to agree with Nietzsche, is likely to miss the undertone of nostalgia that seeps into Nietzsche's aphorisms. With Mann, there can be no mistaking the sense of loss; the long Scholastic arguments that occupy the final third of *Magic Mountain* both dismiss as superannuated and defend as essential the unifying vision of the Middle Ages— the vision that held Europe together, according to Mann, until the catastrophe of 1914. It became fashionable during the decadent years leading up to the Great War for disillusioned intellectuals, their youthful folly spent, to convert to Catholicism (or Anglicanism), finding in Holy Mother Church the meaning that personal liberty could not supply. The reek of incense and the Latin chants of celibate priests guided many thoughtful but unhappy men and women to the oblivion of Faith.

Among those who made the journey back to the Church was Joris-Karl Huysmans, who became an oblate of the Benedictine order associated with Liguge Abby in Poitiers. Huysmans, for years a clerical worker in the French ministry, was of course the author of the scandalous *À rebours* (*Against the Grain* 1884), the literary model for Michel Houellebecq's *Submission*. Huysmans's literary alter ego, Jean de Esseintes, a decadent Parisian nobleman, a Nietzschean aesthete, a dandy who loathes the hollow pretensions of middle-class life, passes his time in pursuit of ever more esoteric sensual and aesthetic pleasures. The tone and mood of the novel are, to put it mildly, overwrought, self-conscious to the point of neurasthenia—in other words, not unlike some contemporary memoirs:

> "When all was said and done, the future was the same for all, and neither one nor the other class, if they had had a particle of common sense, could possibly have desired it. For the rich, it was, in different surroundings, the same passions, the same vexations, the same sorrows, the same diseases, and likewise the same poor satisfactions, whether these were alcoholic, literary or carnal. There was even a vague compensation for all the sufferings, a kind of rude justice that restored the balance of misery as between the classes, enabling the poor to endure more easily the physical sufferings that broke down more mercilessly the feebler and more emaciated bodies of the rich." (Chapter 13)

A bit too didactic, precisely in the voice (whiny, hectoring, self-absorbed) of Houellebecq's narrator. De Esseintes quotes Baudelaire, grows poisonous flowers, and loads a tortoise's shell up with enough gems to crush the poor beast. He drinks too much and ruins his health; mocks the Church, but in the tone of a jilted lover. Throughout the novel the abiding questions revolve around the problem of meaning—what to make of this comfortable modern life of ours? Now that God is dead, superstition is vanquished, reason is triumphant, and "freedom" has been achieved—what do we do until we die? There appear to be only three options: suicide, political engagement (but with Communism dead this option appears cut off), and submission to one of the three overweening monotheisms available to modern persons. Decadents don't do politics and they generally enjoy something enough to stay alive (sex or food or reading), so what's left is the Temple or Church or, in the case of *Submission*, the Mosque.

Baudelaire, who could well have been Huysmans's model for des Esseintes, smoked opium and drank himself to death, proclaiming, like Rimbaud, the "derangement of the senses," also saw fit to take the sacrament of extreme unction on his deathbed, hoping, perhaps, like Pascal, to hedge his bets. This sort of thing is real decadence.

Submission's plot is fairly straightforward: In the near future (the 2020's) a close election and an alliance with the disillusioned French Socialist Party hands the presidency of France to a presentable representative of the Muslim Brotherhood (no talk of *jihad*; Western business attire). The narrator, a disillusioned professor at the Sorbonne, a specialist in Huysmans, a decadent himself, looks on with cynical disinterest as France quietly accepts Islam as its new religion/ideology—an Islam cloaked in terms of traditional family values: women out of the workforce, back into the nursery; a new Mediterranean empire with Paris as its capital (Tunisia, Morocco, Turkey, and the Arab Middle East are quickly admitted to the EU); and an abandonment of secular education. The Sorbonne becomes a center of Islamic scholarship, and all professors must pronounce the *Shahada*. The narrator, a half-hearted atheist, is retired on a generous pension. The trouble is that his life has no meaning. He is alone—his lover has left for Israel, as have many other French Jews—he is friendless, alienated from politics and dismissive of his former life as an intellectual. He still has his prostitutes—there's a generous amount of raw sex sprinkled throughout the book, but it's entirely joyless. Copulating and eating and drinking—like de Esseintes, Houellebecq's narrator finds nothing much to attract him in any pleasure, and mulls over the meaninglessness of life in the style of an angst-ridden teenager, without much belief in his own despair. Eventually, after an abortive journey to the scene of his hero's Benedictine monastery in Poitiers, the nameless narrator is offered a chance to return to the Sorbonne, to revive his study of Huysmans, to take up a well-paid academic existence. Is he interested? Not really. But the other attraction, the lure of submission that is tempting, is almost irresistible. Why think or feel when you can surrender to Creator of the Universe?

Not an especially good book—Houellebecq is more of polemicist than a novelist, and *Submission* is full of the sort of long speeches on the absurdity of life that are a feature of French literature—the book does hold out the attraction of timeliness and painful relevance. It was published in France around the time of the Charlie Hebdo massacre; I read it during the weekend surrounding the most recent

ISIS atrocities in Paris. It's nonsense to accuse Houellebecq of being "anti-Muslim": he's against religion, academics, women, men, and even the pleasures his characters so mindlessly pursue. He is a nihilist, and for the reviewers at the *Times* and other publications to wring their hands over his depictions of sodomy and his mockery of religion (Houellebecq has a "twisted outlook on the sacred" according to Adam Gollner of the *New Yorker*) misses the point. This isn't a book about Islam or even about religion—it's a work of cultural pessimism, a lament for the end of Western civilization, an ending that has been announced often in the past, but never before with as much conviction that *this time* we're not kidding.

I have two immediate reactions to the criticisms of Houellebecq as (frankly) an unpleasant writer and person. First, when did book reviewers become so complacent about the ideas expressed in novels? The main outlets for cultural opinion in this country appear to have tacitly agreed that virtually no work of fiction that is "offensive" can be taken seriously, no matter how serious its intentions. Second is the fact that the media in which these reviews appear are replete with respectful essays on the trashiest products of Hollywood, the misogynistic music churned out by hip-hop artists and the sex-and-violence-laden pulp fiction that graces the *New York Times* bestseller list every week. Put simply, books and movies and music that make money are treated with respect, no matter how ghastly and immoral their content, while literary fiction, committed to awakening readers' senses to some of the difficult truths of life, are dismissed on moral grounds.

Houellebecq insults Islam? He's contemptible, but if he were a member of the Republican Party he could be running for president. Or perhaps the upside-down values of our age are a sign of *our* decadence. Kant's "dare to know" has become "don't you dare," as we close our eyes to what is difficult in favor of what affirms our fantasies.

Reading *Submission*, I kept seeing the benign countenance of Ben Carson, our current Secretary of Housing and Urban Development, in my mind's eye: Carson became Ben Abbes, Houellebecq's Muslim President of France, also a benign-seeming man, whose brand of low-volume politics was pitched exactly right for a France that had (fictionally) tired of the indignities of the contemporary world. Gentle Ben's platitudes, reducing their disguised ideological fervor in the mush of banalities that we seem to prefer. Here's Spengler:

> *"A Culture is born in the moment when a great soul awakens out of the proto-spirituality of ever-childish humanity and detaches itself, a form from the formless, a bounded and mortal thing from the boundless and enduring. . . It dies when this soul has actualized the full sum of its possibilities in the shape of peoples, languages, dogmas, arts, states, sciences, and reverts to the proto-soul." (Part III, "Cultures as Organisms)*

Spengler doesn't mention this, but it seems clear that the universalizing aspirations of the Enlightenment—a French inclination, born in the wars of Louis XIV and at the heart of the Revolution, systematized by Diderot in the Encyclopedia, and detested by Germans like Herder, Hegel, and Fichte—are what led to the "decline of the West." If Culture at its foundation is a set of spiritual aspirations that generate a particular soul (Europe in its golden Roman and medieval periods), then decadence arrives with the rejection of this universalizing spirit in favor of an atomized individual. All of the great decadents are loners—the *flâneur*, the solitary poet wandering the countryside in search of lost gods, the despairing intellectual alone in his chateau with his books and tortoises (Huysmans), or the despairing Frenchman pumping himself dry into a woman he's paid for the privilege. How do we reverse this decline and fall, how do we restore hope if not meaning to the declining West? Find another universal, another great spiritual truth. Ben Carson has the Lord and Houellebecq imagines France with Ben Abba's Allah. Decadence dissolved in the Absolute; Mind in mindlessness; politics in Authority; love in reproduction; thought in blessed ignorance.

All will be well. Only submit.

G.O.

The Dark Terminus of All We Know

Is this what death looks like? A house with nothing in it?

Driven from home by his irate wife, Eva, following her discovery of his affair with a young woman in town, the narrator of Stig Sæterbakken's novel *Through the Night*, a modest Norwegian dentist named Karl Christian Andreas Meyer, has just returned to his sullen and resentful family, when his teenaged son, Ole-Jacob, commits suicide. The pain he feels is overwhelming:

> *Grief comes in so many forms. It's like a light being turned on and off. It's on, and it's unbearable, and then it goes off, because it's unbearable, because it's not possible to have it on all the time. It fills you up and it drains you. A thousand times a day I forgot that Ole-Jakob was dead. A thousand times a day I remembered it again. Both were unbearable. Forgetting him was the worst thing I could do. Remembering him was the worst thing I could do. Cold came and went. But never warmth. There was only cold and the absence of cold. Like standing*

with your back to the sea. Ice-cold ankles every time a wave came in. Then it receded. Then it came in.

An arresting, truly brilliant study of guilt and misgiving, *Through the Night* is the story of one man's deeply affecting struggle to come to terms with his grief. Yet to say this, to state it in such trite, conventional terms, is to gravely underestimate the force of such feeling, as it plays itself out in this novel. Indeed so consuming, so total, is the loss the narrator feels that even of the commonplace objective of his own mental health he remains fearful, unsure: "What will we do, I wondered. When this is over. When we're finished with all the grief. When we've gotten through it, if we get through it, what on earth will we do then."

Perhaps one of the most frightening aspects of grief, as it sprouts and blossoms in this bleakly cogent tale, is its potential to isolate one from others, from the people one knows and loves. C.S Lewis captured this poignantly in his famous book, *A Grief Observed*, a work—written immediately following the death of his wife—in which he, fumbling for the words to portray it, describes the experience of grieving as something akin to fear, though not fear itself, only to add, "At other times it feels like being mildly drunk, or concussed. There is a sort of invisible blanket between the world and me."

And no wonder. Can even someone who has experienced such grief himself truly fathom the grief of another? Is the experience of grief actually relative, commensurable, at all?

Or is it—like its sister, love—in fact stubbornly, intrinsically personal, always and necessarily unique? How else could we bear so many depictions of it in the literature we read, in the films we watch, in the music to which we listen at night, but as signal variations on this dark and universal theme.

As with any fresh depiction of grief, indeed with the successful depiction of any emotion in fiction, the devil lies squarely in the details. One has only to think of Joyce's short story "Araby" with its "high, cold, empty, gloomy rooms," its "dark, dripping gardens," its rusted bicycle pump, and the "brown imperturbable" faces of the houses in the streets to be reminded of this fact. Sæterbakken himself is especially adept at stringing his protagonist's grief upon the nails of so many stark and original details. Undoubtedly the most effective of them for me, that single detail that opened up this man's grief to me, that made me feel it in the pit of my stomach, in the marrow of my bones, is his habit, started almost by accident, of calling his dead son's cell phone number, which continues to glow, to implore him, in the directory of his phone.

Ole-Jakob. I know that you're there. You're there somewhere, and I'll find you.

P.N.

Dysfunctional

Tirza, by Arnon Grunberg

How many books have actually caused you to laugh out loud? I remember laughing to the point of crying at the Major Major sections of *Catch-22*. Vonnegut can still make me laugh in one paragraph and nearly weep in the next; Dorothy Parker's little stories ("The Cradle of Civilization") are quite funny, and while I don't think this is entirely normal, whenever I need to cheer up I reach for Thomas Bernhard—the only writer I know of who can make suicide seem witty—or I'll reread the sections of *Pale King* that reliably do the trick (e.g. David Cusk's sweating episodes). On the other hand I don't find the *New Yorker's* "Shouts and Murmurs" funny, nor do I even chuckle at David Sedaris, Calvin Trillin, or the late Nora Ephron. But I smile when I try to read Heidegger or Hegel—what else can one do?—and so I admit that my sense of humor is quirky and probably says more about the oddities of my character than anything else.

I've been reading *The Island of Second Sight* by Albert Vigoleis Thelen, and it occurred to me at about page 150 that it was the heavy-handed, almost self-parodying irony that, more than anything else, was keeping me from enjoying the book. But irony, deftly deployed, can be funny, as it is, for example, in A.M. Homes's delightfully weird novels. Bernhard's running joke is the same one that made MAD magazine so smart back in its Al Feldstein/William Gaines years, namely the conceit that *everything* is absurd if examined properly, that is, honestly. Irony, of course, is the recognition that the "meaning" (scare quotes *de rigueur*) of experience is slippery at best, that there are no final or definitive correspondences to anything in our relationships and our inner lives; every human exchange has an ulterior motive or is fraught with ambiguity. There's nothing in this formulation that is inherently funny, so that Thelen's pounding away at the quirkiness of his alter ego's experiences isn't funny, while Bernhard's repetitive, Beckettian, over-the-top formulas (the Cone!) do the necessary work of humor, which is to relieve us of the burden of seriousness. Comedy releases us from fate, assuring us that either we are in control of our lives or no one is. I remember reading once that there could be no Christian tragedy; maybe so, but there can't be any Christian comedy either, except in Dante's sense of comedy as transcendence. There is no point in lamenting a world that makes no sense, so one might as well laugh at it. The forbidden is funny, as is the gross, and even the unspeakable can be funny in context, but then all of these things are stupid and embarrassing if not done with intelligence. Tragedy is natural in storytelling—a narrative arc is built in—but the comedic plot presents an altogether difference sort of problem. I respect a writer who does tragedy well; I marvel at one who can do comedy.

> *"One more thing about paranoia and irony: paranoia without irony is unbearable. And the combination of paranoia and irony might still be the best answer to the horror of our times."*

Aaron Grunberg, the Dutch novelist who lives in New York, and who is, I suspect, right at this moment working in his kitchen in Queens (he writes in the morning, in his kitchen, listening to music, and, apparently, hooked up to an EKG as part of a study of the creative process), also writes a blog that I have been enjoying. He has opinions on everything, and they're often good ones: as in the quotation above: *paranoia without irony is unbearable.* You can tell Grunberg has been in the U.S. a while—paranoia has replaced optimism everywhere: we're being watched, and what we're doing, though hardly worth a second thought, is probably illegal.

His novel *Tirza* is set in an upscale enclave of Amsterdam, though its disturbed and disturbing central character Jorgen Hofmeester could just as easily live in Gotham City, though not in Ed Koch's favorite borough—maybe on the Upper East Side—where the horrifying and hysterical (in both senses of the word) unraveling of his family would seem no more absurd that anything else currently transpiring (how's this: "A Generation Redefines Mourning: Millennials have begun *projecting their own digitalized sensibilities* onto rituals and discussions surrounding death," *NYT*, 3/23/14; my emphasis).

Hofmeester's wife has left him, but, spectacularly, returns on the eve of the big party he is throwing for his youngest daughter, Tirza. Mrs. H has been off with a lover or ten, living on a houseboat. She is, it transpires, a slut, while hyper-bourgeois Jorgen has fantasies of "dirty" salesgirls. Hofmeester's reunion with his estranged wife is one of the funniest and most cringe-inducing enactments of marital hatred I have ever read. Ibi, Hofmeester's oldest daughter, loathes her parents and has run off to France. Tirza has what can only be described as unnatural affection for her father—who reciprocates by making his youngest daughter the center of his paranoid and ironic universe. Hofmeester himself has been let go from his job as an editor and passes his days at the airport, acting the role of a person who awaits the arrival of a loved one. He also cooks and cultivates the image, but not the substance, of a concerned father. Tirza has a boyfriend who looks like Mohammed Atta, at least to her father, and is ingenuous to the point of idiocy. The party, which occupies much of the book, is hellish and yet utterly banal—Grunberg excels at depicting the calamity that is everyday life.

Yes, we've come a long way from "Father Knows Best," all the way from bland patriarchy through emasculating feminism to unmitigated domestic horror. But the horror stories no longer require ghosts or vampires or zombies—now everyone is a monster, and the wittiness of a book like *Tirza* derives from the absurd notion that there ever could have been such a thing as a happy family. I won't mention the *Sopranos* here, or Walter White, but what Grundberg does with the nuclear family evokes the sort of rueful smiles of recognition one often had in watching Tony at table with Carmela and Meadow and little Anthony. The post-modern family: no longer is the home a refuge from an unkind world but rather a replica of that world. Cruelty has become the face of love, and aside from the banality of pop fiction and network TV, everyone gets it—from Amsterdam to New York—the family is where we sharpen our claws, nothing but a dress rehearsal for the flaying we are expected to dish out in the "real" world. The roles have been reversed. Now one goes to work to find a modicum of peace and quiet, bracing oneself for the return home, to the horrors of one's family.

> *"Ibi was at a cafe with friends, the wife was painting in her studio and receiving her almost exclusively male models. Jorgen Hofmeester sat in the living room and underlined one paragraph after the other in the informative book about his youngest daughter's disorder, and in her bedroom beside the cello Tirza was busy giftedly starving herself to death. That was how the Hofmeester family lived at the start of the new millennium."*

G.O.

Cerote

For many readers (and writers) like me, the novelist Thomas Bernhard stands, now some twenty years after his death, as a literary prophet, a destroyer of idols, a seer-priest of the secular-humanist world. Relentless in his criticism of his native Austria, of the hypocrisy, dogmatism, jingoism, racism, and philistinism he found in such abundance there, he revered the loner, the scholar (what he called *Geistesmenschen* or "spirit-people"), the eccentrically, brilliantly, mad.

Enter Horacio Castellanos Moya's hero, Edgardo Vega, expatriate professor, returning from exile in Canada to war-torn El Salvador for his mother's funeral. When the novel *Revulsion: Thomas Bernhard in San Salvador* opens we find Vega sitting with an old friend of his, following his mother's wake, in a bar called La Lumbre, where he has been biding his time before returning for good to Montreal. The conversation, a single long paragraph, is charged with urgency, bitterness, and fury. "…I have to chat with you before I leave," explains Vega to his friend, "I have to tell you what I think about all this nastiness, there's no one else I can relate my impressions to, the horrible thoughts I've had here…"

What follows is a dazzling tirade against his native land and the cultural self-destruction of its recent civil war, a virtual apocalypse of greed and violence that laid waste to nearly everything he held dear. Writes Castellanos Moya, "With the relish of the resentful getting even, I wanted to demolish the culture and politics of San Salvador, same as Bernhard had done with Salzburg, with the pleasure of diatribe and mimicry."

Surely he had plenty against which to rail, against which to vent his ardent spleen. The twelve-year Salvadoran Civil War (1979-1992), a struggle for power between the military-led government of General Carlos Humberto Romero and the FMLN (Farabundo Marti Liberation Front), was one of the most violent chapters in the history of Central America, claiming the lives of more than 75,000 people. Wrote Reinaldo Figueredo, in his summary of the conflict for the U.N. Truth Commission, "In examining the staggering breadth of the violence that occurred in El Salvador, the Commission was moved by the senselessness of the killings, the brutality with which they were committed, the terror that they created in the people, in other words the madness, or locura, of war."

Robert Walser once said, "You can't confront your own country with impunity." In the case of Castellanos Moya, he was right about that, for shortly after the novel's publication his mother, still living in San Salvador, received a death threat from an anonymous caller. The author himself was warned never to return, as Salvadorans at large were incensed by the novel, by his unforgiving portrait of them and their country. Even friends and family were enraged by this brief, acerbic tale in which he spared nothing and no one, excoriating them for their *papusas* and their politics, and lambasting their language itself with his sharp and fulsome ire: "...not in vain is *cerote* the most repeated word in their language, they don't have any other words in their mouths; their vocabulary is limited to this word *cerote* and its derivatives: *ceretísimo, cerotear, cerotada.*" *Cerote*—as you might have guessed by now—means "shit".

In what was perhaps a gesture of consolation to his disgruntled compatriots, Castellanos Moya explained "...that some countries would require many more pages to complete their *Revulsion*..." Clearly, he felt that even a back-handed compliment was better than none at all!

P.N.

False Dichotomy

This morning my wife said to me, "This tea is perfect"—she's Irish, so tea in the morning—"it's the perfect temperature; it's just strong enough, and I put in exactly the right amount of milk."

Late last night I finished reading Tom McCarthy's remarkable novel *Remainder*, a book which is about the joy one has, or perhaps the madness one cultivates, in having things "just right." I hesitate to write anything about this novel as Zadie Smith has already written a brilliant review of it for the *New York Review of Books*, but I disagree with Smith's argument that there are "two paths for the novel" and would like to say something about her views as well as a few things about *Remainder*. In her *NYR* piece, Smith argues that the novel might take one of two diverging roads: the old worn out road of traditional realism, as in Joseph O'Neill's *Netherland*, or the fresh macadam of experiment, surrealism, anti-realism, as in McCarthy's *Remainder*. Smith's is a great piece, bristling with ideas, references, provocations, but I wondered if her assignment—reviewing, in tandem, Joseph O'Neill and Tom McCarthy—wasn't a set up for a concocted face-off between two different approaches to fiction. Different, but not, in my view, incommensurable.

It seems to me that Smith offers a false dichotomy. She sets the two novels against one another in every way imaginable—the books are "one hundred eighty degrees apart," but so are the authors (Oxford and Cambridge), and so, most of all, are the philosophical underpinnings of O'Neill's and McCarthy's fictional worlds. O'Neill retains the old, and apparently outmoded, faith in the existence of the self, that Cartesian "mirror of nature," an entity that can sniff out meaning in the events of everyday life or in the colloquies of the mind or in relationships or language. O'Neill's lovely book is fiction before Richard Rorty came along, before Derrida persuaded us that words aren't attached to anything, that selves are passé, or at least impossible to comprehend. Perhaps not even worthy of comprehension, for what does the Self tell us but that we yearn and are hopelessly inauthentic? Authenticity is the overriding concern of Smith's review—who has it and who doesn't—and I couldn't help but think as I read her perfect sentences that 'authenticity' must be a New York-London-Paris intellectual thing—honestly, have you ever felt *inauthentic*? Do you even know what it would feel like to be inauthentic? I confess to being at a loss. Worrying about authenticity seems like the kind of thing Heidegger or Sartre might do, an existential concern with good faith, but nowadays, given the way the world turns, most of us worry more about making ends meet and finding time to read good books. That was my first problem with the 'two paths.'

McCarthy writes in spare prose that disdains fixed meanings, a prose that abjures the traditional conventions of plot, character, theme, and voice for a philosophical reflection on the nature on happiness. Imagine what would happen if Slavoj Zizek were to write a novel. Things, unspecified, fall on the narrator's head; he is gravely injured to the extent that he must learn all over how to perform life's simplest tasks (the description of relearning how to eat a carrot is brilliant and typical). The narrator is awarded a huge sum of money as compensation and is able to use this money to construct a repetitive, fanciful, banal, but utterly satisfying existence.

Zadie Smith asks, in effect, which side are you on? Do you like O'Neill's mainstream but smart story of immigrants and cricket in New York post-9/11, or McCarthy's manifesto-like riffs on the nature of detachment and joy? And, in her intelligent review that almost persuaded me, Zadie found more to praise in McCarthy than in O'Neill—*Remainder* is, she thinks, the future of the novel. In fact, I note that one line of her review made it onto the front cover of the Vintage paperback of *Remainder* saying just this—"the future of the novel." So perhaps she is right.

Or is she? I find it difficult to make such a choice, or to find much validity the assumption that such a choice is required of readers. One might read both George Eliot and Kafka in the same day with equal, if different sorts of pleasure. O'Neill's novel, which I found engaging and thoughtful and well-written (and it led me to learn a lot more about cricket), didn't shake me up as McCarthy's did (I had dreams about *Remainder*, and I almost never dream about what I read) but my responses had nothing to do with the philosophy or future of fiction and everything to do with the fact that *Remainder* made different demands on me, demands that I was inclined to capitulate to and that were in accord with my frame of mind at the time I read it. Fictional meaning isn't Platonic, nor is it solely a function of the writer's intentions or of the novel's success in meeting them. Fiction's power and greatness is contingent upon the reader. It is the reader who appears to be missing from Smith's account of the future of fiction. She writes about the novel as a writer, not as a reader, not as someone who would (as I do) hate the idea of narrowing the future of fiction to two possible 'paths.' Serious readers are, in my experience, promiscuous, requiring different forms of gratification at different times. O'Neill's realism, its respect for the conventions of the novel as a mirror of life, might be just the ticket on days when the ground shifts beneath our feet; on the other hand, McCarthy's repetitions of events, his refusal to acknowledge normative rules of conduct or of expectation, his mordant wit, are qualities that might attract a reader who finds himself in a different frame of mind, perhaps more playful, maybe on vacation, or in love, or alone in Prague—who knows?—in any case less attached to the bourgeois/realist conventions that Z. Smith professes to find confining (or does she? She did, after all, write a wonderful conventional realist novel—after E.M. Forster—*On Beauty*).

Is it absurd to point out that there is no such thing as "the novel"? That courses, articles, sections of bookstores, and blogs that purport to treat of the *Novel* are misleading—that books calling themselves 'novels' are as diversely constructed as human faces, variations on a theme that is as variegated as life itself? This past vacation week I was able to read *Remainder*, Tabucchi's *Requiem*, Jo Ann Beard's *In Zanesville*, and Michael Connelly's new Harry Bosch mystery, *Black Box*. How could one begin to categorize these four diverse books using Smith's 'whither the novel' framework? And each book was wholly satisfying—I loved reading Connelly late at night and then waking up to fifty pages of the smart young woman who narrates Beard's lovely book; and at lunch reading a dozen pages of Tabucchi's dream-like meditation on Portugal and Pessoa, and then late in the afternoon, after a walk, Tom McCarthy, CEO of the necro-nautical society or some such. I don't want one flavor—I want them all. When it comes to books, I don't want two paths—I want them all.

G.O.

Why Literary Fiction Matters:
Not Actually a Review of *To This Day* by S.Y. Agnon

In reading S.Y. Agnon's short final novel *To This Day*, I suddenly understood more clearly why it is that reading literary fiction is such an important complement (if not antidote) to the all but overwhelming glut of blogs, newspapers, magazines, self-help books, and popular fiction that defines the intellectual-literary world of the U.S. today. In the voice of his protagonist, a young Palestinian man (that is, a Galician Jew then living in Palestine) caught in Berlin on the eve of World War I, Agnon writes:

> *This was the job of the press: to distinguish the living from the dead by reporting on the dead to the living. If you were alive you read the newspapers, through which the lifeblood of the times circulated: birth and marriage notices, anniversaries and obituaries, commodities and stock prices, and the like. Moreover, reading a newspaper spared you the trouble of forming your own opinion... In no time you crisscrossed the world and the world was yours for the price of a newspaper."*

While surely exaggerated, while surely tongue-in-cheek, the passage helped to sharpen for me my long-held belief that literary fiction asks of a reader something radically different from the many other more popular forms of print, something essential, more lasting, unique. Unlike with much commercial fiction and non-fiction these days, a novel by Agnon, Bernhard, *Klíma,* Kafka, Sebald, Toer, Bellow, Valenzuela, Naipaul, El Saadawi, Kawabata, Castellanos, Dostoevsky, Rodoreta, Müller, Conrad, Mulisch, Emecheta, Bolaño or Mahfouz will not permit you to be passive, *to be persuaded*, but will confront you with a character or characters, a problem (ethical, moral, spiritual, existential), a world (perhaps familiar, perhaps strange), then force you to think about it, to examine the evidence before you, to draw your own conclusions. It will ask you—after what is often a mighty struggle—*to form your own opinion*. That is the difference posed by literary fiction: the onus is on *you*, and you alone. *You* must decide, *you* must adjudicate or—if too moved, too shaken—you may recuse yourself instead, find a quiet place to think.

Part of what inspired this essay was the fact that hardly a week seems to pass anymore when I don't have at least one intelligent adult tell me that he or she hasn't the time for literary fiction anymore, that when he or she does find the time to read it is almost always non-fiction: magazines, newspapers, blogs, and the latest from Gladwell, Friedman, Gilbert, Sedaris, and Larson. While I genuinely believe that all types of reading are good, and I mean *all*, I also believe that it is important to read widely, eccentrically, *independently*—independent, that is, of such cultural midwives and mediums as Oprah, *Slate, The New Yorker,* and *The New York Times.*

Commercial non-fiction (even the more political and intellectual variety) is largely about trends (spotting them, mapping them, making readers feel a part of them—even creating them, when the conditions are right). As such it is not only (and for all its distinctive urgency) often highly ephemeral in nature (guaranteeing—as with the latest cut in clothes—that whatever it is or implies about the world will soon be replaced) but is likely to be driven in its popularity less by some practical or aesthetic measure of "quality" or "value" than by corporate marketing and the prospect of gain. My contention here is that the world needs more people who are less reliant on the marketplace and more reliant on themselves—on their own wisdom, intelligence, and humanity, readers who genuinely trust themselves *to think*.

Writers invested in complexity (as opposed to profit, demagoguery, fear-mongering, and self-promotion) do justice to us all by refusing to package up the world and tie it neatly with a bow. It is why their work sells so poorly and is harder, often disturbing to read. While surely the best non-fiction *is* complex, forcing us to reckon hard with the matters at hand (and on our own brave and lonely terms), only literary fiction refuses to persuade. It—unlike every other form of prose—has nothing to sell you, nothing to gain.

P.N.

The Gate

How do you like your books? Large or small? Loud or soft? Full of pretense or as plain as a Quaker Meeting-House?

There is the literature of agoraphila: *Moby-Dick* for example, or *Doctor Zhivago*, the open sea or the endless tundra, each swallowing up a human drama that derives, in part, from the vastness of the space where it occurs. Or *War and Peace*, where space and time and the weight of history conspire to create the greatest novel of agoraphila. Victor Serge, *2666* (the world as graveyard), Ha Jin's *War Trash*, Thomas Glavinic's *Night Work* and David Markson's *Wittgenstein's Mistress*—where *-philia* tips into *-phobia* as solitary characters wander aimlessly through a world otherwise devoid of human beings. The agoraphilic novel mostly terrifies as it removes the sense of scale and proportion that was the primary attraction of the genre in the first place. The novel's precursors—epic poems, story collections by Chaucer and Boccaccio, mythic tales of travel—gave way in the eighteenth century to the emerging bourgeois world of domesticity, feminine consciousness, claustrophilia—to Richardson and Rousseau and Goethe.

My own preference is for books about small things, quiet books where nothing much happens—Proust is the demi-god of this subspecies of fiction—also Robert Musil, Robert Walser (*The Assistant*), Georges Perec, David Foster Wallace's *Pale King* (a book about boredom), and nearly every Japanese novel I have ever read—from *Genji* to minimalists like Kawabata and Oe.

Those who love their literature quiet—string quartets rather than symphonies—will love Natsume Sōseki's *The Gate*, a Zen-like story of a married couple, Sosuke and Oyone, who live within the tiny confines of their small house, their garden, and their childless, but loving, marriage. No problem—of money, of filial relations, of health or happiness—is important enough to require an immediate solution. For the most part, Sosuke, a melancholy, fatalistic office-worker, is content to let life go on around him without intervention. He's indolent, Oblomovian, not one to say either 'no' or 'yes,' but always 'not yet.' He believes in destiny, and his is to be no one, and yet he is devoid of envy and rancor. It would be too much trouble to feel such things, and he prefers to watch the world from the comfort of his veranda.

At one point in the novel, Sosuke's younger and far more ambitious brother, Koroku, moves into the tiny six-mat room in Sosuke's house...there isn't money to send Koroku to university, and no one has a clue as to what to do about the young man's future until fate intervenes. Here we have Sosuke, just returned from work, inquiring about his brother:

> *"After a few sips of hot tea Oyone had brought him, [Sosuke] asked, 'Is Koroku home?'"*
>
> *"It was of course certain that his brother was there. But not the faintest sound could be heard from the six-mat room, and it seemed impossible that there could be anyone inside. As Oyone rose to call Koroku, Sosuke stopped her: There was no need to speak to him right now. Then, burrowing under the quilt attached to the portable kotatsu [a low table, covered by a quilt, with a heater underneath], he lay stretched out on his side. Twilight had already made its presence felt in this room, where the shoji all faced the steep embankment. His arm pillowed beneath his head, he simply gazed into the dark, confined space, his mind a blank."*

With Sosuke, one might be tempted to think of Bartleby or Hamlet, but that would be inaccurate: these figures are still and inactive in the midst of activity—Sosuke is the calm center of no storm, of a world that is sequestered, monastic, unchanging. Strangely, the novel culminates in Sosuke visiting a Zen monastery—as if a respite were required from doing nothing. Aside from the neighbor's daughter's piano practice, it appears no one does much of anything behind the gated world of the novel. Perhaps Soseki, who wrote the book in 1910, was nostalgically invoking pre-Meiji Japan, a world before modernization and the urban displacement of traditional Japanese life. Sōseki is also the author of the highly regarded novel *Kokoro,* another quiet book about the conflict between Western values and Japanese culture, as well as several other works of fiction and non-fiction.

The Gate reminded me of a quiet summer I spent just outside of Tokyo as a guest in the home of an older Japanese couple. We could not speak to one another, and, in the evenings, the three of us would sit in unbroken silence, staring out into the garden, bamboo entwined with delicate pink hibiscus, smoking and sipping tea.

G.O.

This Snarl of a Life

The fiercest hearts are in love with a wild perfection.
—James Wright, from a letter to James Dickey
August 12, 1958

I'd like to begin by praising James Wright for having written the only poem about sports I have ever liked, a poem about a high school football game called "Autumn Begins in Martins Ferry, Ohio". The poem is not really about sports, but about hope and despair and the power of language to quicken our blood. My college roommate, Tom Hurley, once took me home with him to Youngstown, Ohio, a once-thriving blue-collar town, which by then, by the early 1980's, was but a shadow of its former self. After an afternoon of drinking beer in a dark old Polish bar, he led me through a hole in a chain-link fence to a point overlooking the wide Mahoning Valley, then still choked, for as far as the eye could see, with the hulking remains of the city's once world-famous steel mills, those of *U.S Steel* and *Youngstown Sheet and Tube*, mills that at their peak had employed as many as 300,000 workers, many of them from Eastern Europe and the Middle East. The silence there was eerie.

It was out of this background, this hardscrabble industrial Ohio, that James Wright made his first appearance on the American poetry scene in 1956 with his collection of formalist verse called *The Green Wall*. Then too began the brilliant, tortured, immeasurably rich and thrilling correspondence between Wright and his friends and fellow poets that comprises the volume, *A Wild Perfection: The Selected Letters of James Wright*. Of friends and correspondents, his were some of the best writers this country has known: Robert Lowell, James Dickey, Mary Oliver, Galway Kinnell, Theodore Roethke, Kenneth Rexroth, Anne Sexton, Louis Simpson, Jack Myers, E. L. Doctorow, Denise Levertov, Richard Hugo, A.R. Ammons, Louise Bogan, J.D. McClatchy, Robert Bly, W.D. Snodgrass, Mark Strand, Hayden Carruth, Tomas Tranströmer, Robert Hass, Stanley Kunitz, Roger Hecht, Diane Wakowski, C.K. Williams, Philip Levine, Donald Hall, and Leslie Marmon Silko.

I have long been ambivalent about reading famous people's letters, just as I have long been ambivalent about reading their memoirs, which have struck me, more often than not, as case studies in vanity and obfuscation. Not so with the letters of James Wright. "In a man's letters," writes Samuel Johnson, "a man's soul lies naked." And so it is with the letters in this marvelous collection, distinguished, on page after page, by Wright's mighty, humble, generous, infinitely hard-suffering voice. At points his candor in the letters is so raw I winced.

Perhaps above all one is struck by the high level of conversation in these everyday missives, by the stakes, by Wright's rare, nearly pious devotion to what he called "the Great Conversation," a correspondence, a dialogue "in which stories and poems and those who love them talk eternally with one another." Poetry—one feels in these letters—is a matter of life or death. And so it is for those who know. One has only to scan the book's index to get a sense of the glorious depth and erudition of this protracted conversation of his. In thinking about poetry and life, he writes with devotion of Catallus and Virgil, of Shakespeare, Dante, Milton, Lorca, Neruda, Jiménez, Whitman, and Baudelaire, as well as about Melville, Forster, Tolstoy, Dickens, Marx, Ramakrishna, Freud, and Camus. His hunger for ideas—and for the language that shapes them—was stupendous.

In his poetry Wright was a perfectionist, working tirelessly to develop his own voice and form, and struggling—with every muscle and sinew in his being—against the unshakable curse of competency, what his friend and mentor, James Dickey, called "the good enough that spoils the world." With the intimate guidance of both Dickey and Bly, he labored restlessly as a poet, and while he often reached dizzying heights in his work and friendships, he was just as often laid low by lengthy bouts of depression and despair. He smoked and drank heavily, both of which destroyed his first marriage and so compounded his nervous exhaustion that at least twice he was hospitalized for it, for what, in one of his letters, he dismisses as just another "mild crack-up." His life was hard, the price of his poetry dear, giving this intellectually dazzling correspondence a dark and tragic weight. Yet for all the emotional turmoil of his life, Wright believed in love, lived love each day as "a kind of miraculous agony" that one struggles in vain to escape.

    P.N.

The Golden Age

The Contemporary American Poets: American Poetry Since 1940, edited by Mark Strand (1969)

The original Golden Age was pastoral—zephyrs and barks plying languid lakes, high clouds reminiscence of Orientalist cities, sun (but not too much), distant peaks and the sorts of views a city-dweller might enjoy from the comfort of her carriage. High summer, one imagines, on Martha's Vineyard, a nice Sauvignon Blanc on the portico, oysters, cucumber sandwiches.

Not that one.

The golden age of American poetry was urban, gritty and unshaven, fueled by whiskey and cheese sandwiches, adjunct jobs at small Midwestern colleges that never quite panned out—booze, or the temptations offered by frisky undergraduates—manual typewriters, manila envelopes, trips to the post-office for stamps, polite phone calls from editors who knew a thing or two about poetry, readings in bookstores—bookstores!—crowds languid with smoke and wine and an unquenchable thirst for words.

The Golden Age. Not, of course, for everyone. Not for Negros (as they said back then), or for women, or for the poor, or for almost everybody else. But still—if you were young and male and white and got to college on the GI Bill, and had been bitten by the unforgettable verses of the King James Bible, or *King Lear*, and had managed to get over T.S. Eliot and W. B. Yeats, and saw the charms of Auden but didn't have the epic impulse—if you were an American romantic, footloose and lyrical, if you'd grown up in a small town but left at once for New York or Chicago, if you didn't give a shit about money—then you just might join the illustrious American post-modernist pantheon of poets.

Post-modernist? That's Strand's view, not my own. No, these poets were somewhere in between the high modernists and what came after, the waves of language poetry unmoored from meaning, the lines that scuttle down the pages of *Poetry* and *The American Poetry Review* and the *Paris Review* like fishing lines atwitch with carp, poems work-shopped to suit the tastes of poets also work-shopped, which is to say poems produced and not written, formed and not felt. The Golden Age was golden for having been produced by men and women who simply had the urge, loved the language, and were confounded by the world around them. That, after all, is the alchemy of art: talent and opportunity come together at a moment when someone—a patron, William Shawn, Harriet Monroe—cares enough about the art to take a chance, when the publisher has taste and not a rabid yearning for profits and fashion.

Roethke and Bishop, Ammons and Justice and Bly, Corso and Creeley, Dugan and Dickey and the great Richard Hugo and sublime Howard Nemerov and Louise Gluck (still going strong), and diminutive Diane Wakoski, and sad Anne Sexton, and the gentlemen James Tate, and May Swenson who always surprises, and lesser known poets like Reed Whittemore and David Ignatow, and tragic ones like Randall Jarrell and John Berryman, and the saintly James Wright, and craftsmen like Richard Wilbur and Anthony Hecht: Donald Hall and John Ashbery, Ginsberg of course, and Le Roi Jones (remember?), and did I mention Philip Levine, Carolyn Kizer, and Charles Wright, X.J. Kennedy whose writing text remains unrivaled, and William Meredith, the discovery of whose work reignited my love of poetry thirty years ago. And many others, ninety-six in all, comfortably residing in the 350 or so pages of this classic collection edited by our finest anthologist Mark Strand (who, modestly, includes only one of his own poems, the haunting "Keeping Things Whole").

I adore these writers, each one of whom has a voice and style and concerns that overlap but never duplicate those of his or her peers. America after the war, America during another and longer war. The place of poetry in a philistine society. The aches and pains of America's emergent greatness (written about with irony, anger, awe, and disbelief, depending on the poet). City streets. Restless searching for meaning, or despair over the lack of meaning—or wondering what "meaning" means. There were no limits on subject matter, no forms that went untried, no lexical shyness—crazy diction by modernist standards, a rejection of academic norms—these poets were often found *in* the academy, but with few exceptions were not *of* the academy. They wore their learning lightly—no pretentious Greek and Latin quotations, though lots of them knew the classics (Charles Olson was an exception, and, sure enough, he's here with "The Lordly and Isolate Satyrs" sounding for all the world like that Satyr Ezra.)

Here's one of my favorites, from 1968:

Degrees of Gray in Philipsburg

You might come here Sunday on a whim.
Say your life broke down. The last good kiss
  you had was years ago. You walk these streets
laid out by the insane, past hotels
that didn't last, bars that did, the tortured try
of local drivers to accelerate their lives.
Only churches are kept up. The jail
turned 70 this year. The only prisoner
is always in, not knowing what he's done.

The principal supporting business now
  is rage. Hatred of the various grays
the mountain sends, hatred of the mill,
The Silver Bill repeal, the best liked girls
who leave each year for Butte. One good
restaurant and bars can't wipe the boredom out.
The 1907 boom, eight going silver mines,
a dance floor built on springs—

all memory resolves itself in gaze,
in panoramic green you know the cattle eat
or two stacks high above the town,
two dead kilns, the huge mill in collapse
for fifty years that won't fall finally down.

Isn't this your life? That ancient kiss
still burning out your eyes? Isn't this defeat
so accurate, the church bell simply seems
a pure announcement: ring and no one comes?
Don't empty houses ring? Are magnesium
and scorn sufficient to support a town,
not just Philipsburg, but towns
of towering blondes, good jazz and booze
the world will never let you have
until the town you came from dies inside?

Say no to yourself. The old man, twenty
when the jail was built, still laughs
although his lips collapse. Someday soon,
he says, I'll go to sleep and not wake up.
You tell him no. You're talking to yourself.
The car that brought you here still runs.
The money you buy lunch with,
no matter where it's mined, is silver
and the girl who serves your food
is slender and her red hair lights the wall.

I like to imagine Richard Hugo trying to place this poem with any of today's publishers.

Or imagine the response to this poem, by Stanley Moss:

Squall

*I have not used my darkness well,
nor the Baroque arm that hangs from my shoulder,
nor the Baroque arm of my chair.
The rain moves out in a dark schedule.
Let the wind marry. I know the creation
continues through love. The rain's a wife.
I cannot sleep or lie awake. Looking
at the dead I turn back, fling
my hat into their grandstands for relief.
How goes a life? Something like the ocean
building dead coral.*

G.O.

Paris, 1944: How Shall We Live?

> The dead are dead; for them there are no more problems. But after this night of festivity, we, the living, will awaken again. And then how shall we live?
> Simone de Beauvoir

When I was young my mother moved her study to the empty milk house on the old farm where we lived on a bluff above the Susquehanna. She had moved her books and papers and electric typewriter there in order to finish her dissertation, a task that had proven too much for her in a house with six kids. Always close to my mother, I used to visit her there while she worked, sitting quietly in the canvas chair beside her and studying the books on the shelves, the pictures on the walls. I remember there were prints by Ben Shahn (one of which I have above my desk right now) and the large, now-iconic image of the young Black Panther, Huey Newton, in a basket-backed chair armed with spear and rifle, a poster given her as a gift from her late friend and admirer (and the subject of her dissertation), the radical historian, militant, and suicide, Robert Starobin. I remember the pictures and I remember the books, the colors of their spines, and my attempts—so much in vain—to decipher their content from their titles alone. There was *The Feminine Mystique*, *Fear of Flying*, *The Wretched of the Earth*, *Women, Race & Class*, and on the shelf by the door a thick paperback copy of *The Second Sex*, a book I wouldn't read for many years to come.

Even so, *The Second Sex* was not my first exposure to Simone de Beauvoir. The first thing I read of hers was her short and sterling work, *An Easy Death*, a brave, nearly day-by-day accounting of her mother's demise. While I knew that de Beauvoir had written fiction as well, I'd simply never read any of it, that is, until recently, when I picked up a copy of her prize-winning, semi-autobiographical novel, *The Mandarins*.

Opening in Paris in 1944, at the end of the Nazi Occupation, the novel follows a group of intellectuals—writers, philosophers, newspapermen, and activists—as they struggle to salvage the future from the ashes and rubble of war. Based in part on de Beauvoir's own experience of that period in Paris in the restless company of Jean-Paul Sartre, Albert Camus, Arthur Koestler, and her one-time lover, Nelson Algren (to whom she dedicates the novel), the story is more than merely anecdotal, more than a just paean to these brilliant, headstrong men. After all, the author calls them *mandarins* (no doubt including herself), after the ancient Chinese order of bureaucrats, meaning also "esoteric" and "consciously superior", if not pretentious, pedantic, effete. As much as the author clearly admired these men, as much as we admire them today, she doesn't pull any punches in telling this tale. For if these men, her characters, are brave, even visionary in their thinking, they are also arrogant, chauvinistic, and vain.

The particular brilliance of this novel stems from the fact that we, the readers, are never locked too long inside the minds of these men, smart, prophetic as they are, but are asked to see the story, first and foremost, through the eyes of a seemingly lesser player in the drama of Paris at the time, the psychiatrist, Anne Debreuilh, who serves as the novel's governing intelligence and emotional keel. It is to her perspective, and to her own trials and tribulations—her relationship with her husband, an imperious Communist party leader; her work with her war-traumatized patients; and her affair with an American writer—that the reader is most closely, most poignantly wed.

Yet what the author achieves with this novel, finally, is much more than that. Thanks to de Beauvoir's extraordinary skill as a writer, to her exceptionally fine ear for dialogue, the reader is transported to Paris itself, in 1944, to sit amidst the crowded tables with these men and women and eavesdrop upon their heady, ever-provocative conversations about politics and war, about loyalty, women, and love. It is a rich, rewarding book that makes me wonder, some days, where such urgency and passion have gone.

P.N.

Small Bombs

The Association of Small Bombs, Karan Mahajan

It happens every single day. Thirty-two thousand seven-hundred people died in terrorist bomb attacks in 2015. Mostly, but no longer exclusively, in the Middle East. A big bomb will kill two hundred, perhaps more. A "small bomb" placed in a car or left in a backpack, five or six, wounding dozens more. We say, "It is terrible." Or, "Madness." Or, "Why did they do it?" And then we forget until the next time, rather as with mass shootings in our own unhappy country. "What can we do?" It turns out that we (that is, those paid to govern) can do nothing. Perhaps we wait our turn, hope for the best, turn off the news, stop reading the newspaper. Maybe elect a president who will do it to them before they can do it to us. That's why they call it terrorism.

What happens to the people who survive a small bomb? The logic of small bombs is that there are fewer victims with whom a survivor can connect and commiserate. Compassion requires a large object: The Holocaust, 9/11, maybe Biafra.

Small disasters evoke curiosity, which isn't yet compassion or even empathy. It takes a lot to wake up sleepwalkers, but a small bomb—for those who have given terror some thought—is a fine way to create ripples of fear and disenchantment. Just the thing if chaos is your ultimate goal. Those merely maimed are basically alone. If the bomb goes off in India (or Iraq, or Syria) the government takes no interest in the victims, or in the perpetrators. What do the survivors feel? How do their lives go on, or do they? You could think about this problem all day long, maybe go a little crazy wondering at the waste of lives. But there's something important for us to consider, and, I admit, I hadn't, at least until I read Mahajan.

Karan Mahajan has asked lots of good questions about small bombs. T*he Association of Small Bombs* is a very smart novel, not only for the compassion it evokes for the innocent victims of terror, but for the honesty with which Mahajan confronts the fundamental fact that suffering is always personal and that the consequences of any political act (it needn't be a terrorist bomb) unfold endlessly. The "association" is both the organization of survivors of a Kashmir-terrorist bombing in Delhi in 1996, and the bonds that forever link the victims, the bombers, the police, and the dozens of others whose own lives are forever altered by a single, relatively low-key political act. And the implication of the novel—searingly revealed in the final pages—is that the Association is rapidly growing to include all of us. The really smart thing I learned from Mahajan is that suffering and chaos unites us in a way that happiness and order cannot. "Unites" might be the wrong word: it is more along the lines of a brother- and sisterhood of suffering creating bonds that would otherwise never have existed. In a strange way the association of small bombs is like the association of believers, a few of whom subscribe to dogmas of violence as central to their creed. The believers create a new dispensation: that of the victims.

Bakunin took up the idea of the "propaganda of the deed" in his struggle against the Tsarist regime in Russia. Revolutionary violence was thought to be more effective than mere propaganda—ideally, the terrorist act stirs revolutionary fervor among the supine masses (Bakunin, Paul Broursse). Modern terrorism may or may not be directed at bringing down a particular state; its purpose may be to draw attention to a particular injustice, to undermine an ideology ("the West"), or simply to spread terror without a definable political goal. Mahajan's terrorists mix all of these motives with a baser alloy: a fascination with terror for its own sake. Murder, it appears, can become a job, rather like engineering or computer programming. Shockie, the bomb builder in TAOSB is a haunted, inscrutable figure. He hates the Indian government for its occupation of Kashmir, but his politics are vague. Mostly he builds and detonates bombs because that is his profession. He doesn't represent the banality of evil, just evil's unreflective nature. Killing innocent people is, for some, a default setting. It's difficult to hate Shockie, even though what he does is terrible. It's a very strange kind of art that can create such a figure, strange and wonderful.

Shockie sets off a small bomb in a crowded market in Delhi in 1996. Two boys, the sons of the Khurana's, are killed; their best friend, Mansoor, survives, but is wounded. The bomb is detonated on page three. What happens next is both a linear description of effects and a multilayered accounting of the complexity of a catastrophic event. The Khurana's lives are, of course, ruined, but not simply torn apart—rather they are blown up slowly, as if in slow motion, briefly healing and then torn open again. Mansoor grows up but he would have been better off if he too had been killed. His suffering is most acutely felt; Mahajan is at his most brilliant in his painstaking stripping away of everything that Mansoor once was, breaking him, as it were, on the rack of his own innocence. The bombers themselves suffer in various ways, but not, I suspect, enough to satisfy any sort of karmic balance. And other characters, not a part of the initial event, are also drawn into the great skein of its tragic consequences. No one survives. That too is why it is called "terrorism." Terrorism is the most acute modern reminder of the fragility of life and the impotence of politics in the face of ideology. You go to work and someone blows you up. Terrorism is the tool of the ideologically inclined, just as peace might have been the natural outgrowth of politics, if politics were motivated by a desire for justice. It's a wonder that a novel so focused on individual peoples' lives could have so much to say (between the lines) about the ordering of everyday life.

Mahajan writes beautifully, with remarkable (he's very young) compassion. I underlined dozens of passages to reproduce here. Let me quote only one. Years after their sons' deaths, Vika and Deepa Khurana establish The Association of Small Bombs, a victims' aid group, though they can do little for the victims of bombings but visit the newly blown up in the hospital. Here is a tender passage whose description turns out to be terribly ironic:

"Together, aged, having experienced so much, [Vika and Deepa] cut warm, comforting, watchful figures in the hospitals. Often, they were observing not the victims but each other. How had they come from marriage to the death of their boys—to this? And yet, it gave them enormous solace to know that their suffering had not been for naught, that they had been able to eke a larger meaning out of it; they felt the closeness couples sometimes experience when they become rich after years of poverty, a mutual appreciation and gratefulness and wonder and an awareness of the depths of the other person—an awareness that is stronger than any affection or love."

G.O.

Wandering Soul

Lifting my gaze, I scan the horizon:
The longed-for return, when will it come?
The bird takes flight to regain its nest:
And the fox, dying, turns to its lair,
Upright and loyal, yet I live in exile,
When shall I forget my fate, what day what night?
                                                Qu Yuan

"French writing continues to emerge from unusual sources," writes John Taylor in his 2008 essay on the matter in the Michigan Quarterly Review, a fascinating piece in which he introduces the reader to the work of three prominent Chinese-French writers, Dai Sijie, Gao Xingjian, and François Cheng, whose extraordinary novel, *The River Below*, is the subject of this essay.

In *The River Below* Cheng "uses the conceit of the medieval *dit* to enable one Tianyi, a Chinese artist, tell the story of his life, as he travels from China (where he was born in 1925) to Paris (where he lived in the 1950's) and then back to Communist China." The *dit* is a form of storytelling believed to have originated in late 12th Century France as a means of distinguishing allegorical tales, tales that concealed a truth within a purely fictional story or *conte*, from other more popular tales. Typically the *dit* signified a moral or instructive story, what soon proved to be a successful compromise "between the heaviness of didactic treatises and the lyricism of courtly poetry…"

No doubt this was precisely what Cheng had in mind when he wrote *The River Below*. As one reviewer describes the novel: "It unrolls like an allegorical scroll, its characters at once individuals and symbolic figures, as in the *I Ching*, in which the individual reflects the universal," making the novel seem both ancient (timeless) and distinctly, significantly modern.

In fact one of the most remarkable characteristics of this layered, deeply sophisticated novel is the constant interplay between these different narrative modes—that of allegory and that of the anxious, modern Bildungsroman. It is the nearly seamless interplay of these different narrative forms that give the novel its unusual resonance, its force.

Early on in the story, the protagonist, Tianyi, in a line straight out of a fairy tale, reflects upon his discovery of the powers of traditional Chinese calligraphy: "…I was won over by the magical power of brush and ink. I sensed it was to be a weapon for me. Maybe the only one I would have to protect me from the overwhelming presence of the Outside."

Now contrast this passage with the novel's modern, distinctly Tristram Shandy-like opening in which, with the same casual disregard with which Tristram's mother—at the very moment of Tristram's conception—interrupts his father at his business by asking him if he remembered to wind the clock, the young Tianyi makes the foolish mistake one night of calling out to a grieving widow in the voice of her dead husband, not knowing that "If by chance someone among the living answers her cry with a yes, he loses his body, which is quickly entered by the dead man's wandering soul that then returns to the world of the living. And the soul of the one thus losing is body becomes in turn the wanderer…" Near the end of this opening section the elder Tianyi, looking back over his long and rootless life, remarks, in words that Laurence Sterne himself might have penned (if with no intended humor): "I was convinced that from then on everything in me would be perpetually out of joint."

And so it is, as we follow young Tanyi in his wandering throughout China, to France, to Paris, then back again to China, a nation torn asunder by the zealotry of Mao Tse-Tung. Juxtaposing an artist's lyrical sensibility against the violent upheavals of revolutionary China, *The River Below* is a subtle, broadly challenging novel of ideas that is rich with rewards for the patient and talented reader.

P.N.

The Blues

Rain in Our Door (Duets With Robert Johnson), poems by Diann Blakely
Escaping the Delta: Robert Johnson and the Invention of the Blues, by Elijah Wald
"I Believe I'll Dust My Broom," Robert Johnson (recorded in 1936)

He was a natty dresser, a ladies man; he always had pocket change, was "a strange dude, a loner and a drifter." He had the kind of long spidery fingers that made it easier to reach for a note; he drank, but he was seldom drunk. Johnny Shines, himself a fine bluesman, spent a lot of time on the road with Johnson, and noted that Johnson "was about the greatest guitar player [he'd] ever heard," an innovator as a slide player and adept at taking old songs, adding verses and sprucing up the guitar parts in ways no one had ever heard before (check out "Terraplane Blues" for a sampling of Johnson's remarkable, innovative style). "I Believe I'll Dust My Broom," based on a blues of Leroy Carr, uses "floating verses"—stock lines that Johnson, like any oral-formulaic poet, popped into his longer tunes to fill out the song. Elijah Wald's reading of this and other great Johnson tunes emphasizes the way in which Johnson used triplets and a boogie-woogie beat to drive the song forward, to give it an urgency that doesn't show up in any early versions. Most listeners know this tune from the Elmore James recording of 1951—it's a remarkable performance and contains what one critic has called the "most famous blues riff" ever recorded. I prefer Johnson's scalding acoustic to James's electric slide, but both songs are the real thing. Johnson wasn't a poet, but listening through the entire body of his recorded work demonstrates his genius for merging standard blues sentiments to stunningly original guitar riffs.

Diann Blakely, like Robert Johnson, died too young. I have admired her poetry since reading her first collection, *Hurricane Walk*, in 1993. Here's the title poem from that collection, typical of Blakely's intense and lyric style:

Hurricane Walk

It was better than sex, the way it relaxed me.
My thighs throbbed for ours, each finger
seemed limp. I lighted
a cigarette, then found it too heavy to lift.
A more comfortable lust would have kept me
inside. Yet I wanted
the wind's touch, to feel its whorled force.
I stood on a bridge, there were no trees
to stop it — I saw thin sheets of water
spin like ghosts from the Charles.
And now, damp from a bath, I feel
honed, quite essential.
This robe seems too big, it abrades
my cleansed skin. The room's warmth
stings my lips; they were left raw and chapped,
almost bruised. It will take days
to heal them, the slightest good-night kiss
is out of the question for weeks.

At the time of her death in 2014, Blakely was working on *Rain in Our Door*, duets that honor, and, in the style of the blues, riff on the songs of Robert Johnson. The blues are stacked deep with meaning: a tag line from a song might reach back to a call and response shouted by a tired field worker on a Saturday afternoon, a man or a woman waiting for the pay envelope and a night at the juke or on the front porch. Johnson and so many other blues players learned their craft from older practitioners; the songs they played were based on traditional tunes, meaning songs whose origins cannot be traced to any composer but are so deeply embedded in the culture as to *be* the culture. The instruments—beat-up guitars, fiddles, banjos, harmonicas, drums—were often found in pawn shops, and the blues voice, more often than not, was honed in a church choir ("devil's music" the preachers called it). Blakely was deeply immersed in this rich tradition of making music out of pain. Her poems, virtually all of them, are full of yearning, and in this collection she brilliantly captures Johnson's moods—not just the words he sang, but the guitar voicings that are often the real attraction.

Here's part of Blakely's syncopated "Stop Breaking Down"

> *"O can I get a witness for this wreckage?*
> *You asked when sweet black angels beckoned*
>
> *And you kicked off the sheets, sweating fresh blues*
> *And dreaming of Friars Point, Memphis,*
>
> *Dreaming of Rosedale and Mound Bayou. The stuff*
> *I get—o sing it now—gon' bust*
>
> *Your brains out baby, gon' make you lose your mind."*
>
> *Lost him like smoke, said Johnny Shines....*

Robert Johnson was always dreaming of someplace else. He lived nowhere in particular. Robert Lockwood shares stories of traveling with Johnson, of splitting the kitty, playing "both sides of the bridge" to make more money for moonshine and smokes, and especially for the women who loved Johnson's look (he was part Indian, with smooth skin and a quick smile, according to Shines).

Blakely replicates the restlessness of Johnson in her poems. They move from blues verses, to fragments of Johnson's life ("Mr. Downchild"), to sad reflections on how race still haunts America ("Rambling on My Mind").

"Truth sides / With history's open veins..." Blakely seamlessly weaves Johnson's lyrics into her poems, or she writes her own blues, following Johnson across his brief, wild life to his dying in agony of poisoned whiskey (or a stabbing, or syphilis, depending on who is telling the story—Wald quotes "Honeyboy" Edwards to support the poisoning story, which is the most credible).

> *"And soon you're brokedown on your knees, mouth full of foam*
> *And blood and curses hurled at God.*
> *Please Mr. Highwayman. please don't block the road.*
> *Three days. Three nights. A borrowed bed*
> *With shrieking metal springs. But first musky confusion;*
> *Your gut becomes a gallows-rope [!]*
> *O play me. Play me. O play me Terraplane Blues...*
> *Strings fray. You're booked and got to go."*
>   —*from* Terraplane Blues

Blakely's chronology of Johnson's life and her remarkable

notes to her poems—not snippets of explanation, but short essays on the life and afterlife of Johnson and the blues—make *Rain in Our Door* more than just an extraordinary collection of poems; the book is a homage to the greatest of the early bluesmen.

I recommend that you read *Rain in Our Door* with Elijah Wald's wonderful account of the Delta blues at hand. Taken together, and with the definitive recordings of Johnson's songs on the stereo, the books provide both poetic and historical insights into one of America's most important cultural creations.

G.O.

Kill Your Television or Titian's Initials (T.V.)

Kill your television. Or maybe just turn it off. That's what the obsessive, hopelessly distracted narrator of Jean-Philippe Toussaint's novel, *Television*, does. Or tries to do. The anonymous narrator, a French academic on sabbatical, has rented an apartment in Berlin in which to commence and complete a draft of what he is confident will be a ground-breaking study of Tiziano Vecellio, the Venetian-school painter best known as Titian. Yet he quickly gets distracted. Within days of living there, he realizes that unless he stops watching television altogether he will never get down to work:

> *I'd decided to spend the summer alone in Berlin to devote myself to the study of Titian Vecellio. For several years now I'd been planning a vast essay on the relationship between political power and the arts. Little by little, my focus had narrowed to sixteenth-century Italy, and more particularly to Tiziano Vecellio and Emperor Charles V; in the end I'd chosen the apocryphal story of the paintbrush—according to which Charles V bent down in Titian's studio to pick up a paintbrush that had slipped from the painter's hands—as my monograph's*

emblematic center and the source of its title, The Paintbrush.

Unfortunately, the project is for naught, that is, unless he can actually renounce the odious habit that has overtaken his life. As he is quick to learn, it is no small challenge. Indeed, more than halfway through the story, the reader discovers that the narrator has still only managed to write the opening two words of his great monograph, "When Musset..." He is so distracted by the television in the apartment that he can't stop thinking about it—even (or especially) when it is off. Every day he sits down to write and every day he gets up. A "first-class rationalizer," "a casuist of rare accomplishment," he reassures himself that *not* writing is as important to the process of writing as writing itself! In fact for *not-writing* he seems to possess a singular gift, whiling away his time in Berlin drinking coffee, reading the newspaper, flipping his computer on and off, watching the neighbors in the apartments across the way (most of them watching television), sunbathing nude by the lake in Halensee Park, and generally neglecting the neighbor's plants, which he has agreed to water according to a strict and particular regimen—all while waxing philosophic about the troubling role of television in his thoughtful, well-meaning life.

Given what I have written so far, it should come as no surprise that what follows in this decidedly quirky novel is not the monograph itself (Who after all was Musset?) nor a humdrum, if heartening account of scholarly creation nor even a comedy of bad manners, say, in the style of David Lodge, but a protracted, ironically amusing, finally deeply unsettling meditation on the effects of watching television, a habit now as ubiquitous in the world as it is disturbing in its effects and implications.

> *I spent hours every day motionless before the screen, my gaze fixed, bathed in the ever-shifting light of the scene changes, gradually submerged by the flood of images illuminating my face, the long parade of images blindly addressed to everyone at once and no one in particular, each channel being only another strand in the vast web of electromagnetic waves crashing down over the world.*

Of course the point (his point, my point) is that a steady diet of video (television, movies, YouTube, TED Talks, advertisements, and pornography, in essence, the internet itself) makes us dangerously impassive—sated, jaded, solipsistic, and remote. Driven by profit, by the frenzied peddling of trends, video culture depends on our willingness to be led by the nose, to cut loose our moorings, to be spectators in our own anxious lives. Indeed it depends on our willingness to *not participate* at all, to *not think, not question, not evaluate* what it is we see on the screen (and by extension in the world around us). The thriving video culture of today is a colossal sleight-of-hand, a vast, impersonal, essentially mercenary conglomeration of forces that thrives by our willingness to feed it, to take what it gives us as meaningful, significant, to accept as real and sufficient the restless tingling of its pulses in our brains.

In his last, uproariously bleak novel *Extinction*, the Austrian novelist Thomas Bernhard has his thinly disguised narrator declare, "Photography is a base passion that has taken hold of every continent and every section of the population, a sickness that afflicts the whole of humanity and is no longer curable. The inventor of the photographic art was the inventor of the most inhumane of all arts. To him we owe the ultimate distortion of nature and of human beings who form part of it, the reduction of human beings to perverse caricatures… Photography is the greatest disaster of the twentieth century." While not explicitly speaking of video, I have no doubt that, were the author still alive, he would be appalled at the virtually unchallenged, now thoroughly dogmatic hegemony of video culture in the world today, astounded and dismayed by our zealous, nearly fanatical subservience to the all mighty screen.

Reading and writing, by contrast, are *actions*, things a person *does*. That is the difference: reading and writing are *creative acts*, while (with perhaps very few exceptions) watching video is not. In time, with exposure, watching video (even the most revered and artistic of films) makes us dumbly acquiescent, for video, by its very nature, is about passivity, about *receiving* information over which we have little or no control. It is about allowing ourselves to be made puppets; it is about permitting our brains to be little more than screens upon which the lives of others are played.

Video culture today is not about connectivity and the democratization of information and knowledge, nor is it about the redistribution of wealth and power, but about its ruthless consolidation. It is about conscription and compliance and consumption. At the risk of overstating it, watching video at the rate we do today is voyeurism and titillation at the price of our souls, a habit and pastime, an obsession now pandemic, that in the gloating guise of reality (and increasingly of "progressive" education) quickly overwhelms our intelligence, our skepticism, our curiosity, our compassion, our courage, and our dissent, not to mention our individuality (about which, ironically, we Americans now seem more boastful than ever). As the late Edward Said puts it: "We are bombarded by repackaged and reified representations of the world that usurp consciousness and preempt democratic critique."

What's worse, what's more, our desperate and ever-more defensive addiction to video erodes our essential optimism about ourselves, our belief (surely a prehistoric one) that the answer to what ails us lies not in sitting captive before a screen, in the political-corporate mediation of our lives, but in our own stubborn agency as *people*, that is, as cultures, communities, and individuals *thinking* and *doing* every day, a trying, hard-won engagement with the world that is, to me, the only truth that matters. Writes Warren Motte in his insightful afterword to the novel: "For as much as anything else, *Television* is about the ways in which novels compete for our attention with other, newer media, in an increasingly unequal dual where some of the most basic terms of our culture hang breathlessly in the balance. And the real hero of *that* struggle, Toussaint suggests, is the novel itself."

P.N.

Idiots and Imbeciles

Adam Cohen, *Imbeciles: The Supreme Court, American Eugenics, and the Sterilization of Carrie Buck*
Don Carpenter, *Hard Rain Falling (a novel)*

That's Carrie on the left, with her mother, Vivian, both institutionalized at the Virginia Colony for Epileptics and the Feeble-Minded. Carrie, as the world knows, was sterilized via salpingectomy by Dr. John Bell. Here is Adam's Cohen's account of the crime against Carrie Buck:

> *"The first legal sterilization in Virginia began promptly on that Wednesday morning [October 19, 1927]. Carrie, who was now twenty-one years old, was taken to the infirmary in the colony's Halsey-Jennings Building at 9:30 a.m. The surgeon who would be performing the operation was no stranger to the patient: it was Dr. John Bell, who had conducted Carrie's physical examination on her arrival at the colony, and had given his name to the Supreme Court case. Carrie was anesthetized, and the operation began. Dr. Bell, working with another surgeon, removed an inch from each of Carrie's fallopian tubes. Her tubes were then ligated, or brought together, and the ends cauterized using carbolic acid followed by alcohol." (p. 283)*

At the Nuremberg trial of the Nazi war criminal Otto Hoffmann, head of the SS Race and Settlement Office, the defense was based in part on Hoffmann's citation of the notorious opinion of Dr. Oliver Wendell Holmes, Jr. in Buck versus Bell ("Three generations of imbeciles are enough"). The *Rasse- und Siedlungshauptamt der SS* was responsible for "safeguarding the Racial Purity of the Reich." Oliver Wendell Holmes, Jr., whose mustachioed visage appeared on the cover of *Time Magazine* on the occasion of his 85th birthday, was considered "the greatest jurist in American history" by none other than Walter Lippmann. He was also, as Cohen's painstakingly researched book shows, a racist and eugenicist, a not unusual combination of views among America's educated classes during the Progressive period. Progress meant purity and the dissemination of American bourgeois values by every means possible, through settlement houses, education, war, and eugenics. The irony of Cohen's title—one can't miss it—is that the "imbeciles" weren't Carrie and Vivian Buck— Carrie was a normal girl who had been raped while working as a virtual slave in the household of the family that had taken her from her birth mother—but Drs. Holmes, Buck, Albert Priddy, and the rest of the cast of eugenicists whose delusions of racial purity based on pseudo-science and social prejudice antedated and inspired the Nazi campaign to rid the world of "undesirables." Hitler, praised by the American eugenicist Clarence Campbell in 1935 ("that great leader"), was moved by America's example in pursuing his own mad dreams of Aryan race hygiene. Even the horrors of the Holocaust didn't deter American eugenicists: as late as 1958 Virginia hospitals were sterilizing inmates against their will. "Deviates, criminals, idiots, morons, and imbeciles."

What explains this obsession with racial purity? Carrie Buck did well in school, but she wasn't allowed to continue beyond sixth-grade. Her family was poor and powerless; as a result she was adopted by the Dobbs family when she was a toddler. "Less a daughter and more a housemaid," a cousin of John Dobbs raped Carrie when she was seventeen. Pregnant, unmarried, and therefore immoral, Dobbs had her committed to the Virginia Colony. The moral of this tale isn't difficult to discover: at a time when American society was changing dramatically under the twin pressures of industrial capitalism and immigration, traditional white and Protestant

Americans discovered in "scientific" racism a defense of their values, of Anglo-Saxons, race hygiene, and Christian sexual mores. Carrie wasn't sterilized for being feeble-minded—she was an average, but poor and friendless young woman—but for representing the caste of down-and-outs whose presence in the landscape of early twentieth-century America was troubling to those who make the rules—to academics, scientists, judges, ministers, and politicians (the only institutional opponent of forced sterilization was the Catholic Church, but not for the right reasons). The Supreme Court's decision in Buck versus Bell has never been overturned, although Virginia and a handful of other states have issued apologies for the practice of forced sterilization.

We all know that Portland is the coolest place in America, but in Don Carpenter's *noir* novel of 1964 Portland is a squalid town, full of grifters, hustlers, pool-sharks, gamblers, hookers, and thugs. Carpenter's novel, *Hard Rain Falling* is the bleak story of Jack Levitt, a brutish but introspective loser whose existence in the prosperous booster culture of post-War America was an affront to the dominant *ethos*, much as some white Americans today find the "browning" of American society deeply disturbing ("Make America White Again" is a slogan that showed up at the Trump rally here in majority-Hispanic Albuquerque). Levitt is the sort of kid who would have been sterilized had he born a decade earlier, the kind of person spawned by the thousands in a society of winners and losers, a nobody whose life comes to an inevitable nothing. This is a novel that is especially valuable for its sociological and historical insight into the lives of the poor and the incarcerated. Carpenter, who lived most of his life in Mill Valley, California, is among that group of largely unknown writers who drifted back and forth between Hollywood script work and writing serious books. Thanks to biographers and scholars, we know of Faulkner's catastrophic stint in Hollywood, but what of Cornell Woolrich, David Goodis, and Charles Williams—all writers of popular and, in some instances, excellent *noir* fiction who supplemented their income writing for (mostly B) films? All are writers worth reclaiming and reading.

The power of these writers lies in their having glimpsed—reveled in—the darker side of American life. Their hard-boiled realism challenged the facade of mainstream culture, the happy endings, the preoccupation with the rich and famous, the moral posturing that dominates much of American popular fiction. Carpenter spares the reader no horror in peeling away the psychological torments endured by Jack Levitt as orphan, reform school kid, inmate at San Quentin, and parolee. Carpenter's description of Levitt's long sojourn in solitary confinement in reform school—three months spent naked, in utter darkness in a tiny concrete cell, subsisting on a single meal each day (food laced with soap designed to induce diarrhea) is a *tour de force* of naturalistic style. Carpenter's sharp prose, his ability to show Levitt transformed by his ordeal, reminded me of passages in Alexander Solzhenitsyn's *One Day in the Life of Ivan Denisovich* and Dostoevsky's *House of the Dead*, the touchstones for novels dissecting the psychological effects of imprisonment. As more Americans find themselves slipping from respectability into debt and marginality, and for 2.2 million of our fellow citizens in prison, the insights of writers like Carpenter, a marginal figure himself, assume greater weight.

But Carpenter doesn't believe in the triumph of the human spirit, and Levitt isn't transformed into a saint by his ordeal. He's a thoughtful and complex figure, but loutish—the offspring of a society that puts the highest premium on wealth and breeding while denying to most individuals the means of attaining either one. Levitt exists in a moral limbo, a world that has its own rules and rituals, but a world from which there is no escape, where following the rules keeps one alive but not much more. The rule of American naturalistic fiction is that one's genetic predispositions and socio-economic circumstances cannot be overcome through the exercise of will or through love, money, God, or anything else. As was the case with poor Carrie Buck, Jack Levitt is condemned by a society that has no use for his kind—no romantic outlaw, Levitt is among the many victims of the great American hustle.

G.O.

Not All of the Ravages

Not all of the ravages caused by our merciless age are tangible ones. The subtler forms of destruction, those involving only the human spirit, are the most to be dreaded.
Paul Bowles

Sometime just after finishing graduate school in New York, I (like thousands of other young men of my background and temperament) found myself bewitched by the life and work of Paul Bowles. So lost, so aimless, so claustrophobic did I feel in that city, did I feel in my skin, that I all but inhaled his keenly wrought stories of American alienation, psychic disintegration, and exotic (sometimes erotic) encounters with the foreign, the cryptic, the strange. I smoked, I read avidly, I wandered the lonely streets of New York some days, praying for a vision, a sign, some encounter that would open up the world to me, that would force me to commit myself to something meaningful at last. If that sounds melodramatic it *is*, I *was*. "Who am I? What am I to the world?" I wondered daily, a question to which Bowles (at least in his fiction) was quick to reply: "Not much."

It was the humbling I needed. After all I was broke; I

wrote poorly, pretentiously; I had no real prospects at all—at least none that beckoned me. At the time I was working fifty-one weeks a year as an assistant editor at a local publishing house. My title, so it turned out, was meaningless: my job had nothing to do with editing, little to do with books, with their content anyhow. I was a factotum, plain and simple, so that most of my days were spent trying to look busy, filing papers, managing correspondence, and paginating by hand the many manuscripts submitted to us by authors who hadn't bothered to number the pages. Still a change was in the offing; I could feel it. I grew restless, more determined than ever to get out of the country for a while, to test myself, to travel. That was when I met Annie, my wife-to-be, an aspiring printmaker and painter. We became inseparable, when one day she asked me to travel with her to Japan.

It was there in Japan that summer that I read Bowles' novels, *The Sheltering Sky*, *The Spider's House*, and *Let It Come Down*, and suddenly my future was plain: I would travel and write. Indeed over the following nine summers, with the money we earned as teachers, Annie and I travelled widely—to India (twice), South Africa, Swaziland, Mozambique, Mexico (multiple times), France, Italy, Germany, Belgium, Holland, Sweden, Costa Rica, Venezuela, China, Hong Kong, Bali, Nepal, and Thailand, where—more in love than ever—we got married in a civil ceremony in Bangkok, passing that hot summer night with Thai friends aboard one of the popular dinner cruises there, laughing, drinking Thai whiskey, and admiring the ancient, flood-lit temples along the busy Chao Phraya River.

It was upon our return from that summer in Japan that I resolved to write to Bowles himself. Why not? What did I have to lose? At once I crafted a letter to him and sent it off to his publisher, praising his work and taking the opportunity (in all my youthful presumption) to tell him about a novel of my own, a distinctly Bowlesesque tale involving a disaffected young American couple adrift in Japan, which I'd entitled *The Shadow Eaters*, after an essay on Buddhism by Lafcadio Hearn.

Many months passed with no reply, so that I soon forgot about the letter. Then one day I received a surprise:

```
                                                    1/viii/88

Peter Adam Nash,
101 East 91st Street,
New York, N. Y.

Dear Mr. Nash:

        Thank you for your affable letter. It's always pleasant
to hear laudatory words about one's work coming from a fellow
writer. Your suggestion of my being able to give you advice
on your project is meaningless, however, since I'd be speak-
ing in a vacuum. And as for my own writing, the last thing
I want to do is make comments about it, even though you do
specify The Sheltering Sky. The only comment I can make about
writing in general is that one mustn't think about it; that's
an occupation as useless as thinking about swimming if one
wants exercise.
        I hope to have the pleasure of reading The Shadow Eaters
when it appears.

                                        Sincerely,

                                        Paul Bowles
```

While I had no faith that *The Shadow Eaters* would ever appear in print, he—Paul Bowles—had written me back! What's more he'd referred to me as a fellow writer. No one had ever called me that. For the first time in my life I felt an urgency, a connection to some greater human project, that compelled me to read and write with an intensity and purpose I had never felt before.

In the ensuing months I read every story of his I could find, only to work my way, with insight and pleasure, while taking copious notes, through his autobiography, his essays, his poems, as well as his translations of the work the Moroccans Mohamed Choukri and Mohammed Mrabet. To top it off I read the singular fiction and letters of his brilliant and ailing wife, Jane Bowles—an adventure, an experience, I would recommend to everyone.

It was Bowles' short story "A Distant Episode" that most impressed me. Recognized widely as his "*ur*-tale", that work that speaks most directly to his vision of life, it is a chilling story about a European linguist who travels to Morocco in search of new dialects only to be captured by some villagers who—in an act as symbolic as it is brutal—cut out his tongue. "It certainly takes its place," writes James Lasdun, "as one of our civilization's more disturbing premonitions of its own breakdown." Be sure to brace yourself for this one.

P.N.

The Mirror of the World

Divan of Ghalib, Nachoem M. Wijnberg

*The human
image remains imprisoned
in the mirror of the world.*
Ghalib

Mirza Asadullah Baig Khan, whose *takhallus*, or pen-name, was Ghalib ("most excellent"), was born in Agra during the twilight of the Mughal Empire, though he lived most of his life in Delhi. Ghalib's traditional divan contains 234 ghazals as well as Urdu poems in other styles. Ghalib also composed poetry and prose works in Persian, including a history of the 1857 Mutiny. Virtually all translators and commentators (over one hundred commentaries on Ghalib's ghazals exist) agree that the task of translating Ghalib is a "doomed mission" [Frances W. Pritchett], and agree that Ghalib was *mushkil-panand*—a lover of complexity.

I have spent parts of the past few days admiring a handful of the ghazals in various translations (Niazi, Ahmed Ali, as well as adaptations from other European languages by W.S. Merwin, Adrienne Rich, and others). I also reread Nabokov's 1941 *New Republic* article, "On the Art of Translation," written as the polyglot novelist revised his version of Pushkin:

> *"We can deduce now the requirements that a translator must possess in order to be able to give an ideal version of a foreign masterpiece. First of all he must have as much talent, or at least the same kind of talent, as the author he chooses. In this, though only in this, respect Baudelaire and Poe or Joukovsky and Schiller made ideal playmates. Second, he must know thoroughly the two nations and the two languages involved and be perfectly acquainted with all details relating to his author's manner and methods; also, with the social background of words, their fashions, history and period associations. This leads to the third point: while having genius and knowledge he must possess the gift of mimicry and be able to act, as it were, the real author's part by impersonating his tricks of demeanor and speech, his ways and his mind, with the utmost degree of verisimilitude."*

No doubt Nabokov considered himself *nearly* up to the task of *Eugene Onegin*—but to render Ghalib's subtle and delicate love poems from Urdu to English—to have assimilated not only the languages but the "author's manner and methods," his "social background," his "demeanor"—who could achieve so much, and how might we, as readers without Urdu or any other Nabokovian qualification, hope to make sense of this great poet?

While I was reading Nachoem M. Wijnberg's poems for (in honor of, as homage to, based on, etc.) Ghalib in David Colmer's fine translation, I had in mind this sentence from the collection's forward, written, presumably, by Colmer: "[*Divan of Ghalib*] is a book of English translations of the Dutch poems Nachoem Wijnberg wrote for Ghalib and with Ghalib and to Ghalib." This clarification—if you can call it that—at first I thought White Pine had sent me a collection of translations of Ghalib by a Dutch poet translated into English by an Australian—not only enhanced my interest in the book (beautifully gotten up, as all WP books are) but let me off the hook: no need to fret about the accuracy or spirit of the translations. This was a straightforward literary transaction: a book of poems Englished from a comfortable (bourgeois!) language from which even I could wrestle some words, a *hommage* (of sorts) rather than another attempt to climb the mountain of Ghalib's esoteric genius.

This is familiar territory for me, this realm of the poetic *transformation* rather than translation. I have enough German to know that Rilke's sublime *Duino Elegies* are untranslatable (William Gass has a book on the subject of not translating Rilke), and Kenneth Rexroth's versions of Tu Fu—among my favorite poems—have always felt more like Rexroth channeling Tu Fu than surmounting the multiple Nabokovian hurdles to rendering a man as little known to us as, say, Lao

Tzu. Rexroth worked with the Chinese scholar Ling Chung on his versions of Chinese poetry; but of course Rexroth had many languages, and he was among the last poets to have read *everything*. I also love reading and comparing various versions of grad school standbys like *Beowulf,* wondering all the while if Michael Alexander, Burton Raffel, and Seamus Heaney had even read the same poem. But then there's John Gardner's wonderful *Grendel*, and that, patient reader, brings us at last to Wijnberg's Ghalib.

G.O.

An Algerian Doll's House

*Today I believe in the possibility of love; that is why
endeavor to trace its imperfections, its perversions.*
                                            Franz Fanon

How very sad it is that Ali Ghalem's novel *A Wife for My Son* is out of print, indeed long out of print, as it is one of the most complex, most moving explorations I've ever read of what it means to be a Muslim today, in this case an Algerian Muslim woman struggling hard to define herself amidst the competing claims of traditional Islam and those of the modern, European world. Originally published in 1979 as *Une femme por mon fils*, it is a charged, highly nuanced treatment of the twisted, often crippling ways in which men and women are taught—thus fated—to relate to one another through the traditions that bind them.

A Wife For My Son, writes critic Doris Tentchoff (and so trenchantly I must quote her at length), "underscores the observation that the personal is political and links the personal struggle to the world stage as it chronicles the story of seventeen-year-old Fatiha's determined struggle to gain control over her life after a traditional arranged marriage to an Algerian who toils in France as a guest worker. Drawing on the multiplicity of strands that constitute the plight of this pair, Ghalem weaves a revealing portrait of working-class life in contemporary Algeria. And because he probes intimate family relationships, the books confronts the intransigent problem: how to transform structures at the core of society—the relationships between women and men? Given Ghalem's unflinchingly feminist stance, the novel is remarkable for its lack of rancor, for the compassion with which its main characters are depicted. Concern is not with an abstract good and evil, but with human beings who, for historical reasons, are locked into vastly disparate and unbridgeable worlds, each predicated on different presuppositions and operating according to a different cultural logic. The yawning gap in perceptions, expectations, and aspirations between middle-aged working-class parents on the one hand, and their offspring on the other, produces spiraling rounds of misunderstanding, conflict, and crisis."

The story, with its fearless exploration of the relationship between the personal and political, is further intensified when one considers it against the backdrop of recent history, namely that of the French colonization of Algeria, a century-long period of tyranny and exploitation that culminated in a frenzy of bloodshed and destruction in the French-Algerian war.

At the heart of this national self-determination, a struggle writ small in the character of Fatiha, were such philosophers and political lions as Franz Fanon and Albert Camus, who helped to flesh out the tensions between France and Algeria that persist to this day.

Compared by one critic to Ibsen's revolutionary play, *A Doll's House*, *A Wife for My Son* treats the condition of modern Muslim women, and of women in general, with even greater frankness and depth. Not only does Fatiha slam the door on her husband, so to speak, but she renounces the entire patriarchal system by leaving him and his home, determined to live by her own terms, to raise her newly born child alone. As a final act of hope she names her daughter Noura or "light".

P.N.

Vampires, Lumps, and Curlicues

I was already dyspeptic, feverish, out of sorts this morning when I came upon Michiko Kakutani's review of Karen Russell's new book, *Vampires in the Lemon Grove*. I said to my dogs—"Guys, why does the lead book-chat person of the *New York Times*—arguably the most influential critic in America—devote her column to yet another book about the undead?"

> *"A vampire couple who live in an Italian lemon grove, a pack of girls sent away by their werewolf parent to be educated by nuns, a minotaur and his human family joining the great westward American migration . . ."*

Not that I dislike vampires—not when one of the greatest actors of all time, Klaus Kinski, gave life (so to speak) to the dead in the 1979 Werner Herzog remake of my all-time favorite horror film, *Nosferatu, eine Symphonie des Grauens*, the genuinely freaky 1922 German Expressionist version of Bram Stoker's *Dracula* directed by F.W. Murnau, starring the positively blood-curdling Max Schreck as Count Orlok (I thought, *a great name for a pug*). But these guys—Kinski and Schreck were *real vampires*—they weren't pretty boys and nubile starlets with a dribble of fake blood on their chins— these two were the stuff of nightmares, all those odd-ball Herzog close-ups, and that limbic shadowland Murnau used to evoke the Freudian netherworlds of human fears come to life. Kinski gave me the creeps in everything he was in—he looked like a demented David Bowie—and in make-up he was my id come to life.

It's bad enough that even vampires have to be metrosexuals now, but then Ms. Kakutani goes on to criticize Russell's *style—style?* I said to the dogs: "This is a book about vampires and we're worrying about *style?*"

> "*Vampires in the Lemon Grove shows Ms. Russell more in control of her craft than ever: the occasional curlicues of language that distracted the reader's attention [!] in her earlier books have been tamed in these pages, and the structural lumps in 'Swamplandia' have given way here to finely hammered stories that have* an organic shape and speed." [my emphasis]

Organic speed? Hammered stories? I liked Karen Russell's *Swamplandia!* and even enjoyed the "curlicues of language"—that is, the style and voice—in which the book was written. I mentioned to Rosie, our heeler, that language and "lumps" are *the whole point* –"What's this woman want? Who doesn't *like* a lumpy story?" What would Ms. Kakutani make of any random sentence from Kertesz or Bernhard or

Robert Walser—talk about lumpiness! I remember when MK trashed David Foster Wallace's *Infinite Jest* for being too long, self-indulgent, *inorganic*. Why do we read if not to be scared out of our wits by great prose, by style and language that clots up like the blessed little formless dough balls in our oatmeal? Do we want our vampires well groomed, with two hundred dollar haircuts? Boys and girls out of Vogue and GQ? No: I want creepy Klaus, drooling out of the deformed hole that was his mouth, sniffing around his victims like a rabid dog—talk about lumps!

So I put the paper down, went to work, and as soon as I could, I reread a story by the great Dutch writer Nescio (Jan Frederik Grönloh, 1882-1961) called "Insula Dei." This story is collected, with a handful of Nescio's other writings, in *Amsterdam Stories*, published by New York Review Books. No vampires are to be found in this little gem of a tale about finding God in wartime and trying to find meaning in memory:

> *"You want to do something, make a difference. But these aren't the first eventful times I've lived through and if I'm granted even more years then with God's help I will most likely get to my third war. The silent course of things takes its silent, implacable course, the little man who is a hero today will tomorrow, when peace comes, be scolded in his stupid little job or maybe won't have a job at all and will turn back into the useless piece of clockwork he used to be."*

Not all sentences go straight, not all writers eschew lumps, not all readers want their prose forged.... Not all of the undead are vampires.

Grönloh was born in Amsterdam, was director of a trading company, had four daughters, and wrote just a handful of short tales in what is considered, by those who know Dutch, to be the finest modern examples of that language. The NYRB has a nice introduction by Joseph O'Neill whose *Netherland* (2008) is splendid—a novel about New York City and cricket.

G.O.

Haitian Alphabet: One Soul's Rising

Tired of zombie stories, movies, television series, and video games? If so, try Haitian Jean-Euphèle Milcé's searing short novel *Alphabet of the Night*. It may be the antidote you need. Set in the smoke-blackened capital city of Port-au-Prince during the dying days of the Duvalier regime, in the very land where the zombie (*zonbi* in Haitian Creole) was born, this story—for all its zombies and voodoo, for all its bloodshed and violence—offers little titillation for those weaned on Hollywood, Max Brooks, and AMC. What it offers instead is a portrait of a gravely wounded man and nation haunted by corpses, the missing, and the walking, still-talking dead.

After the daylight murder of his lover, Lucien, Jewish shopkeeper Jeremy Assaël decides to leave his cursed and lawless homeland for good, but not before discovering the fate of his childhood friend and one-time lover, a mulatto named Fresnel, who mysteriously disappeared. By the time the novel opens, the Duvalier family has ruled the country for nearly thirty years through a strategy of corruption and terror: an estimated 30,000 Haitians have been murdered by "Papa Doc" Duvalier's security forces, thousands "disappeared", and tens of thousands more exploited, terrorized, and finally forced to flee the country with nothing—quite literally—but the clothes on their backs.

Jeremy Assaël's quest to learn the fate of his missing friend and lover takes him on a journey through the hell of contemporary Haiti, in the course of which he encounters a broad sampling of the Devil's disciples: government henchmen, foreign aid workers, Catholic priests and Brothers, Protestant missionaries, Rotarians, and even a German Consul General. Commencing his journey on All Souls' Day, an important Catholic holiday of alms-giving and prayers for the dead trapped in purgatory (Dante, by contrast, begins his journey through Hell on the day before Good Friday), the narrator has first to make his way through the raucous celebrations, celebrations which, while ostensibly Catholic, are in practice something more. Indeed in Haiti, All Souls' Day has a special resonance for the descendants of African slaves, mixed with voodoo, as it is, and informed by the deep-seeded fear that one's deceased loved ones have becomes zombies, dead people who cannot get across to *lan guinée* (literally Guinea, or West Africa), the leafy-green paradise of their ancestors. Only through the intervention of a voodoo priest and the execution of an elaborate series of rituals can the dead be so freed.

Near the end of the novel, the narrator himself meets a *hougan*, a voodoo priest, who helps him to complete his quest. For like his black compatriots, Jeremy Assaël yearns to discover, if only in a secular sense, if his lover, Fresnel, has become a *zonbi* or crossed safely to *lan guinée*.

P.N.

Hell

The Theory and Practice of Hell, Eugen Kogon
Life and Fate, Vassily Grossman
The Kindly Ones, Jonathan Littell
Stalingrad: The Fateful Siege, Antony Beevor

"We ourselves, even if we must rise up from the grave,
will deal with those who break the oath I take -
baffle them with disasters, curse their marches,

> *send them hawks on the left at every crossing -*
> *make their pains recoil upon their heads."*
> (*The Eumenides*, 779-784, Trans. Robert Fagles)

In his brilliant novel *Life and Fate*, Vassily Grossman—a Jewish journalist who reported from inside Red Army units throughout the war—explores the events that surrounded the fateful Battle of Stalingrad with an eye for historical detail that reminds one of Tolstoy. Every one of the hundred or so characters in his sprawling novel of one of history's greatest battles is a victim of fate. No one escapes the war, the Holocaust, the enforced starvation imposed by Stalin on the Ukraine, the torture chambers of Beria and the NKVD, or the execution squads of the *Sonderkommandos*. In the Great Leader's mad dystopia every janitor spies on her building's residents, loyal workers turn in their bosses for off-handed criticisms of the regime, and parents casually consider ratting out their own children when they stray from the Party line. For Grossman, the structure of bureaucracies, the requirement of unquestioning obedience, is what makes mass murder possible. The Party, as a fascist organization, has systematically stripped away the concept of a shared humanity, confiscated the "traitors'" government-issued identification cards, turned ordinary men and women into non-persons, and then—what else?—killed them. As we know from Antony Beevor's study of the Battle of Stalingrad, in the midst of the June invasion Stalin was busy ordering the deaths of as many members of his armed forces as the invading Germans were massacring in the one-sided battles of that first summer. Retreat in the Red Army was punishable by death; capture was treasonous; questioning an order, no matter how insane, was the end of an officer's career and likely his life. Stalin ordered the murder over 36,000 officers in the purges of 1937-1938. What occurred in 1941was a continuation of the regime's *modus operandi*. Beevor informs us that two million Soviet soldiers and an uncounted number of civilians died during the first three weeks of Barbarossa. Here is a number I cannot comprehend, so I scroll through as many photographs of soldiers and civilians as I can find on the internet (there are many). I force myself to look at pictures that will keep me awake. Two million.

Look around your peaceful house and yard (or the view from your apartment window). Then try to imagine this world, evoked so devastatingly by Jonathan Littell:

> *"If the awful massacres of the East prove one thing, paradoxically, it is the awful, inalterable solidarity of humanity. As brutalized and habituated as they may have become, none of our men could kill a Jewish woman without thinking about his wife, his sister or his mother, or kill a Jewish child without seeing his own children in front of him in the pit. Their reaction, their violence, their alcoholism, the nervous depressions, the suicides, my own sadness, all that demonstrated that the other exists, exists as an other, as a human, and that no will, no ideology, no amount of stupidity or alcohol can break this bond, tenuous but not indestructible." (The Kindly Ones).*

When Littell's novel was published to acclaim in France I was eager to read it. When it was translated by Charlotte Mandell in 2009 (the French edition came out in 2006) the American reviews were mostly negative. Famously panned by both David Gates (whom I respect) and Michiko Kakutani (whose literary taste I don't share) in the *Times*— "obscene," "disgusting," "hopeless," "executed by a sadist," and so forth. I wondered if any of the book's severest critics had ever read a Greek tragedy where sadism, incest, and murder are commonplace. Or if Ms. Kakutani, upset by the graphic depiction of Holocaust atrocities, had read Raul Hilberg's or Saul Friedlander's meticulously researched histories of the war in the East? Or seen a Quentin Tarantino film. *The Kindly Ones* is deeply upsetting, but Littell's literary intelligence should be apparent to any serious reader. Not only has he told in tedious and banal detail (one thinks of Hannah Arendt's ill-considered subtitle, her story of Eichmann, indeed a banal figure, a character who has a cameo in *The Kindly Ones*) the horrifying story of the massacres of Jewish, partisan, gypsy, and Slavic populations across the Eastern front, and then, when you think you can't take any more, goes on to describe the living hell of Auschwitz, the bureaucratic world of the camps so chillingly rendered by Eugen Kogen in his autobiographical *Theory and Practice of Hell.* In other words, Littell provides a graphic account of the *Rassenkampf* on the Eastern front.

But that isn't the whole of it. *The Kindly Ones* is also a deeply moral story—and I'm surprised that most critics didn't see this—for Maximilien Aue, the monster at the heart of Littell's novel, is the mouthpiece for a story that probes the Hobbesian assumption of a war of all against all. Few of the monsters of Aue's tale are sadists. Most are the "ordinary men" of Christopher Browning's books. Though Aue narrates his tale of horror and genocide after the fact, and while he is by no means a credible witness to his own actions, the novel relates the evolution of human degradation in a way that is not so much believable as fated. Aue takes mincing steps toward embracing his corrupt soul, or perhaps, better, his authentic self. He is appalled, sickened, by the first murders he witnesses—he vomits continually, drinks to dull the pain, and engages in a ceaseless rationalizing dialogue that invokes duty, honor, philosophy, and history. But never politics. Aue hasn't a political bone in his body; he never speaks of Hitler except in reporting another officer's opinion of the Führer. Gradually, over hundreds of pages and thousands of murders, Aue is able to rationalize his clerk's role in the unfolding genocide. But even this much wouldn't make *The Kindly Ones* a great novel—there's sadism enough in contemporary literature. At the heart of the novel is something worse than depictions of mass murder, serial sodomy, incest, and matricide—this is a novel that succeeds in negating all of the assumptions of Western rationality and Christian morality. Littell sets out to show us that what took thousands of years to build was destroyed in the ravine of Babi Yar on three September days. Aue might have been a character plucked from Thomas Mann: an educated German bourgeois, but one who, in Littell's version of the world, finds himself stepping over dead people, delivering the *coup de grace*.

What is the duty of a writer when faced with monumental historical events? Should fiction release us from the discomfort of terrible truths or immerse us in them, forcing us to come to terms with the past, to make sense of it as best we can, and if we can't, well, as Michael Korda crudely put it in his review of Littell, "tough shit." Should we have to squirm and flinch and feel nauseous ourselves? Has Littell gone too far?

> *"[Littell] isn't trying to make you feel good about yourself, or feel morally superior to the Germans, or come away from the book with the feeling that anything has been gained or proved by the murder in cold blood of six million people. Most of the people who did it got away with it, like the hero of this novel, and didn't lose a night's sleep over it, and the people who were murdered are—dead. Deader than dead, actually, because all over the world there are people who refuse to believe that they were ever killed in the first place, not just among jihadists, or in the Arab mainstream press, or in the tattooed ranks of the Aryan Nation, or Catholic bishops, but also among otherwise respectable people and educators who still don't get it that perfectly ordinary Germans committed mass murder, then, when the war was over, went home and got on with their lives, and even collected their pensions." (Korda, The Daily Beast)*

Neither Littell nor Grossman lets the reader off the hook. After two novels totaling 1700 pages the lesson is that...there is no lesson. "We should learn about the mass murders of the Second World War—in Kiev, in Nanjing, or, for that matter, in Dresden and Hiroshima so that events like these don't happen again."

Really? I'm afraid I've lost my faith in history's catechism.

Here's Aue:

> *"Why couldn't an SS-Obersturmbannfuhrer have an inner life, desires, passions, just like any other man? There have been hundreds of thousands of us whom you still judge as criminals: among them, as among all human beings, there were ordinary men, of course, but also extraordinary men....I started out within the bounds of my service and then, under the pressure of events, I overstepped these bounds.... Those who kill are humans, just as those who are killed, that's what terrible...I tell you, I am just like you!"*

I applaud Littell for not resorting to Nietzschean nonsense—the Superman above others who must fulfill his romantic destiny by killing a bunch of women and children—and for taking the time to make Aue's monstrosity if not credible at least not trivial. Aue devolves from a man into a demon, but must we accept the moral of the story to be something stupid like "There but for fortune go you and I?" We know that many men refused to participate in the *aktions*. War is hell, but some wars are more hell than others. Beevor argues that a significant proportion of the Wehrmacht's officers posted to Stalingrad were not in sympathy with National Socialist ideology, and yet they knew about, and did not protest, the reprisals undertaken against Ukrainian and Soviet civilians, partisans, Slavs, and Jews. Grossman is especially good on this point. *Life and Fate* is full of men and women who capitulate out of a terrible fear of not doing so. Party members sell their souls to Stalin. Soviet commanders sent thousands of men to their deaths rather than question an order. Germans and Red Army soldiers alike ignored the suffering of civilians. Not life and fate, but life against fate.

Here's a lesson: it isn't a fair fight.

Many years ago, when I first began to read serious books, I was hoping to discover a unique form of enjoyment, one that bound my reason to my feelings. As I got older I read serious books in order to understand something that I could never pin down. Now, in my late age, I read to be confounded, nothing less. Here are four books to do just that.

G.O.

The Troubles

"*Ils ont les chagrins qu'ont les vierges et les paresseux,*" quotes Elizabeth Bowen from Proust's *À la recherche du temps perdu* for the epigraph of her monumental novel *The Last September*, in this way preparing the readers for the sorrows and heartbreak to come. Set in Ireland, in the year 1920, the story centers upon a lonely teenaged orphan named Lois Farquhar living with her wealthy uncle and aunt, Sir Richard and Lady Myra Naylor, in their country home in County Cork. Still reeling from the wounds and uncertainty of the Great War, from its material and spiritual depredations, the characters in this novel are forced to confront the civil unrest in Ireland itself, the Irish War of Independence or *Cogadh na Saoirse* (1919-1921), with its rapidly escalating violence between the British forces and the Irish rebels, the IRA, who remain determined—to the last man and woman—to drive the English out of Ireland for good. It is an anger and hostility directed not only at the British soldiers, the Black and Tans, as they were known, but also, indeed especially, at the wealthy Anglo-Irish gentry or "Protestant Ascendency", people like the Naylors, who for centuries, and for all of their loyalty to England, have been happy to call Ireland their home.

Such country estates or "Big Houses" as owned by the Naylors and their class (which class included Bowen's own family with their house called Bowen's Court) had flourished throughout Ireland since the mid-eighteenth century, built with the easy profits that came of cheap land and cheap labor, making them a potent symbol of English exploitation and an easy target for the rebels who burned down, blew up, or otherwise destroyed more than 275 of them in the years between 1920 and 1923.

This is the very danger that threatens the Naylors in *The Last September* who struggle, throughout the story, to maintain the illusion of happiness and security by throwing dinner parties, playing tennis, and generally carrying on as if their fate—the signs of which are everywhere apparent—is not yet sealed. Only Lois, their niece, has the chance to escape this doom, if only she can get free. This simple story, in the hands of Elizabeth Bowen, achieves a moral depth and complexity, an artistic resonance, that has earned it the distinction of being one of the great novels of the twentieth century. For a High Modernist like Bowen, at least half of the tale is in its telling, in its style and language, which is sharp with angles and rich with metaphor and symbol, so that the novel is as poetic in its prose as it is compelling in its plot.

Differently, if equally affecting, is William's Trevor's short, melancholy novel *The Story of Lucy Gault*. Set in the same time period as *The Last September*—indeed under almost identical circumstances—in an Anglo-Irish manor house called Lahardane, this haunting story opens upon an evening when Captain Everard Gault, the latest in a long line of Irish-born Gaults, fires upon a trespasser whom he suspects is a Catholic rebel trying to burn down his house, triggering a chain of events that proves tragic for him, his wife, and his daughter, Lucy, as they are forced—each in his or her own way—to pay their history's dues. A spare, finely-felt tale, it was described in the *San Francisco Chronicle* as "A perfect Irish ballad in prose: sad, fateful and impossible to get out of your head."

P.N.

The Man With the Golden Pencil

Nelson Algren, *Chicago: City on the Make*

He was the son of Polish Jews, born in Detroit. Like Joseph Mitchell, Pete Dexter, Mark Royko, A. J. Liebling, Luc Sante, and a handful of others, Algren wrote about urban life without mentioning the swells. Chicago, where he lived for most of his life, provided him with his subject matter—the hard lives of working-class men and women, the scams of grifters and politicians, the tragedy of bad choices or of no choices at all. His best-known novel, *The Man With A Golden Arm* possesses the same foreboding sense of doom as James T. Farrell's Studs Lonigan trilogy—the city's dynamics, its teeming inner life, bring out some of what is best and all of what is worst in everyone. Survival is possible, but at great cost, and much that other writers think of as growing out of our ethical nature, in fact depends upon blind chance. In other words, Algren, like many of the other naturalists of the period just before and just after the Second World War, worked within the social Darwinian framework exploited for different purposes by racists like William Graham Sumner and Theodore Roosevelt—the difference being that Algren and his journalist/novelist brethren felt compassion for the victims of an economic and social system that exploited everyone's worst instincts.

He had an affair with Simone de Beauvoir in the late 40s and early 50s (Algren is "Lewis Brogan" in *The Mandarins*), was investigated by the FBI (a badge of honor in those days; Algren never joined the Party, and though he was a man of the Left, he wasn't especially political), and he was condemned by his own Chicago Polish community for his novel *Never Come Morning*. His 1956 novel, *A Walk on the Wild Side,* has the distinction of being the darkest of *noir* writing—the plot reads like an Elizabethan revenge tragedy—drunks, prostitutes, pimps, orphans, and murderers (dark enough to inspire Lou Reed). Algren at his best makes Jim Harrison seem upbeat. Algren disliked fiction that tipped over into propaganda or sociology. His characters are real, if unimaginable. I picked up *Naked Lunch* the other day to see if there was any Algren in Burroughs. Not a drop. Algren brings the purity of art to his stories. Burroughs rambles on like Falstaff—a junky jester.

Not precisely the home of the Blues, but close enough, Chicago's African-American population has known/knows a thing or two about hard living. (See Wayne F. Miller, *Chicago's South Side, 1946-1948*). The lyrical element in the music of someone like Jimmy Davis is reflected in Algren's prose, especially in the essay under review here. *Chicago: City on the Make*, like many a blues lament, is a love-hate song:

"My baby done me wrong, but I can't live without her..."
Here's a sample:

> *"Chicago keeps two faces...one for sunlit traffic's noontime bustle. And one for midnight subway watches when stations swing past like ferris wheels of light, yet leave the moving window wet with rain or tears."*

> *"When chairs are stacked and glasses are turned and arc-lamps all are dimmed. By days when the wind bangs alley gates ajar and the sun goes by on the wind. By nights when the moon is an only child above the measured thunder of the cars, you may know Chicago's heart at last:*

> *You'll know it's the place built out of Man's ceaseless failure to overcome himself. Out of Man's endless war against himself we build our successes as well as our failures. Making it the city of all cities most like Man himself—loneliest creation of all this very old poor earth."*

In Algren's hands Chicago becomes what it is in geographic terms—the middle ground dividing us. Saul Bellow loved Chicago but yearned for New York. Algren was all about the odd perch of Porkopolis on Lake Michigan. Chicago is our grasping nature, our vulnerability, our indifference to others, our rare but genuine compassion, our imagination and our banality. In the end, what wins out depends on the man or woman. The City, any city, has a life of its own, disconnected from ours ("like the indifferent stars" as Algren puts it). The city is the theater in which we act out the tragicomic existence of human life. The Mandarin herself found Algren (at first) charming, hard-edged, a man of conviction—perhaps unlike her Parisian lover. Later on he bored her, or perhaps he acted badly—probably he did act badly. He sometimes did.

He was hardly a writer's writer. In a Paris Review interview (1955) Algren disavows connections with just about every other writer, including Hemingway, though he grudgingly admitted to admiring Hemingway's style. Algren says a lot of interesting things about the craft of writing, including this:

> *"I do have the feeling that other writers can't help you with writing. I've gone to writers' conferences and writers' sessions and writers' clinics, and the more I see of them, the more I'm sure it's the wrong direction. It isn't the place where you learn to write. I've always felt strongly that a writer shouldn't be engaged with other writers, or with people who make books, or even with people who read them. I think the farther away you get from the literary traffic, the closer you are to sources. I mean, a writer doesn't really live, he observes."*

*A writer doesn't really live...*though Algren did live, richly. Does one choose to write, or does writing choose you? Algren had no choice—writing was his means of living, of making a living, but also the way he made sense of the world. I suppose he's a footnote in American literary history; his early books are just coming back into print. It's a shame—he should be better known since his world and this one aren't all that different.

Algren died in, of all places, Sag Harbor, on Long Island, in 1981.

G.O.

Death In (Not Venice but) Rome

"*Death in Rome* is the most devastating novel about the Germans that I have ever read," writes translator Michael Hofmann in his introduction, a case he makes persuasive even before one considers the tale itself.

In the aftermath of World War II, German writers were forced to pick up the pieces of their world, while somehow coming to terms with the murder and destruction that they (and their parents and grandparents) had wrought. As the losers and "villains" of the war, villains of a stripe not seen in Europe before, their task was markedly different than that of, say, the French intellectuals and writers in Paris, whom I touched upon in my earlier essay on Simone de Beauvoir. Some German writers, writers such as Arno Schmidt and Günter Eich, found it too much or not useful to confront the past directly, choosing instead to explore German racism, violence, and guilt through means more symbolic and abstract.

Then too there was the need, the desire, to forget, to start afresh. After a brief (some would say unconscionably brief) period of moral scrutiny the country was ready to move on, an instinct, a compulsion, that soon gave rise to the post-war "German Miracle" or *Wirtschaftswunder*, a surge in economic growth and cultural regeneration, a "phoenix act," for which many German writers (not to mention German politicians) were happy to write the script. As Hofmann remarks, the *status quo ante* 1933 was not restored after the war: "Instead, the story was one of discontinuity. It was as though the literature had been bombed as the cities had been."

Indeed many of the new generation of writers, like those of the controversial *Gruppe 47*, chose to make a clean break from the country's literary-historical past, as represented by Thomas Mann, to turn their backs on the war, the results and verdict of which seemed clear enough. As Aaron Dennis Horton writes, "This group of writers believed their work represented a new beginning for German literature, just as 1945, the so-called "zero hour," allegedly signified the start of a new era in German history, separate from the Nazi past." Writing what came to be known as *Trümmerliteratur* or "rubble literature," they were determined to start with a clean slate, their focus the here and now, the future rising fast before their eyes. This is not to say that these writers denied or attempted to ignore German culpability in the war, only that they were sometimes conflicted in their aims. Most notable among them were Alfred Andersch, Heinrich Böll, Siegfried Lenz, and Günter Grass, all of whom served under Hitler but were ardently anti-Nazi. With two Nobel laureates among them, they are undoubtedly some of the best-known German writers in the world.

Then there were the lonely, lesser-known writers like Wolfgang Koeppen whose relentless condemnation of the new Germany, with its collective amnesia and devotion to Mammon, now rings like a bell. Shaped by the works of Proust, Kafka, Faulkner, Woolf, and Mann, he came of age as a writer in the 1930s then fled. In the words of Hoffman, "He went abroad. He wasn't a Nazi. He returned." Unfortunately the cultural landscape had changed, so that his novels of the 1950s, "works of memory and continuance and criticism," were met with widespread reproach and contempt, savaged by "the modish and dirigible German public" for their often brutal candor at a time when Germans were just beginning to like themselves again.

Of those novels, *Death in Rome* is an especially trenchant look at the sickness and psychology of post-war Germans. Focusing on the reunion of a large German family in Rome in the early 1950s, a story of fathers and sons, husbands and wives, cousins and cousins, the real *Geist* of the story is the megalomaniacal, "unreconstructed and unkillable SS man" Gottlieb Judejahn, who—on the run and uncover of false identity papers—storms about the ruins of Rome, addled by dreams of Valhalla and the certain redemption of *Grossdeutschland*.

The title's echoing of Mann's *Death in Venice* is particularly apt. Written (as was *Death in Venice*) with a combination of what Mann called "myth plus psychology," *Death In Rome* is densely layered with allusions to Scandinavian mythology (so dear to the Nazis) and to the near-mythical German history in Rome, from Alaric the Goth to the Holy Roman Emperor Charlemagne to "Der Führer," Adolf Hitler. That Mann's novella—shot through with contagion and death—was also a study in moral responsibility must surely have appealed to Koeppen as well.

Of the author, finally, Hofmann writes, "There is something implacable, almost vindictive—like one of his Furies—about his pursuit of the Germans post-war, post-Holocaust, post-division, turning away from their crimes towards rehabilitation and their EC, once again exporting their goods and their culture and themselves. He shows them to us. All of them." Like his Austrian counterpart, Thomas Bernhard, Koeppen was never afraid to dirty his own nest.*

* For his vociferous criticism of his homeland, Austria, Bernhard was frequently criticized as a *Nestbeschmutzer*, one who dirties his own nest.

P.N.

Distant Fathers

A Distant Father, Antonio Skarmeta

This illustration is "The Death of Adam," from Piero Della Francesca's great fresco on the Western wall of San Francesco Church in Arezzo. There are three narratives here, and, following the model of most medieval storytelling, they are juxtaposed within the flattened picture plane of this single image.

On the right, seated, is Adam, father of us all, who is sending his son Seth to the Archangel Michael. In the background you can just make out the angelic meeting, while, on the left, the now-deceased Adam is laid to rest, surrounded by his family, some of whom prefer not to wear much clothing, Piero's way of incorporating classical motifs in what is an otherwise sacred picture (see Heinrich Zimmer, *The Survival of the Pagan Gods* on this convention). The text that inspired this depiction of Adam's dying—our father, who art of earth—is found in the *Golden Legend* or *Legenda Sanctorum*—compiled in the thirteenth century by Jacobus de Voragine. Any reader of Chaucer is familiar with some of this material. The Second Nun's Tale of St. Cecilia (Englished by William Caxton in 1486) and a portion of the Physician's Tale of Virginius, whose roots are ultimately in Roman literature, have connections to the Golden Legend. The Tree under which Adam was buried provided the wood for the True Cross; it is under this same tree that one finds the opening to hell—this spot is the *omphalos* of Christian legend.

> *"And in the end of his life when he [Adam] should die, it is said, but of none authority, that he sent Seth his son into Paradise for to fetch the oil of mercy, where he received certain grains of the fruit of the tree of mercy by an angel. And when he came again he found his father Adam yet alive and told him what he had done. And then Adam laughed first and then died. And then he laid the grains or kernels under his father's tongue and buried him in the vale of Hebron; and out of his mouth grew*

> *three trees of the three grains, of which trees the cross that our Lord suffered his passion on was made, by virtue of which he gat very mercy, and was brought out of darkness into the very light of heaven. To the which he bring us that liveth and reigneth God, world without end."*

I love the line: "Adam laughed first and then died." And: "...out of his mouth grew three trees..." Fascinating iconography. Here is Christ crucified on the Tree of Life, with the serpent still in residence. This is a confusing reading of Genesis as it was the Tree of the Knowledge of Good and Evil that tempted Adam (Gen. 3: 22-24); it was to keep Adam and his suggestible companion away from the Tree of Life that our primordial parents were banished from Eden. We need to recall that medieval and Renaissance artists relied as often on legendary texts for their iconography as on Scripture, which is, of course, full of its own ambiguities. (e.g. Gen. 4:17)

The primal father in the three monotheistic religions (Adam shows up in the Qu'ran not only as the first human being, but as the person who has taught us all we know, the source of civilization and culture—Prometheus—see Sura II) is a complex figure. Progenitor and renegade; beloved of God and cursed by Him; awarded Paradise and banished to the realm of the fixed stars. In Dante, see *Paradiso*, Canto 26—the constellation that Adam shares with St. Peter is Gemini, Dante's own, which I take to be a demotion. Catholic theology's mansion has too many rooms, and Adam, who, let's face it, neither asked to be created nor solicited temptation, got a raw deal. But don't fathers always fare poorly in the mythopoetic literature? Perhaps they deserve to be nothing more than fixed stars, eternally rotating to a tune played by God and his Divine Mother (*l'amor che move il sole e l'altre stelle...*)

***

Distant Fathers: are there any other kind? The heavenly version, to be sure, is the archetype of the earthly—silent, absent, obsessed, it appears, with His own concerns. Mine worked late and took long naps on the couch while, miraculously, smoking a cigarette. Then, as sometimes happens, he disappeared altogether. In Antonio Skarmeta's charming mini-novella (I read it in an hour and a half), the narrator's father goes away unexpectedly—presumably to Paris, leaving Jacques and his bereft mother alone in their backwater Chilean village, lost without a man who, given the condensed nature of the narrative, has no real substance. The mythical father, shortcomings aside, is the very best kind: e.g. attentive and tender Leopold Bloom, childless, father to Stephan Daedalus. Or, from my reading this morning, Philip Roth's portrayal of his father in *Patrimony*. Skarmeta's Jacques, who is a schoolteacher enamored of the younger sister of one of his pupils, stumbles upon his past on his way to the bordello in a neighboring town. Fictional boys wishing to become fictional men must lose their virginity to a whore who is sexually condescending. Does this sort of thing ever happen? My hometown had a YMCA but no bordello (alas). Little more can be said plot-wise without ruining the story—this small tale, a tidy Fathers Day present of a book, an uplifting tale to be stuffed into Dad's backpack as he sets off for the Sports Bar—hinges upon a plot twist worthy of Chaucer. The book is nearly artless, and that is its art. There isn't any psychological complexity to deal with, no mysteries: Jacques seeks his father and....well, he *might* find him.

Antonio Skarmeta wrote the novel and the screenplay for the popular film "The Postman." I didn't see the film but it is easy enough to see that Skarmeta is the sort of writer who could easily write screenplays—*A Distant Father* would make a nice film. Skarmeta is *not at all* your typical Latin American—especially Chilean—writer. He is fond of every character in this book, he works outside the usual political boundaries of Chilean writing, and deploys not an iota of irony in telling a story that is engaging and uplifting. It turns out that the lost father might be found and returned to us without a drop of blood being shed.

G.O.

Marriage

When I finally put down Zeruya Shalev's novel, *Husband and Wife*, I was trembling. Described in *The Scotsman* as an "emotional white-knuckle ride," this story plunges the reader deep into the heart of a rapidly disintegrating marriage in present-day Jerusalem. In prose so accomplished, so stirring, at times so achingly beautiful that one is tempted to drop one's guard, to sit back, relax, and surrender oneself to its rhythms, Shalev is relentless in her determination to draw the reader inside the very skin of her protagonist, a mother and social worker named Na'ama Newman, as she registers the bruising daily trauma—each banal and horrific detail—of her imploding love life and family.

The simple plot is set in motion one morning when Na'ama's husband, Udi, a healthy, active man, wakes up at home after a solitary outing in the desert to discover that he cannot move his legs. Unable to find a physical, medical explanation for his paralysis, they are forced to recognize that the problem lies elsewhere, in their marriage itself, their once-happy life together attacked from within by an aggressive emotional cancer. From there, their relationship quickly spirals out of control, fueled—as fire by gasoline—by years of pent-up disappointment, longing, recrimination, and fear.

Told from Na'ama's acute, often startling perspective, *Husband and Wife* is the story of one woman's desperate, exasperating, sometimes valiant attempt to save her marriage and family, to check the momentum of what at points seems as terrible, as implacable as fate. While the novel might just as well have been set in Shanghai, Durban, or Madrid, so little do we see of modern Israel, so broadly human is the story's appeal, one cannot help but suspect that this tangled and septic relationship is somehow reflective of the anguish and violence of Jerusalem itself.

Grim, depressing as this sounds—and *is* (Why would anyone but a masochist read such stuff? Or recommend it?), the novel is also singularly exhilarating in its pacing and candor, in its fearless, thereby hopeful depiction of relationships and love. "*Husband and Wife* is not a book for the faint-hearted," writes critic Jamie Jauncey, "but for anyone prepared...to experience with almost hallucinatory vividness the complex and conflicting emotions of a modern woman dealing with a disintegrating relationship, there can be no finer opportunity." Indeed if, like Kafka, you believe that a book should be an axe for the frozen sea inside us, then pick up a copy of this one. It will crack you wide open.

P.N.

Seasons and Writers

Walt Whitman, Henry David Thoreau, David
Reynolds, Rebecca Solnit

Does it seem to you as it does to me that some writers have their seasons? Just as a nicely chilled Pinot Grigio served with gazpacho on the back porch seems perfect for hot summer days, so do Walt Whitman and Henry David Thoreau seem the perfect literary companions. I could no more read Thomas Mann—say *Doctor Faustus*—in July than I could sit down to a pot roast. Nor could I reread *Paradise Lost* or, heaven help us, a single stanza of *The Faerie Queen*, or dip into Shakespeare's problem plays on a 101-degree afternoon than I could consume a plate of fettuccine Alfredo. American writers, and I mean the originals, not derivative figures like Fenimore Cooper or the ruthlessly sententious Ralph Waldo Emerson (our Plato), or Joseph Conrad's pale cousin Herman [An absurd judgment, but it was the mood of the moment, and I leave it intact. G.O.] but true originals like Whitman, Dickinson, and Thoreau, each of these originals has a season. Like the Hudson River painters, our great romantics offer the promise of sunny skies, cool mornings and languid afternoon walks, long evenings of conversation and light fare—exactly the three writers I pack on hikes or take to the beach.

Rereading the first (1855) edition of *Leaves of Grass* this past week, I was struck yet again by the felicity of Whitman's eye; truly he is not only the greatest poet of democracy, but the most philosophical American writer, Jefferson with a soul.

> *"All goes onward and outward...and nothing collapses, / And to die is different from what any one supposed, and luckier."*

What a line! You could brood on these words all afternoon, staring at the cumulus clouds bunching on the horizon, and not feel as if you'd wasted a minute. Or this piece of American Platonism, so much more digestible than Emerson, whose platitudes unfold like a bolt of cloth:

> *"If I and you and the worlds and all beneath or upon their surfaces, and all the palpable life, were this moment reduced back to a pallid float, it would not avail in the long run, /*
> *We should surely bring up again where we now stand, / And as surely go as much farther, and then farther and farther...*
> *See ever so far...there is limitless space outside of that, Count ever so much.... there is limitless time around that.*
> *Our rendezvous is fitly appointed...God will be there and wait till we come."*

Old Walt, the sly sensualist. Remember the line from Ginsburg? *"I saw you, Walt Whitman, childless, lonely old grubber, poking among the meats in the refrigerator and eyeing the grocery boys,"* written, I am certain, with wry affection, though Whitman, alone in Camden, wasn't the same man as the would-be seducer of Brooklyn, the man who wrote this beautiful line: *"For me lips that have smiled, eyes that have shed tears,/ For me children and the begetters of children."*

I hadn't read any of Whitman's prose since college, but then came upon this passage in *Spiritual Laws*:

> *"A man is a method, a progressive arrangement; a selecting principle, gathering his like to him, wherever he goes. He takes only his own out of the multiplicity that sweeps and circles around him.... Those facts, words, persons, which dwell in his memory without his being able to say why, remain, because they have a relation to him not less real for being as yet unapprehended. They are symbols of value to him, as they can interpret parts of his consciousness which he would vainly seek words for in the conventional images of books and other minds."*

These few sentences offer a remarkably astute analysis of how poetry works, Whitman's included. The real poet isn't merely crafty with words, but is able to draw from memory and experience those "symbols of value" that help him and the reader interpret parts of consciousness that might otherwise remain inaccessible. *A person is a method...a selecting* principle. And the artist, the writer, is especially this, sorting through experience not for its Meaning, but for the way in which individual experiences tie the world together, the way in which they bind people, rich and poor, black and white, gay and straight, together—yes, the finest democratic poet, perhaps our *only* democratic poet—a democratic vista rooted not in ideas but in the body, the source, as Whitman shows us, of all meaning.

The only critic of American literature I have read who recognizes the wit as opposed to the sagacity of Thoreau is David Reynolds, author of a very fine study designed to bring F. O. Matthiessen's magisterial *American Renaissance* up to date. In *Beneath the American Renaissance*, an investigation of what he calls "the subversive imagination," Reynolds writes: "Thoreau was confronted with a problem which faced several other major American writers of the period: theoretically committed to incorporating popular idioms, he nevertheless recoiled from the directionlessness and devilishness that characterized these idioms as they usually appeared in the popular press." Thoreau found beneath, or within, the crude wit of American popular literature an unhappiness, a despair, that he addressed in the first chapter of *Walden*. American *angst*, as Reinhold Niebuhr would later point out, was attributable to materialism, precisely the point made by de Tocqueville, Harriet Martineau, and other dispassionate observers of 19th century American life.

This combination of sociological insight, humor, compassion, and social criticism make Thoreau the perfect companion for a long walk or a quiet hour in the hammock. While I love *Walden*, my favorite summer reading in Thoreau, an essay that I come back to again and again, is "Walking," found in the perfectly backpack-sized Modern Library edition (with a nice introduction by Brooks Atkinson) of *Selected Thoreau*, a book first published in 1937—think of that—which I have owned since 1968. Then last summer, at 57th Street Books in Chicago, I came upon *Wanderlust: A History of Walking*, by Rebecca Solnit, a writer of whom I knew nothing.

Ms. Solnit has this insight into Thoreau's essay: "For Thoreau, the desire to walk in the unaltered landscape no longer seemed to have a history, but to be natural—if nature means the timeless truth we have found, not the historic specific we have made." This is a smart rewording of Thoreau's wonderful opening sentence: *"I wish to speak a word for Nature, for absolute freedom and wildness, as contrasted with a freedom and culture merely civil,—to regard man as an inhabitant, or a part and parcel of Nature, rather than a member of society...."* and then the wit of which Reynolds speaks takes over. *"I wish to make an extreme statement, if so I may make an emphatic one, for there are enough champions of civilization: the minister and the school-committee and every one of you will take care of that."*

And here the two strands of our complicated history, our two most original writers, and our summer season come together. As Perry Miller noted many years ago, taking his title and theme from a famous sermon, "Errand into the Wilderness," by Samuel Danforth (1670), America was at first seen as a great opportunity, as a divinely inspired project, a utopian settlement designed to glorify God's works, a City Upon a Hill. But as Miller points out, the aspirations of the first generations of New England settlers ran aground on the realities of the wilderness, a wilderness that proved to be both physical and moral. How, the Puritans and America's most original writers asked, can one balance the spiritual errand into the wilderness (purification, temptation, preparation) with the material wealth this wilderness bestows and the rapaciousness this wealth inspires? Whitman's genius was to discover what was universal in American life—to lift the body electric out of greed and war and slavery and into the benign fantasy of his imagination. Thoreau walked away (with a scathing look back). He walked into the woods, along the Concord River, across the beaches of Cape Cod—to escape the din of the school-committee's "civilization."

G.O.

The Open Mind of Lafcadio Hearn

The year my girlfriend (now wife), Annie, asked me to spend the summer traveling around Japan with her, I didn't know what to expect. Of course I'd eaten sushi, teriyaki, and tempura, and had seen a couple of Kurasawa films—if with the bright unknowing of a pilgrim at Plymouth Rock. I was as ignorant of the country as I was happy and eager to explore it.

Annie, a student of East Asian Studies in college, did her best, in the months preceding our trip, to prepare me for the adventure to come, lending me books about Buddhism and Shintoism, pressing me to read the various travels guides she'd collected, and speaking with wonder about her own first trip there the previous summer to visit a close college friend. Just before we left for Japan, Annie's stepfather, the late sociologist Robert Nisbet, gave me a book to take with me, Lafcadio Hearn's *Writings From Japan*, a number of the essays of which he had read and liked very much when he was stationed on Saipan during World War II. I thanked him kindly for the gift and packed it away.

It wasn't until we'd been in Japan for some weeks, settled for a spell, after our first stint of travelling, in a handsome old house in the town of Hayama, overlooking the long, wide curve of Sagami Bay, that I actually opened the book and read. What I discovered in those pages not only transformed the country I saw before me each day, but kindled in me an affection for Japan—for the dreamlike strangeness of the land, its people, and its past—that haunts me to this day.

My initial hours in the country were a glorious, intoxicated blur, an experience perhaps best captured by Hearn himself when he first set foot in the country, in nearby Yokohama, nearly a hundred years before me, in the spring of 1890:

> *It is with the delicious surprise of the first journey through Japanese streets—unable to make one's kurama-runner understand anything but gestures, frantic gestures to roll on anywhere, everywhere, since all is unspeakably pleasurable and new... 'Tis at first a delightfully odd confusion only, as you look down one of them [the streets], through an interminable flutter of flags and swaying of dark blue drapery, all made beautiful and mysterious with Japanese or Chinese lettering. For there are no immediately discernable laws of construction or decoration: each building seems to have a fantastic prettiness of its own; nothing is exactly like anything else, and all is bewilderingly novel.*

By the time of Hearn's arrival, Japan had been visited and written about at length by writers as esteemed and varied as Pierre Loti and Rudyard Kipling. Following the invasion of Commodore Perry and his fleet of American warships in 1853, the modest, introverted, once-insular Japan had been overrun by westerners, by "diplomats, advisers, teachers, businessmen and journalists", each armed with something new to teach the Japanese, something by which to draw them out (meaning *westward*) into the bright and "civilized" world.

Lafcadio Hearn was different, precisely in that regard, encountering all he saw before him in the country with a child-like wonder, with a mute and goggling awe. Yet in his thinking he was hardly simplistic, naïve. Indeed his critical acumen in these essays (his extraordinary ability *to see*) is unmistakable, buoyed—though it nearly always is—by his enchantment, his humility, his glee.

What followed for me, that long, chimerical summer in Japan, were weeks of reading and rereading the essays in this collection, and of wandering the nearby towns and villages with my intrepid guide and girlfriend, Annie. Together we delighted in the shops and temples, and in the local festivals (*Tanabata* and *Obon*), while admiring the gardens and grave-yards and shrines—and all through Hearn's deeply observant, deeply affectionate eyes.

Surely a part of the charm of Hearn's work for me that summer was the house in which we happened to be staying, a traditional Japanese house on a narrow street above the bay, complete with a *genkan*, *tatami, shoji*, and a *tokonama*, as well as a free standing teahouse from which we'd had an unobstructed view of Mt. Fuji.

We could hardly believe our good fortune, our luck. Tired, our resources already strained by the cost of living in *ryokans* and hostels, we'd all but stumbled into taking care of the house for a retired U.S. Navy nurse, then on emergency medical leave in the States, a distinctly Hearn-like woman who, since her arrival in Japan at the end of WWII, had come to love the country so much that she'd made it her home. Not surprisingly, the house was filled with Japanese antiques—porcelain, screens, various *tansu* or chests, woodblock prints, and a fantastical array of Buddhist statues. If that were not enough to set the scene for that magical summer of ours, we'd received a letter one day, from the owner herself, thanking us again for taking care of her house and encouraging us to have a look at her collection of *netsuke* in the shoeboxes beneath the guestroom beds. *Netsuke*? we wondered. What in the world were *netsuke*?

Nestuke—so we learned (so many of you know)—are small, sculptural objects made of porcelain, ivory, wood, boar tusk or stone that were traditionally designed to prevent one's purse from slipping through the belt or *obi* worn over one's *kimono*. Both functional and aesthetic, *netsuke* were commonly designed after people, plants, and animals, after gods and religious symbols, after folkloric figures and mythological beasts.

The *netsuke* we found in the shoe boxes that summer left us speechless for their strangeness and variety, as well as for their extraordinary workmanship and beauty—charms, tokens, of a long-gone, bygone age. Purchased by the owner of the house from the many desperate Japanese she'd encountered in Tokyo and Yokohama immediately following the war, men and women often on the verge of starvation and madness, she'd collected the *netsuke* in the shoe boxes beneath her guestroom beds for close to a decade, originally knowing little or nothing about their function or worth. Was it kindness or simple opportunism that had motivated her to buy them, these extraordinary artifacts? We didn't know; not having met her before, we couldn't even guess. Only later, in a follow-up letter that same summer, when she'd nearly recovered and was planning her return, did we learn that, years before, and whatever her initial motive for collecting them, she had willed the entire collection, appraised at over a million dollars, back to the nation of Japan, to the country and people she loved. It is something Hearn himself would have done.

Of course Hearn (the writer and ethnographer, the avid devotee) made his own fine bequest to the Japanese people— his nearly countless essays and observations about a Japan now largely vanished beneath the flash and clamor of the modern world, so that today even the Japanese themselves rely on his writings to revisit and remember who they were and what they valued, to reacquaint themselves with their once-singular customs and ways.

Surely one of my favorite passages from this collection of essays, one I'd like to leave you with, is Hearn's awestruck description of a legendary sea-cave near Matsue, which he had heard about upon his arrival in the city and had hoped dearly to see:

> *Few pilgrims go thither there by sea, and boatmen are forbidden to go there if there be even enough wind "to move three hairs." So that whoever wishes to visit Kaka must either wait for a period of dead calm—very rare upon the coast of the Japanese Sea—or journey thereunto by land; and by land the way is difficult and wearisome. But I must see Kaka. For at Kaka, in a great cavern by the sea, there is a famous Jizo of stone; and each night, it is said, the ghosts of little children climb to the high cavern and pile up before the statue small heaps of pebbles; and every morning, in the soft sand, there may be seen the fresh prints of tiny naked feet, the feet of the infant ghosts. It is also said that in the cavern there is a rock out of which comes a stream of milk, as from a woman's breast; and the white stream flows forever, and the phantom children drink of it. Pilgrims bring with them gifts of straw sandals—the zori that children wear—and leave them before the cavern, that the feet of the little ghosts may not be wounded by the sharp rocks. And the pilgrim treads with caution, lest he should overturn any of the many heaps of stones; for if this be done the children cry.*

P.N.

For Tony

Hotel Europa by Dumitru Tsepeneag

It is now a decade since we lost the inimitable Tony Judt, the finest historian of Europe of our generation. His magisterial *Postwar: Europe Since 1945* stands as the most incisive work of historical scholarship and humane erudition produced in recent memory. Judt wore his learning lightly, wrote lucidly, judged according to clear and rational standards of historical conduct, and remained remarkably untainted by the ideological distortions that have diminished the writings of so many contemporary historians. What reader of the *New York Review of Books* or of the *London Review* hasn't marveled at Judt's ability to distill a career ("Goodbye to All That? Leszek Kolakowski and the Marxist Legacy"), demolish the useful idiots of the early 2000's ("The Silence of the Lambs: On the Strange Death of Liberal America"), or cut to the heart of a complex contemporary political question ("The Country That Wouldn't Grow Up")? Well, plenty of them. Because he refused to climb on board any bandwagon and was equally critical of all parties guilty of self-serving mendacity and gross stupidity, Judt had plenty of enemies—those blindly loyal to Israeli policies in the Occupied Territories, supporters of the intransigence of the PLO under Arafat, unreconstructed Marxists, the editors of the *New York Times* who supported W. Bush's war in Iraq, those who adored Pope John Paul ("A Pope of Ideas?" one of the most devastating essays ever written about the pretensions of papal power), and anyone hoodwinked by the fatuousness of Thomas Friedman. Even when I didn't agree with Judt's viewpoint on some question it was difficult not to be charmed and persuaded by his prose, his deep and humane learning, and his ethical sincerity.

All of which is a prologue to the tale of *Hotel Europa* by Dumitru Tsepeneag. *Hotel Europa* (a bit of a joke I think: Bucharest is closer to Istanbul than to Paris) was published in Romanian in 1996, not long after the political events it depicts, translated by Patrick Camiller, and issued by Dalkey in 2010, by which time the sclerotic memories of Romania's descent into chaos (from somewhat greater chaos) had already fallen into the black hole of forgetfulness that the zombies of the informationless age inhabit. This is one thing among many I loved about Tony Judt—he knew everything worth knowing, he thought it was *important* to know everything, and he appeared never to forget what he knew. Even in his dying from ALS he dictated a book to his secretary (*Ill Fares the Land*) that puts every other book about our nation's predicament to shame.

And what are some of the things Judt hadn't forgotten? The unspeakable crimes of Ceaușescu for one thing.

The torture centers, the extra-judicial murders, the violence against dissenters, the lies he told to hoodwink three or four American presidents. Ceaușescu was a critic of the Soviet leadership during the Cold War and thus an ally of Richard Nixon, Henry Kissinger, and others. Despite his brutality—for example, in an effort to increase the "pure Romanian population," beginning in 1966 both birth control and abortion were prohibited in Romania, a draconian measure which resulted in the deaths of at least 10,000 women. In spite of such Stalinist madness, Ceaușescu was granted IMF loans that he repaid on the backs of the poorest people in Europe, MFN trade status, membership in GATT, a state visit to London, and fawning attention by Western politicians who should have known better.

Dumitru Tsepeneag is among the most popular writers in Romania and highly regarded in his adopted nation of France. In the 1960s he was among the founders of the Oniric group of Surrealists—indeed his books have a strong surrealist strain. They are dreamlike, fracturing space and time, dispersing with chronology and causality, jumping from fiction to purported fact, from autobiography to novelistic invention. Tsepeneag had his Romanian citizenship revoked by Ceausescu's government in 1975 and in that year emigrated to Paris. At first he published in Romanian, and then, as he puts it, his publisher asked him to write in French to save money on translation. His most popular novel thus far, *The Vain Art of the Fugue* was his first to appear in his adopted language—it's a good place to start with this difficult writer.

Hotel Europa tells the story of the 1990 revolution in Romania through the eyes of both the narrator (who is trying to get away from Paris and his French wife in order to write the book that we are reading) and a group of students victimized by the riots of that year. The novel is full of mordant playfulness—witty exchanges on the forever twinned subjects of politics and sex, not unlike those that fill *Hopscotch,* replace traditional plot lines. Who, for example, is Ion, whose principle role appears to be the mouthpiece of the author, but a most uncooperative one?

> *"Ion [the novel's main character, a student] might accuse me [the novelist] of speaking more about myself in this novel than him, despite the fact that he's the main character. Of course it would be easy for me to reply that he doesn't decide who the main character is. . . But that, I admit, would be unworthy of an author who hates appearing to his readers as a god or a father in relation to his characters. . ."*

Although he wrote a generation earlier, I thought of Tsepeneag's countryman Eugene Ionesco as I read *Hotel Europa*. The two exiles had a lot in common, including residence in Paris, a love-hate relationship with their country of birth, and the adoption of the French language. I remember my first reading of Ionesco's brilliant absurdist play *The Chairs,* a farce not unlike *Waiting for Godot* but darker—Tsepeneag doesn't unhinge reality in quite the way that Ionesco did, but the comparison is apt. Both writers, coming from a country where, as Tony Judt pointed out, there has been an "obsession with identity," confront the facts of displacement and a lack of rootedness. Tsepeneag's books place his characters in predicaments that consistently undercut their sense of gravity. No one *belongs*; no set of circumstances feels fixed beyond the moment, and political violence sweeps up everyone—all that is solid melts into air.

> Back to Tony Judt: *"'Some countries,' according to E.M. Cioran, looking back across Romania's twentieth century, 'are blessed with a sort of grace: everything works for them, even their misfortunes and catastrophes. There are others for whom nothing succeeds and whose very triumphs are but failures. When they try to assert themselves and take a step forward, some external fate intervenes to break their momentum and return them to their starting point.'"*

This is from Judt's essay "Romania Between History and Europe," included in the collection *Reappraisals*, published in 2008.

G.O.

The Uses of History

"I'll tell you," she said, in the same hurried and passionate whisper, "what real love is. It is blind devotion, unquestioning self-humiliation, utter submission, trust and belief against yourself and against the whole world, giving up your whole heart and soul to the smiter—as I did!
                                                            Charles Dickens

True history, insists historian J.H. Plumb in his 1969 book *The Death of the Past*, is basically destructive in the way that, by its very nature, it attacks those mythical, religious, and political interpretations of the past by which cultures and nations sanctify themselves, cleansing "the story of mankind from those deceiving visions of a purposeful past." It is a passage that might very well be used to describe certain types of literary fiction as well, novels—like *War and Peace* and *The Man Without Qualities*, like Fernando Del Paso's magisterial *News from the Empire*—that not only cleanse the story of mankind from those deceiving visions of a purposeful, mythical past, but enrich and complicate it by adding flesh and feeling to its bones. History—as novelists know well—is a deeply human, deeply personal thing.

"In 1861," writes Del Paso in his prefatory remarks to his operatic novel, *News from the Empire*, "Benito Juárez suspended payment on the foreign debt of Mexico. This suspension was the pretext that the Emperor of the French, Napoleon III, used to send an army of occupation to Mexico with the purpose of creating a monarchy there, at the helm of which would be a European Catholic monarch. An Austrian, Ferdinand Maximilian of Hapsburg, was chosen. He arrived in Mexico in the middle of 1864 accompanied by his wife, Princess Charlotte of Belgium. The book is based on these historical facts, and on the story of the tragic end of this ephemeral Emperor and Empress of Mexico."

Maximillian I, for all his honest and liberal intentions, proved particularly ill-suited to the post, to the demands of successfully contending with both the international intrigues that had brought him to power there and the increasingly violent divisions within Mexico itself. Preferring to "chase butterflies" on his summer home on the grounds of the ancient Borda Gardens in Cuernavaca, not far from where Malcolm Lowry's fictional character, the British consul Geoffrey Firmin, in his novel *Under the Volcano*, is murdered by the local police chief them dumped, like so much garbage, into the barranca below:

¿LE GUSTA ESTE JARDIN?
¿QUE ES SUYO?
¡EVITE QUE SUS HIJOS LO DESTRUAN!

Maximillian's death by firing squad was hardly more dignified.

What is particularly remarkable about this novel, aside from its often extraordinarily fine prose, is that, for all its historical sweep and grandeur, it is rendered up for the reader on a decidedly human, decidedly intimate scale, filtered as it is, in large part, through the mad and fevered reveries of the aged, long-widowed Carlota, an embittered, broken-hearted, Miss Havisham-like figure who passes the time, following her inglorious return to Europe, in "mercurial madness," pining daily for her late husband and true love, Maximilian, and berating the world for its indifference to such refined, once-noble fates.

The novel opens with her haughty, still imperious voice:

> *I am Marie Charlotte of Belgium, Empress of Mexico and America. I am Marie Charlotte Amelie, cousin of the Queen of England, Grand magister of the Cross of Saint Charles, and Vicereine of the Lombardo-Veneto Provinces, which Austria's clemency and mercy has submitted under the two-headed eagle of the House of Habsburg. I am Marie Charlotte Amélie Victoria, daughter of Leopold, Prince of Saxe-Coburg and King of Belgium, known as 'The Nestor of Europe,' and who would take me onto his lap, caress my chestnut tresses, and call me the little sylph of the Castle of Laeken. I am Marie Charlotte Amélie Victoria Clémentine, daughter of Louise Marie of Orléans, the saintly*

queen with the blue eyes and the Bourbon nose who died of consumption and of the sorrow caused by the exile and death of Louis Philippe, my grandfather, who, as King of France, showered me with chestnuts and covered my face with kisses in the Tuileries Gardens. I am Marie Charlotte Amélie Victoria Clémentine Léopoldine, niece of Prince Joinville and cousin of the Count of Paris; I am sister of the Duke of Brabant, who became King of Belgium and colonized the Congo, and of the Counts of Flanders in whose arms I learned to dance, at the age of ten, under the shade of flowering hawthorns. I am Charlotte Amélie, wife of Ferdinand Maximilian Joseph, Prince of Loraine, Emperor of Mexico and King of the World, who was born in the Imperial Palace of Schönbrunn, and who was the first descent of the Catholic Monarchs Ferdinand and Isabella to cross the ocean and tread on American soil; who built a white palace for me with a view of the sea on the shores of the Adriatic; who later took me to Mexico to live in a gray castle with a view of the valley and the snowcapped volcanoes and who, on a June morning, many years ago, was executed in the city of Querétero. I am Charlotte Amélie, Regent of Anahuac, Queen of Nicaragua, Baroness of Matto Grosso, and Princess of Chichén Itzá. I am Charlotte Amélie of Belgium, Empress of Mexico and America. I am eighty-six years old and for sixty years now I've quenched my lunatic thirst with water from Roman fountains...

Rounding out this singular voice and perspective are those of a wide variety of contemporary players, both distinguished and prosaic, ranging from Napoleon III, Count Metternich, Emperor Maximillian, and Benito Juárez to a patriotic camp follower, a cuckolded palace gardener, and a randy Basque priest. For those with a fondness for Mexico, *News from the Empire* is a demanding, if exceptionally rewarding tale.

    P.N.

Beautiful Cortázar

"The problem for an engagé writer, as they call them now, is to continue being a writer. If what he writes becomes simply literature with a political content, it can be very mediocre. That's what has happened to a number of writers. So, the problem is one of balance. For me, what I do must always be literature, the highest I can do . . . to go beyond the possible. But, at the same time, to try to put in a mix of contemporary reality. And that's a very difficult balance."

Cortazar, from the Paris Review Interview

He was a beautiful man—there's a little of Chet Baker in his face, though Cortázar was darker and his face had more sadness in it. Chet would catch up in the sadness department, pretty quickly. In my office I have lots of pictures, but only one image of a writer—Julio, bearded, smoking of course, looking off into the distance, looking, perhaps, for La Maga in some Parisian cafe, or thinking about a philosophical paradox posed by Gregorovius, that spinner of paradoxes. Oh, to have lived in that Moveable Feast, Paris in the Fifties, cheap wine and jazz and conversations that lasted all night! When I dip back into *Hopscotch* I almost weep at the beauty of it—the gorgeous writing, the flow of ideas, the lost world, the riffs on politics and love and art that follow Oliveria/Cortázar as he wanders the streets in his lumberjack coat and leaky shoes, looking for, or trying to forget, La Maga, that life-force, that enigma, who just happens to be a woman.

He was a poet, a poet in prose, like so many other writers in Spanish. This morning, reeling from half-a-dozen poems from *Save Twilight*, I was thinking that, for sure, no language has more beautiful writing than Spanish— Cortázar, Márquez, Bolaño, Vila-Matas, Abad. Russians and East Europeans do politics better than anyone; the French have no peer when it comes to *malaise*; the Brits are the great chroniclers of imperialist regret; Anglophone Indian writers are the best storytellers (Rohinton Mistry), and Americans *own* bewildered self-regard—but literature in Spanish, whether peninsular or colonial, is by far the most poetic and passionate and beautiful.

From section 25 of Hopscotch:

> *"Gregorovius thought that somewhere Chestov had written about aquariums with a removable glass partition which could be taken out any time and that the fish, who was accustomed to his compartment, would never try to go over to the other side. He would come to a point in the water, turn around and swim back, without discovering that*

the obstacle was gone, that all he had to do was to keep on going forward..."

He tosses this sort of thing off on every page—emblems of deeper truths, hints at the inner lives of his characters (who we know to be real people, thinly disguised). Cortázar/Oliveria is this fish, walking and smoking and talking in riddles to his *cercle intime*—and then traveling back to Argentina to work in a circus that is an insane asylum and in an insane asylum that is a circus (yes, the glass partition can be removed and the fish never tries to go to the other side). There is a yearning in Cortázar for truth and clarity that I find brave and touching and deeply moving; he is one of the greatest philosophers among writers, far more bracing than Dostoevsky because he is far less willing to capitulate to dogma or to divide the world up at all—Julio/Horacio swallows life whole, just as it is and must be.

Look, I don't ask much,
just your hand, to hold it
like a little frog who'd sleep there happily.
I need that door you gave me
for coming into your world, that little chunk
of green sugar, of a lucky ring.
Can't you just spare me your hand tonight
at the end of a year of hoarse-voiced owls?
You can't, for technical reasons. So
I weave it in the air, warping each finger,
the silky peach of the palm
and the back, that country of blue trees.
That's how I take it and hold it, as

if so much of the world
depended on it,
the succession of the four seasons,
the crowing of the roosters, the love of human beings.

This is "Happy New Year." In interviews, like the one given to the *Paris Review*, Cortázar often made the point that the real and the surreal are one and the same thing—I think he felt the glass partition between consciousness and the unconscious to be porous, or non-existent. His novels, like *62: A Model Kit* aren't at all like dreams, but they are dreamy, the prose languorous rather than sharp. There's nothing business-like about Cortázar's writing, and he's never eager to take the reader to some destination of plot or character development. Things pop up in the stories embedded in *Hopscotch*, like that marvelous long account of Horacio/Julio wandering into an eccentric piano recital by the deluded impresario Berthe Trepat—this is writing as jazz, Charlie Parker put into words, and Horacio/Julio is, in La Maga's words, "like a glass of water in a storm."

He was a beautiful man who died too young (at 69), possibly from a blood transfusion. He was born in Brussels, taught elementary school in rural Argentina where he began to write, then moved to Paris in 1951. He offended the Peronists who ruled his native country and wasn't welcome—and that was all right since Paris was his natural home. He translated for UNESCO, played the trumpet, collected books and art, wrote and thought and lived.

Julio Cortázar died in Paris in 1984. I visited his grave in Montparnasse. It was covered with flowers.

G.O.

Trotsky's Sink

For years now, I've been fascinated by the life and times of the Soviet revolutionary and Marxist theorist, Leon Trotsky, particularly by the time he spent in exile in Mexico City, in Coyoacán, where he befriended the radically leftwing painters, Diego Rivera and Frida Kahlo, before being murdered with an ice axe by his secretary's boyfriend, a young man named Ramón Mercader, one of Stalin's faithful agents. At the time, Trotsky was hard at work on his biography of Stalin himself.

If you've never been to Trotsky's house in Coyoacán, now a modest museum, it is well worth a visit, whatever your politics. The original entrance on Avenida Viena has been bricked up; now one enters the house and grounds from the other side, through a larger, salmon-colored, partly glassed-in façade. There, straight ahead, one finds a gallery, in which rotating shows are hung. To the left, in a small room, clearly part of the original structure, is where one pays one's admission. There too are books for sale, mostly in Spanish, and a small glass case in which one finds a surprising (and somehow pleasing) variety of Trotsky paraphernalia: Trotsky T-shirts, Trotsky lighters, Trotsky key chains, bookmarks, and mugs.

Once admitted, one enters another small gallery filled with photographs of Trotsky and his wife, Natalia Sedova, and of their many and varied friends, along with a sampling of his personal possessions in plexiglass frames and cases. From there one follows a short and narrow hallway out into the yard and garden—a bit of paradise behind the high, fortified walls.

Starting in May of 1939 Trotsky and his wife lived in this house until his death shortly after on August 21, 1940. He'd recently parted ways with Diego Rivera and Frida Kahlo (they'd bickered over politics; he and Frida had had a brief affair) whose now world-famous house, La Casa Azul, was only blocks away. By then he knew that his days were numbered: his health was failing and Stalin's assassins were hot on his heels. In May of that same year, their house was sprayed with machine-gun fire, an attack believed to have been led by the Stalinist painter, David Alfaro Siqueiros, one of the three great Mexican muralists of the time, along with Diego Rivera and Jose Clemente Orozco. There, in his bullet-proof vest, surrounded by armed guards in their makeshift brick towers, Trotsky lived a life of veritable seclusion, reading, writing, and attending to his beloved rabbits, which he kept in the hutches he'd built in the yard.

So, what is it that so intrigues me about this man and his life? To be honest, I'm not sure, though over the years I've not only read a great deal by him and about him, but he and his house, there in Coyoacán, have somehow found their way into my last two novels (three, if I include the one

I'm working on now). Certainly, his politics appeal to me, if mainly on a cultural-historical level; I particularly admire his position with regard to the role of art and literature in the mounting revolution, which he, unlike virtually all of his Marxist contemporaries, did not believe should be shackled to the cause, as he described clearly in his 1924 book, *Literature and Revolution*:

> *It is not true that we regard only that art as new and revolutionary which speaks of the worker, and it is nonsense to say that we demand that the poets should describe inevitably a factory chimney, or the uprising against capital! Of course, the new art cannot but place the struggle of the proletariat in the center of its attention. But the plough of the new art is not limited to numbered strips. On the contrary, it must plough the entire field in all directions. Personal lyrics of the very smallest scope have an absolute right to exist within the new art. Moreover, the new man cannot be formed without a new lyric poetry.*

Perhaps, that's it; perhaps that's what most moves me about him—his aestheticism, his sentimentality, his unwillingness to sever all ties with the past, to embrace, as his rival Stalin seemed eager to do, a Soviet version of Italian Futurist Filippo Tommaso Marinetti's famous cry to "Destroy the museums. Crack Syntax. Sabotage the adjective. Leave nothing but the verb." In the end, and for all his zealotry and narcissism, he has always seemed human to me.

Which brings me back to his house itself, to the museum in Coyoacán. Unlike a visit to the homes of other great thinkers and writers, say, that of Virginia Woolf in Rodmell or Marcel Proust in Paris, in which two places the authors had always felt at home, Trotsky's house is not a home at all, but the haunted refuge of a pariah, an exile, a Jew. One has only to walk the gloomy rooms, with their armored windows and doors, to stand at his desk, the desk at which he was murdered, and to peer into his bathroom, with its simple sink and tub, to feel the terrible human weight of his pain.

P.N.

Her Last Day on Earth

AVA, by Carole Maso

> "*Where is the ebullient, infinite woman who, immersed as she was in her naiveté, kept in the dark about herself, led into self-disdain by the great arm of parental-conjugal phallocentricism, hasn't been ashamed of her strength?*"
>
> Helen Cixous, "The Laugh of the Medusa"

Many of the ideas of Cixous are rather more elegantly expressed in the great classic work of feminist aesthetics, *A Room of One's Own*. My friend and I have discussed the question of a uniquely "women's writing" (*ecriture feminine*) at some length. I have expressed the view that there is a form of literary expression unique to women, and though I am unable to specify what I mean, my view is that women's novels and poetry in the modernist and post-modernist mode encompass a sensibility that no male writer could duplicate. By coincidence, I reread parts of Kate Millet's *Sexual Politics* this past week and found that she shared my view—Millet also asserted that there is a "writing of the body" that belongs to women (and to Jean Genet).

My friend has hesitated to accept this viewpoint and yearns to believe that gender can be overcome, that empathy and full identification with others is possible. I wondered, foolishly as I now see it, if a man could write *Sense and Sensibility*; my friend rightly reminded me of Trollope and of George Eliot, writers whose male and female characters are equal in psychological depth and (in Cixous's terminology) bodily verisimilitude. My counterpoint to the argument from fictional realism was to cite the great modernist novel *Mrs. Dalloway*, a book I cannot imagine a man could write, but then, of course, there is Michael Cunningham's *The Hours*, a more than competent piece of ventriloquism, a book that, once again, forces me to wonder about my thesis—that men cannot write women and that Cixous is right to find in women's fiction a unique form of expression, a literature freed from the phallocentricism—to use a convenient, if awkward and demeaning bit of shorthand—of Western culture.

Then I read Carole Maso's novel *AVA* and felt vindicated: surely this is a book that no man could write (I asserted, phallocentrically).

Ava Klein is dying of a "rare blood disease." The novel is a recording, or perhaps an opening, of the rich contents of Ava's mind, the vestiges of her flickering consciousness, as it alights on memories, dreams, desires, and illusions, evoking lovers, travels, ideas and associations, as well as plenty of banalities, just in the way one imagines the diminishing consciousness of any person (of you or I) dancing among sentences that are mere representations of who we once were. A few pages into *AVA* and I thought I was in for another take-off on the *Tractatus*—a fictionalized rehash of those aphoristic paradoxes Wittgenstein offered as the end of philosophy. But after twenty pages I felt myself fall into Ava herself. There was no need to make comparisons or to think of some other writer or character. In her dying, Ava became gloriously alive.

It's pointless to review-quote *AVA* since the impact of the novel is cumulative. Any one page seems meaningless or at least too cryptic to bear much significance by itself. This novel isn't just "stream of consciousness" in the Joycean sense but something subtler. Maso recreates ("pictures" is, I think, just the right word, in a Wittgenstein mode) the horrible reality of dying, the sheer intensity of one's desire to cling to life through the exercise of memory. *AVA* is all *eros* and no *thantos*.

"Who gave me life/Continues to give me life."? This is the novel as poetry. Fragments of thought that are broken and reassembled a few lines later, tropes repeated over two-hundred and fifty pages, themes that need to be recomposed by the reader, theories of feminist literature (Cixous), Schubert's brief life and works, the streets of Paris, the Holocaust, the difficulty of writing...Maso breaks consciousness down to the level of *aide-de-memoir*: *"The poet writes love; the poet writes death,"* or the single word, "Treblinka" repeated over and over in slightly different contexts and therefore each time possessing a unique resonance.

Maso, like David Markson, breaks the traditional

narrative down into its most basic unit—the sentence. No, that isn't quite right. In fact, Maso's text has a staccato quality that makes Markson seem long-winded. There are 5,000 or so individual bits of Ava Klein's memory in *AVA*—words, sentence fragments, sentences, short paragraphs. Naturally as I read the book I thought of the unlikelihood of any traditional venue reviewing such an odd duck of a novel. Where's the plot? The character development? And at the same time I was stirred by the possibilities for fictional expression Maso opens for those who find the realist novel stultifying. In an interview given to the editor of "Rain Taxi," Maso says this about traditional narrative forms:

> *"The kinds of mysterious, hypnotic, lyric leaps that happen in the first two books become the method of AVA. To me all my work is of a piece. I feel slightly perplexed I must say when I hear AVA is not narrative. I think it just redefines narrative, reformulates it. It's like where Ava says somewhere 'and if not the real story, then what the story was for me.' I don't think it's such a good idea to assign to old definitions of what narrative is to new work. The worst thing of all, and I've probably already said this, is to emerge already constructed. Somewhere most writers entered a pact, some weird silent agreement was made as to what story is, character, time, all of that. What passes for narrative in most fiction I just find senseless. Literally, I cannot make sense of it. For me, narrative does not reside in these old, artificial notions. Narrative in AVA is refigured; I think that is true."*

I love her comments on the "weird silent agreement." A narrative must be whatever it needs to be to convey the mystery of character or the depths of the story. Honestly, is life lived as stories or as shards of memory? How do we go through the day? Do we think in rational arguments, mystical koans, or bits of trivia mixed in with images of the past that express our longings and desires? Are we screens onto which are projected Aristotelian rising action, *denouements*, tragedies, and climaxes, or the bearers of mostly incoherent bits and pieces of memories and dreams? I can't speak for anyone else, but my internal life is far more closely allied to Ava Klein's than to Nathan Zuckerman's.

Then there remains the question—could a man have written this *AVA*? I wish I knew.

G.O.

The Joys of Duty

*The joys of doing one's duty are so varied...that
it always pays to put them in the proper light.*

Under Nazi rule the German people were nothing if not dutiful. The historical record is clear on that. Thanks in large part to the work of such groundbreaking scholars as Robert Gellately, Ulrich Herbert, Christopher Browning, Omer Bartov, Robert Ericksen, and—perhaps most famously—Daniel Goldhagen, it is now widely accepted (though surely the precise degrees will always be debated) that, during the war, German citizens were not only well-informed about the Third Reich's policies and atrocities (receiving regular bulletins about them on the radio, in the movie theaters, and even in church, as well as reading about them in the daily papers), but were willing, often active participants in the horrors themselves. It is a growing body of evidence that negates, perhaps once and for all, the oft-made claim that "they [the German people] were only following orders, just "reacting to the extreme duress of a totalitarian state," the Nazi reign of terror less the will and product of good, hard-working people than the sinister machinations of an aberrational clan of "cold-blooded technocrats dispassionately organizing mass disappearance on an industrial basis." Sadly, wholesale German complicity is closer to the truth.

In the years immediately following the war, young German writers, especially those like Gunter Grass, Heinrich Böll, and Alfred Andersch (all of whom had worn Wehrmacht uniforms in their youth) found themselves "standing on the edge of an abyss." They had few real choices: they could confront the Nazi horrors head-on, including their own complicity in them, or they could avoid the subject altogether, seeking their voice and vision in the abstract, allegorical, and ideal, groping their way back through the centuries toward a charmed and mystic past. Then there were the writers, surely the best of them, who sought to define a vision somewhere in between the two extremes, a vision of *then* and *there*, but with a twist, writers like Grass with his novel *The Tin Drum*, Böll with his novel *The Clown*, and Andersch with his novel *Efraim's Book*. Instead of directly confronting the monstrous, arguably ineffable phenomenon of the Nazi years, especially from that proximity, all three authors chose to approach it more obliquely (as one might study an eclipse by its projection alone), and therefore, in that way, "By indirections find directions out." Of all of the novels of the post-war years I have read, I can think of none that describes the period, the culture, and its fateful psychology as successfully—with such clarity, depth, and integrity—as Siegfried Lenz' extraordinary novel, *The German Lesson*.

Told in retrospect, not long after the war, through the eyes of a juvenile delinquent named Siggi Jepsen who, as punishment, has been confined to his cell to write an essay for his German lesson called "The Joys of Duty" ("die Freuden der Pflicht"), the story proper unfolds during the war in a remote German town on the North Sea, a bleak, storm-struck village of windmills, peat bogs, and dykes called Rugbüll where the narrator's father was "the most northerly police officer in Germany." Charged by Berlin to stop a local Expressionist painter (his own childhood friend) from practicing his "degenerate" art, Siggi's father, Jens Ole Jepsen, carries out his duty with a doggedness and consistency that proves deeply revealing in its implications for the people of the modest, taciturn town. Writes Goldhagen, in his controversial and award-winning study *Hitler's Willing Executioners*, "All 'obedience,' all 'crimes of obedience' (and this refers only to situations in which coercion is not applied or threatened), depend upon the existence of a propitious social and political context in which the actors deem the authority to issue commands legitimate and the commands themselves not to be a gross transgression of sacred values and the overarching moral order." Sure enough, this proves true in the remote little town of Rugbüll, this simple village drama a brilliant microcosm of the insidiously destructive power of the Third Reich itself.

While at first resistant to the idea of writing this obligatory essay, the narrator Siggi Jensen, soon finds himself enthralled by the normally humdrum subject of duty, inhabiting the past in all its richness, sorrow, and detail, and filling notebook after notebook with his descriptions of his intense, if largely refracted experiences of the war as a child in Rugbüll—of the many eccentric characters in the village there, of his friendship and complicity with the local artist, Max Ludwig Nansen, and of his ultimate defiance of his father, the dutiful policeman and proxy for the State. Told in some of the freshest, most evocative language I have read in years, I would be remiss if I didn't offer you a little taste of it, this from the opening of Chapter 2 called "No Painting Permitted":

> *In the year '43 (to get going somehow), on a Friday it was, in April, in the morning, perhaps around midday, my father, Jens Ole Jepsen, policeman, who manned Rugbüll, the northernmost police station in Schleswig-Holstein, got himself ready for a daily trip to Bleeckenwarf, in order to deliver to the painter Max Ludwig Nansen, who the people round about simply called — 'The Painter', an official order form Berlin by which he was forthwith forbidden to paint. Unhurriedly my father gathered together his rain-cape, field-glasses, uniform belt and torch; he busied himself at his desk, obviously with the intention of delaying his departure, buttoned up and unbuttoned his tunic for the second time, eyed the miserable spring day and listened to the wind, while I waited for him, muffled up and motionless. It was not merely wind one heard; this north-westerly, besieging the farms, the hedges and rows of trees, tumultuously skirmishing, testing their*

resistance, was what shaped the landscape, a black, windy landscape, crooked and tousled and charged with some incomprehensible meaning. It was this wind of ours, I think, that made the roofs keen of hearing, made the trees prophetic, caused the old mill to grow larger, swept across the ditches so that they became delirious, or attacked the peat-barges, despoiling their shapeless loads.

When our wind was out and about, one was well advised to put some ballast in one's pockets—packets of nails, or bits of lead piping or even a flat-iron— to be a match for it. Such a wind is part of our lives and we could not argue with Max Ludwig Nansen for bursting his paint-tubes, taking furious violet and crude white to make the north-westerly visible, this north-westerly that belongs to us and which we know so well—the wind to which my father was listening with deep suspicion.

P.N.

Hard Streets

The Other Paris by Luc Sante
The Matthew Scudder novels of Lawrence Block

Whenever someone stops me on the street to ask me what "neoliberalism" means—you'd be surprised—I suggest that the questioner Google some images of Times Square in the 1970s and then compare the gritty pictures of New York's *demimonde* (prostitutes, peep shows, pretzel stands, porn theaters, pizza by the slice, bucket-of-blood bars) with today's corporatized/Disneyified version—a mind-numbing onslaught of digital advertising, cleaned up by a succession of neolib mayors who wanted "the center of the universe" to cater to consumers rather than to the unwashed and, let's be honest, libidinous masses. "Family friendly," meaning no working girls, boys on the make, nobody nodding in doorways, no black guys with boom boxes—the smell of burnt chestnuts replaced by the smell of money. The lowly hot dog, slathered in mustard and affordable for all—the great democratic street food of America—now sets you back a five spot at least, and the guy who hands it to you is wearing plastic gloves and *not* smoking a cigar. In other words, New York, once a place where a person could at least dip his or her toe in the real world has been gentrified and commodified out of existence. That's the meaning of neoliberalism.

New York in the Wagner-Lindsay-Beame era of grit and sleaze (of the best sort) is brilliantly captured in the Matthew Scudder novels of Lawrence Block, among the finest writers of *noir* fiction, a dozen novels set in New York in the Iron Age before Giuliani and Bloomberg forged the World of Oz. I want to get to Sante but just a word about Block, whose books should be better known. His Matt Scudder series follows the life of an alcoholic ex-cop (he quit the force after accidentally shooting a young Puerto Rican girl), who has moved out of his Long Island home and settled into a hotel room in what was once Hell's Kitchen but is now, appropriately, called Clinton. Scudder's lady friend is a call girl he met while trolling the streets around Times Square. Scudder isn't a detective, but he survives by doing favors for various people, including the ominous Mick Ballou, an Irish mob figure who is among the more interesting bad/good guys in all of genre fiction. Scudder walks around the city, attends two or three AA meetings each day, and with minimal help from NYPD puts some very bad people in jail. But the finest part of Block's books, the irresistible sections, are his descriptions of that old New York. On a walking tour of Hell's Kitchen a few years back I looked for Scudder's hotel and for Armstrong's, his favorite watering hole. Both are still there, but *spruced up*. I went so far as to have a bourbon and coffee in Armstrong's *Pub* (Scudder's drink of choice before the black-outs got too bad), but it was no good—there were yuppies and ferns and a bartender who didn't want to talk.

I loved that older, gritty New York, the new one, not so much. I never knew the old Paris, the one about which Luc Sante, our poet/scholar of the underside of urban life writes so brilliantly in *The Other Paris*. I've read everything I can about the Paris of Baudelaire and du Beauvoir, of Henry Miller and Hemingway, of Dabit and the witty Elaine Dundy. But the world opened for us by Sante is of an altogether different sort. Perhaps Henry Miller's wonderful *Quiet Days in Clichy* comes closest to evoking the city hidden with the City, the world of the underclass, the proletarian subbasement of a wealthy world-class metropolis, the wine bars and bistros and cafes and bordellos and back alleys, *flâneurs* and prostitutes, faded dandies, transvestites, and brawlers.

The great historian of the rich life of Paris was of course Walter Benjamin, whose *Arcades Project* presents an unrivaled inventory of the great city, especially of its inner life. But Luc Sante has done something original, and perhaps even more enlightening in *The Other Paris*. Sante, whose *Low Life* is a great accounting of 19th century New York, has performed a similar service for those who would know the "low life" of Paris—he's opened up neighborhoods and previously closed doors, and shown us lives that reveal a Paris quite different from that of the Michelin guides. As a bonus, he's also filled the text with hundreds of black and white photographs.

> *"The dance halls of Montmartre were by that point [when the Impressionists began to paint them] as showcases for prostitution, but there were dance halls in most other neighborhoods...In Charonne stood the Bal des Lilas, known as the Bal des Punaises (cockroaches or bedbugs), which had, tucked away behind the orchestra, a bench reserved for women too drunk to dance, and those who lacked shoes..."*

The sections on little known artists and artistes are brilliant. Here's Frehel, the great chanteuse who died in 1951:

> *"Her charisma and strength of personality, in addition to the map of her life in her face—her big eyes and full lips remaining as proof of lost beauty under the palimpsest—got her cast in movies, sixteen of them, mostly in the 1930's...In her last years she sold vegetables on the street. Her landlady said, 'She scared me. She was like a bull.' In 1950 a group of young admirers that included Jacques Yonnet [author of Paris Noir: The Secret Life of a City] and Robert Girand, working-class poet and journalist] got her to perform one last time...a year later she was dead in Pigalle."*

There are hundreds of anecdotes like this one, of forgotten singers, of poets and painters not on the A list, of dance halls and cafes now vanished to make way for offices and apartments. My favorite chapter, "Insurgents," surveys a territory unknown to me—the underground political/criminal history of France's capital, from the Commune (Louise

Michel) to the notorious career of Edouard Carouy and the gang of which he was a part, a group immortalized (after a fashion) in Emile Michon's *Un peu l' ame des Bandits* (*A Little of the Bandits' Soul*)—apparently no relation to Magritte's painting of the same name.

And who cares? A forgotten New York, a Paris that is hardly present. Perhaps the point of reading Sante's marvelous *hommage* is to be reminded that the city, far from being a place of commerce, a monument to the egoism and elitism of the marketplace, was for most of its history simply a place where people of all kinds lived and worked and loved and died. In other words, a democratic and egalitarian space where one could hardly avoid rubbing shoulders with different sorts of people. Of course, that still happens, but in the city within the City the rubbing took a more intimate form, defining the lives of citizens in a way that is no longer the case.

G.O.

Dictatorship of Flies

*When the trumpet sounded
everything was prepared on earth,
and Jehovah gave the world
to Coca-Cola Inc., Anaconda,
Ford Motors, and other corporations.
The United Fruit Company
reserved for itself the most juicy
piece, the central coast of my world,
the delicate waist of America.*

*It baptized these countries
Banana Republics
and over the sleeping dead,
over the unquiet heroes
who won greatness,
liberty, and banners,
it established an opera buffa:
it abolished free will,
gave out imperial crowns,
encouraged envy, attracted
the dictatorship of flies...*

Pablo Neruda
from "La United Fruit Co.",
Canto General (1950)

Modeled after the brutal Guatemalan dictator and corporate henchman for the American-owned United Fruit Company, Manuel José Estrada Cabreras (1898-1920), the nameless tyrant of Nobel laureate Miguel Ángel Asturias' most influential novel, *El Señor Presidente*, achieves a nearly mythical stature in this surreal and brawling tale as an aloof and evil god, the mysterious source of all suffering and death. What we learn of him we learn principally through the eyes and mouths of the poor and mad and dispossessed, as well as through the political jockeying of his many sycophants and jackals. Alternately praised as "Beloved Deity," "First Citizen of the Nation," and—in a single breath, without a trace of irony—"Constitutional President of the Republic, Benefactor of the Country, Head of the great Liberal Party, and Liberal-hearted Protector of Studious Youth," this reclusive tyrant—with his toothless gums, pendulous cheeks, and pinched eyelids—is compared daily by his wretched subjects to none other than Pericles, Jesus Christ, and "the Sun King at Versailles."

Yet ultimately this novel is a less a satire of a particular man and regime, a particular Banana Republic* (for which Asturias had no shortage of choices, most notably Jamaica and nearby Honduras) than a broader, artistically ambitious study of the brutal effects of plutocracy, no matter the era, the people, the place. Indeed if one were to change the names, switch the props, adjust the lighting here and there, this novel could be set almost anywhere today (forget Iraq and North Korea and Iran; think of China, Russia, and Germany, think of England and France, think especially of the U.S.A.)—any place where, in the hallowed name of This or That, the elites of business, politics, and the military have gladly joined hands.

In a story reminiscent of the gory productions of the popular, turn-of-the-century Parisian theatre, the Grand Guignol, there is one character, a man known as Miguel Angel Face (Miguel Cara de Ángel), who serves as a lifeline for the reader throughout the novel's many twists and convulsions and turns, a moral, starkly human gauge of the corruption and tyranny that reigns supreme in this unnamed Central American nation.

Known as one of the first "dictator novels" (see also *Fecundo* by Domingo Faustino Sarmiento and *Nostromo* by Joseph Conrad), a genre that would inspire such other Latin American greats as *Autumn of the Patriarch*; *I, the Supreme*; and *The Feast of the Goat*, *El Señor Presidente* is additionally remarkable as a novel for its clear break from the historic and realist style that dominated the period, both in Europe and Latin America. Cleary influenced by surrealism, Asturias, in his effort to more deeply probe the human psyche under tyranny, achieved a new style at once mythical, dreamlike, and incantatory, an innovation soon to inspire the "magical realism" boom of the 1960's and 1970's, for which the literature of Latin America remains widely, if imperfectly known.

* The term was coined by coined by American author O. Henry around 1904, following his travels in Honduras.

P.N.

The Falling of the Dusk

The Blind Owl, Sadegh Hedayat

Hegel's profound insight into our historical blindness has been affirmed again and again in recent decades—understanding comes too late, history preempts reflection and therefore wisdom. The Owl of Minerva flies with the falling of the dusk.

But in one respect Hegel was incorrect. Some persons do see the truth, as it were in advance of its unfolding. There are false prophets to be sure, usually hawking a future that will bring them riches and power, but there are genuine prophets as well. Hedayat was one such. Long before the fateful combination of autocratic power and fundamentalist religion (the creation, in part, of foreign meddling and Western greed) conspired to undo Iran's historical and cultural greatness, Hedayat foretold the event in his writings.

The tension between Western ideas and the cultural traditions of the rest of the world—the subject of so much great literature—manifested itself in the life and art of Hedayat, the finest of Iranian modernist writers. He was obsessed with the novelists and poets of his generation who were expanding the boundaries of fiction and the understanding of the psychological turmoil imposed on ordinary men and women by progress, urbanization, and war. Hedayat read Kafka and Chekhov, Rilke and Poe, while at the same time immersing himself in Persian literature, folklore, and history. His literary works seek a balance between tradition and the tumultuous change that was the touchstone of his age (he was born in 1900). He believed in the power of literature to awaken his countrymen to the dangers of complacency, the risks inherent in obedience to a monarch and to a clergy that dominated intellectual and emotional life in Iran. He felt unheeded and ignored, and was driven to despair, exile, and, in 1951, suicide.

The Blind Owl is Hedayat's only novel and a classic of modern Iranian fiction. It is a strange, hallucinatory book, overwrought and almost mystical in style and content. The story—as much a dream as a traditional plot—focuses on the obsessions of a solitary Iranian artist (he decorates pen cases) with a woman who haunts his wine- and opium-induced visions. As I read the *The Blind Owl* I kept thinking of Poe's "Lenore," and finally found the lines in Hedayat's strong predecessor that I had been dimly recalling:

> *"Let no bell toll!—lest her sweet soul, amid its hallowed mirth,*
> *Should catch the note, as it doth float up from the damned earth."*

This sentiment, and the mysterious Lenore, are typical not

only of Poe but of dozens of European romantics who haunt *The Blind Owl*. She is the mysterious woman who dies in the artist's garret and who possesses the sublimity and inexplicable power of the tubercular Clavdia Chauchat in Mann's vision of cultural decay or of Maria Timofeevna in *Demons*—insubstantial (diseased!) women whose proximity to death raises their value as objects of sexless adoration. To love the dying (or dead, in the case of Poe) Feminine is to slip free of a world that is horrifying in its banality and coarseness. One can find rich studies of this construct of ideas in Leslie Fiedler or Camille Paglia.

> *"I often used to recall the days of my childhood in order to forget the present, in order to escape from myself."*
>
> *"Sometimes I imagined that the visions I saw were those which appeared to everyone who was at the point of death. All anxiety, awe, fear and will to live had subsided within me and my renunciation of the religious beliefs which had been inculcated into me in my childhood had given me an extraordinary inner tranquility. What comforted me was the prospect of oblivion after death.....I had never been able to adapt myself to the world in which I was now living."*
>
> (from *The Blind Owl*)

Romantic modernism. The second half of *The Blind Owl*—actually a novella thematically linked to the first half of the book that reprises the same themes at an even higher pitch—evokes not only Poe but T.S. Eliot, especially *The*

Four Quartets:

> *Where is there an end of it, the soundless wailing,*
> *The silent withering of autumn flowers*
> *Dropping their petals and remaining motionless;*
> *Where is there an end to the drifting wreckage,*
> *The prayer of the bone on the beach, the unprayable*
> *Prayer at the calamitous annunciation?*
>   *("The Dry Salvages" II)*

What is going on here? It's facile and reductive to point to Hedayat's despair and suicide, to his inability to live in a present that mocked the things he believed in—individual autonomy, the dangers of religion, vegetarianism (yes, Hedayat is among the most ardent defenders of animals), the sanctity of art. The weight of personal despair plays a role in Hedayat's work and gives it much of its power, but more important is the fact that he was a committed cosmopolitan, a believer in the universal value and transformative power of literature at a time when only blood and iron and money and nationalism stirred the masses of men. The romantic modernist isn't just nostalgic for a vanished past; he has recognized that there can be no compromise with the present without losing one's soul. Better to die, or remain silent (same thing if you are a writer) than to rage against the inevitable.

Stefan Zweig, Nietzsche, Kafka, Robert Walser, and, reaching back further, Leopardi, Trakl, Novalis—Hedayat is in their company, a man out of time, in the wrong place, feeling too deeply and being too unwilling to give up the things for which he lived. Until cynicism came along to save us from being serious, the deep thinkers and great souls had no choice but to succumb to the machines. To the 'bots' as we now affectionately call them, to the Shahs and Ayatollah's, to the gruff liars and self-seekers. I'm not fond of the notion of the "rabble," but I don't know Persian so I will let Hedayat's translated words stand:

> *"What relationship could exist between the lives of the fools and healthy rabble who were well, who slept well, who performed the sexual act well, who had never felt the wings of death on their face every moment—what relationship could exist between them and one like me who has arrived at the end of his rope and who knows that he will pass away gradually and tragically?"*

G.O.

Palestinians at Sea

The "Ship of Fools" trope has been an important allegory in Western art and literature for at least five hundred years. Typically involving a pilotless ship packed with fools of every kind, it is the story of a journey to nowhere, an apologue, a parable, that has been traced to actual practice in Renaissance Europe. As described by Michel Foucault in his book *Madness and Civilization*, there was a tradition—no one knows how rare or widespread—of ridding a city of its lunatics by crowding them onto a ship then turning it out to sea.

I first learned of this allegory when I happened upon a copy of Katherine Anne Porter's 1962 novel, *Ship of Fools*, a story about a motley collection of Mexicans, Germans, Americans, and Jews bound from Veracruz, Mexico, aboard a German freighter called the *Vera*, to Europe on the eve of World War II—a journey to nowhere indeed! Clearly Jabra Ibrahim Jabra had something similar in mind when he wrote his novel, *The Ship (al-Safinah)*, if with some bold and compelling variations. Set shortly after the creation of the State of Israel in 1948, what Palestinians refer to as "The Catastrophe" (al-Nakbah), the novel follows an assortment of Palestinian exiles—writers, professors, artists, and intellectuals, as well as a smattering of Lebanese, Iraqis, and Europeans—on a journey aboard the passenger ship *Hercules* as it plies the Mediterranean en route to London. Drinking, dancing, debating, declaiming, the travelers pass their days in a state of restless limbo, a sort of floating Purgatory between East and West, neither here nor there. Into this crucible Jabra pours all of the hopes and dreams, all of the anger, frustration, and despair of the Palestinian people, as well as that of the Arab world itself. According to translators Adnan Haydar and Roger Allen, "Palestine is the microcosm of the Arabs' defeat, of their failure to determine their destiny in their own lands. The fall of Palestine is not an incidental event; it is the tragic fall of the whole Arab world, a product and a result of Arab acquiescence to a reality before which they are helpless. Palestine is the land, the soul to be reclaimed…"

What is so striking about Jabra Ibrahim Jabra's novel, about his particular version of the allegory, is that for all its nods to the West, its rich and numerous allusions to nihilism and classical Greece, to Bach, Freud, Goethe, Balzac, Eliot, Le Corbusier, Dostoevsky, Kafka, and Thomas Aquinas, the novel hardly feels Western at all. For we read also—and to equal effect—of Ibn al-Arabi, Ahmad Shawqi, and the Arab history of Palestine, hear the haunting, incomparable voice of Umm Kulthum. Told from a variety of perspectives, in a series of dramatic, sometimes internal monologues, the novel feels far more like a modern version of *Tales from the Thousand and One Nights* than a remaking of Porter's *Ship of Fools*. Distinctly

Arab in style, distinctly Palestinian in longing and grief, the novel represents a dexterous bridging of East and West that springs directly from the identity of the author himself. Born to a Syriac Orthodox Arab family in Bethlehem in 1919, Jabra Ibrahim Jabra came to be one of the finest ambassadors of his time between the Arab and European worlds. Novelist, poet, translator, sculptor, painter, art collector, playwright, and critic, his work and interests knew no boundaries. Sadly, as noted by the late Anthony Shadid in a 2010 article for *The New York Times*, "His [Jabra's] secular notion of identity has withered before the ascent of sectarian and religious forces. In an asymmetric conflict, at times cartoonish, an aggressive West faces a seething East."

P.N.

Worship

The Age of Atheists, Peter Watson
Ostend, Volker Weidermann
I and Thou, Martin Buber
The Name of God is Mercy, Pope Francis
The Quest of the Historical Jesus, Albert Schweitzer
"What Binds Us," Jane Hirshfield
Music by Igor Stravinsky and Steve Reich

"In the day to day trenches of adult life, there is actually no such thing as atheism.
There is no such thing as not worshiping. Everybody worships. The only choice we get is what to worship."

David Foster Wallace

I'm listening to Steve Reich's "Tehillim" on vinyl as I write, a recording I bought in 1981 at a record shop in Providence, a possession as valuable to me as my copies of Plato's *Dialogues* or Shakespeare's plays. "Tehillim" is the Hebrew word for Psalm; Reich chose the well-known lines from Psalm 19 that begin "The heavens declare the glory of G-d,/the sky tells of his handiwork," and the lovely lines from Psalm 34, "Who is the man that desires life, /and loves days to see good?/Guard your tongue from evil, / and your lips from speaking deceit. / Turn from evil, and do good. / Seek peace and pursue it." The B-side covers Psalms 18 and 150. The music is incantatory, hypnotic, like the plainsong one hears during the recitation of the Hours in a monastery. The voices intone each Hebrew syllable with equal stress, as though reaching through the words toward the divine: *Ha-sha-my-im, meh-sa-peh-peh-rim ka-vohd-Kail.* Reich was among the remarkable collection of artists gathered by Manfred Eicher at ECM in the 70s and 80s—I own dozens of records from this era by musicians like Ralph Towner, Jan Garbarek, Gary Burton, and Pat Metheny. Eicher allowed Reich and the rest to experiment with long, loosely structured compositional forms, non-traditional arrangements, and unexpected concatenations of instruments.

The sublime series of Keith Jarrett's improvisational piano works is also part of the ECM catalogue. These performances stir in me a sense of awe at the beauty of the sonic world. Like Reich's "Tehillim," like the sublime poetry of the Psalms themselves, they evoke a feeling that must be akin to worship.

Don't be alarmed. This won't be a Judaeo-Christian apologetic, or an apology for any other religious persuasion. Like sex, religion is private, or should be. Public sex is pornographic; so are public ravings that purport to describe one's private conversations with the deity (*de rigueur* for any American aspiring to public office). We really do need to revive the idea of reticence, of a divide between our public and performative selves (high drama!) and our silent, solitary, authentic selves. But that's another topic, for another time.

The impetus for this essay was some reading I've done this past week in Buber and Schweitzer, in Peter Watson and in the short historical essay *Ostend* by Volker Werdermann. I often read in themes. This week's theme was cultural despair, informed in part by the American presidential election. Werdermann's little book on Joseph Roth and Stefan Zweig in the resort city of Ostend in the middle 1930s is a deft and affecting lament for Europe's second collective suicide of the twentieth century. Roth, a more cynical and worldly figure than his romantic and somewhat naive friend Zweig, understood what would transpire with the Nazi seizure of power. Zweig came to see the future as well, and perhaps, in his sobriety rather more clearly than Roth, though not before he'd convinced himself that Europe's humanistic traditions would prevail over fascism. By 1936 such a belief in humanistic traditions was farcical, suicidal, and Zweig decamped to Brazil where he and his wife Lotte took their own lives (a tragic story brilliantly retold by Peter Nash in *The Perfection of Things*.)

After *Ostend* I ventured into the intellectual history of Peter Watson's *The Age of Atheists*. Watson is a breezy and readable intellectual historian—his encyclopedic *The German Genius* (2010) pays homage to a remarkable tradition of artistic and philosophical achievement, while at the same time lamenting the rapturous mass destruction of those very traditions—and of much else besides.

Watson's thesis isn't original, though he examines it with care: with the "death of God" proclaimed by Nietzsche, Western persons yearned to fill a spiritual void in their lives. Without the promise of transcendence, without the rich symbolism of religion, without the moral guidance of Scripture, Western life devolved into violence and chaos, *Being and Time*, the narcissism of Sartre's existentialism, into nihilism, preening aestheticism, war and genocide, greed and consumerism, mad science and bad science, and then, of course, right back into the arms of wacko fundamentalists. Watson isn't put off by the emptiness of most of the failed sources of meaning he describes—on the contrary, the age of atheists is mostly depicted as level-headed, devoid of delusions, married to progress. In other words, as liberal, the secular city upon a hill.

Everybody worships according to the now suspect but still, for me, quotable DFW—but what exactly? Watson aside, if you subtract God or Truth, or Meaning—all metaphysics, all general nouns, then, be honest, there isn't much left to provide us with hope and comfort. History is a blood-bath. Philosophy, which abandoned the project of meaning (or Meaning) with Nietzsche, has devolved into technical arguments whose arcane vocabulary has closed the discipline to all but specialists. Politics has surrendered the common good for dramas of self-aggrandizement, and therefore accepted the pragmatic necessity of pandering to the basest instincts of an increasingly ill-informed electorate. And theology, particularly Catholic theology, persists in repeating ancient fairy tales and demanding faith in place of understanding. A sorry spectacle, and one whose discontents have not been eased by the alternative beliefs outlined by Watson. I adore Joyce and Proust and Joseph Roth and Zweig, but their effect on my soul, my inner life, is fleeting, narcotic, comforting, but no substitute for belief in...what? I love literature, but can I *worship* it?

I find the "new atheists"—unlike the intellectually astute "old atheists" like Bertrand Russell—to be a sorry lot. Dawkins, Hitchens, and Dennett mistake what can be said about believing in God for the actual experience of believing in God. Their mockery of the tall tales that fill the Bible and other religious books feels cheap, rather like laughing at the sentimental banalities of a greeting card or mocking someone who really enjoys Elizabeth Barrett Browning's "How Do I Love Thee"—as if a heartfelt wish for joy or an expression of love is diminished by words that can't live up to the feeling. As if the feeling doesn't come first.

The truth is simple: all deep feeling, every profound conviction, any belief that isn't merely a passing fancy—dammit, *everything that matters* lives in us in a place that language cannot penetrate, does not even belong. Who came up with the idea that language defines the limits of truth?

Martin Buber is among the theologians I still read. I

cannot endure Catholic theology, though I have browsed the admirable Pope Francis's little book *The Name of God Is Mercy* (sorry *Papa*, I'm not seeing it), as modest and lovely a Q and A on faith as you will ever find—and as ecumenical a book as I have ever read, touching in its sincerity. However, Francis is unique. With rare exceptions, his parish priests and conservative bishops have never outgrown Augustine's self-loathing or Paul's horror of the body. Jewish and Protestant theologians are another matter. Especially German theologians, a point that Watson makes in *The Age of Atheists*. With great finesse and astonishing erudition—they all read Hebrew, Greek, Aramaic, and Latin as well as all the modern languages—men like Buber, Hershel (a Pole), Schweitzer, Tillich, Niebuhr (American born, of German descent), Oscar Cullmann, Karl Barth (Swiss) and many others, revitalized theology as a legitimate intellectual pursuit.

Buber theologizes Kant's profound ethical idea of the categorical imperative (there are several versions, but they all stem from the same insight). The greatest moral imperative we have is to treat others as ends in themselves, never as means to an end, never as objects, never in a way that we couldn't imagine conceptualizing as a universal moral law, binding on everyone, always. Concise and intuitively appealing, central to any ethics, the entire point, one would hope, of Judaism and Christianity. The lonely, alienated "I" of *Being and Nothingness* become an I-Thou relationship in Buber's theology. Rather than focus exclusively on human perception, as most philosophy since Comte has done, Buber privileged relationships—to things, to the world, to other people, and, through other people, to God. Buber's theology appears to have been deeply influenced by Husserl, by the phenomenological insight that perception and experience are relational, and that consciousness is inherently creative. Human beings, in Buber's view, desire "to possess God," long for "a continuity in space and time" that comes with possession of God. Communal life and the desire for salvation, that is, for deep relationships, constitute the core of Buber's I-Thou relationship. There's a gentleness and humanity in Buber that appeals to me, a sense I also get in reading Spinoza that I am witness to a profound intellect yearning for truth. I don't understand everything, or even much, but reading Buber is not unlike a walk in the woods: you may not be able to name all the trees and plants, but you feel refreshed by the exercise.

I won't attempt to summarize Schweitzer's classic *Quest*, or his life, which was extraordinary in every respect. Had he only written this volume of historical theology, or his magisterial book on the life and music of J.S. Bach, or done nothing but found a hospital in what is today Gabon (French Equatorial Africa), his life would have been remarkable, even saintly. When I think that Schweitzer shares the honor of a Nobel Peace Prize (1952) with the likes of Henry Kissinger and Barak Obama I have to laugh to keep from weeping. Schweitzer used his prize money to found a hospital for lepers.

The historical Jesus is a mode of dealing with one of the fundamental problems of Christianity, namely the fact that the founder and his contemporary disciples saw their faith as apocalyptic, that is, they believed time was coming to an end, and that the events prophesied in Daniel and Isaiah were close at hand (Mark 13). Schweitzer took up the challenge of historicity through a brilliant critical survey of Protestant theology, and a reconceptualizing of Jesus's message. Specifically, Schweitzer focuses on the paradoxes, contradictions, and indecipherability of Jesus's words. And the greatest of these paradoxes, plain to anyone who reads the Gospel of Mark (the source of the other three) is the idea of predestination. In Mark, chapter 4, verses 10-12, Jesus explicitly says that his teaching in parables is done to keep the message of salvation closed to those who are not among the chosen. If the message weren't esoteric, "*they might be converted and forgiven,*" clearly not a desirable outcome. Nor did the Parousia, the Second Coming of the Son of Man, occur as prophesied, so that the fundamental beliefs touted by Christians have at their core what is at least a paradox, if not an outright contradiction. A religion of *ending*, St. Paul had to reinvent the faith as a religion of *waiting*—this was a tall order, and if one reads Paul objectively, it is easy enough to see that he failed. Modern theology, Schweitzer observes, with its emphasis on what is universal in Christianity, distorts the historical facts and the nature of world-negating message of the founder. There is much to admire in Jesus, but there is much to be confounded by as well. Schweitzer as musicologist, physician, and humanitarian was committed to seeing clearly and to telling the truth as he saw it.

What should we make of these arcane arguments, these attempts by theologians to create a form of meaning that doesn't mock history or human reality? I am persuaded by Schweitzer's earnestness, his willingness to debunk a century and a half of theological preconceptions, but his Jesus is no more appealing to me as an object of worship than the "Lord" invoked by Rev. Falwell. In the end I return to Watson's thesis: we're trying to fill a void left by the death of God. Some fill it with art and some with a rereading of ancient religious texts. In either case the effort falls short, the crude handprint of wishful thinking is everywhere evident.

***

By this point I have moved on from Steve Reich and am listening to Stravinsky conducting his "Symphony of Psalms," composed in 1930 for Serge Koussevitzky and the Boston Symphony Orchestra. The text of the first movement is from Psalm 38: *Quoniam advena ego sum apud te et peregrinus sicut omnes patres mei,* "Like my fathers, I am a stranger to You, and a wanderer," or perhaps better: "You are a stranger to me, just as You were to all my fathers—and I am a seeker." Which pretty much sums up the case.

Why so coy, so hidden, so cruel, at least within the ethical terms human beings are permitted to understand? Why, *contra* the good Pope, is there so little justice and virtually no mercy? Couldn't it be, shouldn't it be, otherwise? Imagine an invisible and unknowable lover leaving opaque notes lying about a vast desert and then enjoining us, on no evidence whatsoever, to love her unconditionally. Absurd. Beyond a "leap of faith," a catapult into the void.

So, if David Foster Wallace is correct, and I believe that he is, what do we choose to worship? Or, since it's none of my business what you do, what should I worship?

I have no idea. My prayers these days—what I call the words cast into the Great Void like bars of Bach's Goldberg's (performed, FYI, by Glenn Gould) set adrift on NASA's probes for intelligent life—are full of thanks for family and friends, for mountains and the Gulf of Mexico, for great books and stirring music. As a kid I asked for stuff: "Lord, please can I have new ice skates?" Older, I merely wish to record my gratitude for this lucky chance, for a shot at being human (as the Buddhists put it). As for worship, let's say I'm open to suggestions.

I'm going to give the redoubtable Jane Hirshfield the last word in this long post; Jane H., a modern mystic—it's "What Binds Us," and is from the early collection *Of Gravity & Angels*. Try to find a Hirshfield poem that isn't as deep as scripture:

> *There are names for what binds us:*
> *strong forces, weak forces.*
> *Look around, you can see them:*

the skin that forms in a half-empty cup,
nails rusting into the places they join,
joints dovetailed on their own weight.
The way things stay so solidly
wherever they've been set down—
and gravity, scientists say, is weak.
And see how the flesh grows back
across a wound, with a great vehemence,
more strong
than the simple, untested surface before.
There's a name for it on horses,
when it comes back darker and raised: proud flesh,
as all flesh,
is proud of its wounds, wears them
as honors given out after battle,
small triumphs pinned to the chest—
And when two people have loved each other
see how it is like a
scar between their bodies,
stronger, darker, and proud;
how the black cord makes of them a single fabric
that nothing can tear or mend.

G.O.

Into Africa

It was Nadine Gordimer herself who recommended to me and my wife Annie that we stay at Letaba Rest Camp in the heart of Kruger National Park. We had—by a seemingly miraculous convergence of forces—found ourselves sitting face to face with the world-famous author and her husband, Reinhold Cassirer, one evening in their modest, if eclectically tasteful home at 7 Frere Road West in Johannesburg, South Africa. The year was 1990, a year that proved a curious window in time for us, as it was not only the year that Nelson Mandela was released from prison on Robben Island, what was surely the death-rattle of the apartheid regime, but was just months before Nadine Gordimer was awarded the Nobel Prize for Literature, after which point it is unlikely I would have had the chance to meet her at all, let alone in such an frank and convivial way.

It had started at a faculty lunch table in the small cafeteria of the independent school in Manhattan where my wife and I were teaching high school. Lunches in hand, we'd joined a colleague of ours, a woman named Judy Platt. As usual we'd talked of school, of students, when she, knowing how we loved to travel, had asked us what we had planned for the summer vacation, which was due to begin in a matter of weeks. After three successive summers of traveling in South East Asia, we'd told her that were planning to go to southern Africa instead, to South Africa in particular, where we looked forward to staying with a couple we knew in Johannesburg before commencing our travels in the region. "South Africa? I love South Africa!" she'd exclaimed. "One of my best friends lives there, in Jo'burg. Perhaps you've heard of her, Nadine Gordimer." I remember gasping at the name. "Heard of her!" I'd exclaimed. "Why, she's one of my favorite writers in the world!"

I wasn't exaggerating, for I'd fallen in love with her fiction—her short stories and novels—for their heady mixture of acute psychological insight and Chekhovian refinement of language and theme, as well as with the author herself for her morally courageous chronicling of apartheid in its most complex and pernicious forms. Elegant, cosmopolitan, a passionate reader of Gramsci and Proust, she was no ivory tower intellectual, but struggled daily in the trenches themselves, regularly berating the white Nationalist government in essays and editorials and letters to the editor, marching in protests, signing petitions, joining boycotts, and generally doing her best as an active and avid member of the ANC, Nelson Mandela's outlawed African National Congress.

Facing her there in her own home that evening was nearly too much for me to believe. Together we talked about

New York, a city she loved, and about her friend Judy, and we talked about her books, her writing, so that soon (and with a considerable amount of whiskey) the four of us were conversing and laughing with ease.

After it grew dark, and fearing for our safety at that time of night, she drove us back to our hotel in the once-Bohemian, then run-down, often violent neighborhood of Hillbrow (in fact we were awakened by gunshots that same night). Having made plans for her husband to pick us up tomorrow and show us his art gallery in nearby Rosebank, we thanked her and said our goodbyes.

Surely one of the highlights of that extraordinary evening for me, one I could hardly have anticipated, was the very car in which she'd driven us back to our hotel, a yellow Volkswagen "Thing" (remember those?), which—in what is perhaps my favorite of her novels, *July's People*—she used as the model for the Smales family's car in their escape into the countryside under the care and protection of their servant, July, a vehicle, a symbol of wealth and power and mobility, referred to repeatedly in the story as the "yellow bakkie", so that it had felt to me that night, as she'd driven us back through the dark Johannesburg streets, as if I were riding through the novel itself!

Of all Gordimer's short stories, surely one of the most poignant for me, for reasons I will explain, is her story "The Ultimate Safari". Set largely in Kruger National Park, where we spent a few nights upon her recommendation, a wildlife reserve of more than 7,500 square miles in the northeastern part of the country that, by the time we'd arrived in South Africa, had become a treacherous no-man's land between the Republic of South Africa and the neighboring country of Mozambique, then shattered by a violent civil war that had set tens of thousands of people on the move, each of them desperate to escape the fighting between the South African-sponsored Rhodesian rebel group RENAMO and the Marxist government forces known by the acronym FRELIMO. Gordimer herself had secretly sheltered some of these refuges in her home.

Of course the bitter irony of this, this situation, an irony deftly exploited by Gordimer in this story, is that what this meant for these many desperate Mozambicans was that, in order to escape the country with their lives, they had to cross the vast Kruger Park on foot, a park designed and rigorously maintained by white people so that white people could enjoy the African wildlife—a dense and dangerously congested population of hippos and lions and elephants, of antelopes, jackals, and zebras, of giraffes, wildebeests, hyenas, and snakes—as it once must have been. As with virtually everything she wrote, it is a deeply humane tale, a story both simply and beautifully told.

My admiration for the works of Nadine Gordimer quickly lead me to seek out the work of other South African writers. I read Alex La Guma, Alan Paton, Bessie Head, Miriam Tlali,

Peter Abrahams, J.M. Coetzee, Andre Brink, Dennis Brutus, Olive Shreiner, Zakes Mda, Richard Rive, Elsa Joubert, Breyton Breytenbach, Es'kia Mphahlele, Laurens van der Post, Rian Malan, Zoe Wicomb, and Damon Galgut. While in Johannesburg my wife and I had the pleasure of seeing Athol Fugard's play *My Children! My Africa!* at the famous and revolutionary Market Theatre, a production directed by the great playwright himself. This reading lead me to cast my net even more widely in the years to come, reading the literature of writers throughout the African continent. Here, for your consideration, is a list of some of the African authors I read (so many of them made available to the west by the remarkable Heinemann Press): Naguib Mahfouz, Buchi Emecheta, Chinua Achebe, Wole Soyinka, Sonallah Ibrahim, Amy Djoleto, T. Obinkaram Echew, Narrudin Farah, Mariama Bâ, Ousmane Sembène, Amos Tutuola, Laila Lalami, Ayi Kwei Armah, Bessie Head, Ama Ata Aidoo, Alifa Rifaat, Tsitsi Dnagarembga, Albert Memmi, Yusuf Idris, Tahar Ben Jalloun, Mohamed Choukri, Mongo Beti, Camera Laye, Mia Couto, Assia Djebar, Tayeb Salih, Mongane Wally Serote, Leópold Sédar Senghor, Ali Ghalem, Ngugi wa Thiong'o, Abdul Razak Gurnah, and Ben Okri—yes, why not start with Ben Okri's brilliant novel *The Famished Road*—the perfect means by which to find your way in.

P.N.

Bildungsroman

My Brilliant Friend, Elena Ferrante

> *"My Brilliant Friend is a large, captivating, amiably peopled bildungsroman."*
>
> James Wood

I must confess that I didn't share Mr. Wood's enthusiasm for *My Brilliant Friend*—I found the novel neither large nor captivating—and as for 'amiably peopled,' I wonder if Mr. Wood means that Ms. Ferrante felt amiable as she drew her characters or that he found the characters to be amiable as literary creatures—impossible to say. For my part, I found the scores of individuals who adorn what is essentially the *pas de deux* of Elena Greco and Lila Cerullo to be neither amiable nor fully conceptualized. They act only as foils for what really interests Ms. Ferrante, which is the complex friendship (hateship, loveship) of two girls who grow up in a rough and tumble working class neighborhood of Naples. Elena tells the story. It is her version of her life with Lila. We have no information about Lila's inner life, nor do we know much about Elena's. If this is a *Bildungsroman*, it is one with an astonishing lack of psychological depth or even authorial curiosity. It's a made-for-Masterpiece Theater sort of novel, one that could be filmed without loss of motivational depth or character analysis. What you see happening is what happens, the world of Naples in 1950 nicely fits with the liberal view that everyplace is anyplace when it comes to entertainment—really it's all the same, Upstairs and Down. If Universal Studios picks up the Ferrante franchise there will be gondolas and knife fights, handmade shoes and widows in black dresses. *The Godfather*, told from the children's perspective. A Catholic neighborhood without priests, lust without sex, learning without knowledge. The novel is like a watercolor, a miniature on an enormous canvas.

My favorite *Bildungsroman* are these, in no particular order: *To Kill A Mockingbird*; *Look Homeward, Angel* (Thomas Wolfe); *Stoptime* (Frank Conroy); *Great Expectations* and *David Copperfield*; *Portrait of the Artist*; and *Of Human Bondage* (Somerset Maugham). Is *Huckleberry Finn* a *bildungsroman*? *Invisible Man*? *Harry Potter*? Some would say yes, but I wonder if the key to the sub-genre isn't an epiphany of some sort—not merely "growing up," since a child narrator, over time, will inevitably do that, but a coming-into-consciousness, a seeing more clearly, a revelation of some deep truth. Most biographical novels will have elements of the *Bildungsroman*, but my sense of the thing is that the focus will be on a romantic encounter with the soul or the self—a real insight into something universal about being human— Joyce's *Portrait*, I suppose, fits my sense of the *Bildungsroman* best of all. I'm not persuaded that just any book about growing up makes the cut—Henry Roth's sociological narrative *Call It Sleep*, or James Farrell journalistic Studs Lonigan trilogy feel like artful documentaries, but their insights are social, material, and impersonal. Though I dearly love picaresque novels like *Tom Jones*, *Tristram Shady* and *The Adventures of Augie March*, stories of growing up, and, perforce, of acquiring experience and a degree of self-knowledge, I'm not sure they intend to offer the kind of universal insight into the human predicament that figures like Scout Finch, Eugene Gant, or David Copperfield offer.

I feel churlish about *My Brilliant Friend*. Everyone loves it. I have volume two on my desk and plan to read it (later). MBF was entertaining (in places), and I understand that it is the sort of novel that is a million times better than the average *Times* bestseller. But there are things about the book that were puzzling to me, even off-putting. Take, for example, this scene, late in the novel. Lila, who was skinny, ugly, and slightly unhinged as a child, metamorphoses—overnight—into Gina Lolabridiga, a real looker, the kind of Italian woman who drives (as the story goes) Italian men to murder. Here she is on the beach—the scene is narrated by Elena:

> *"One of those times [on the beach] I looked up for a second and saw a tall, slender, graceful girl in a stunning red bikini. It was Lila. By now she was used to having men's gaze on her, she moved as if there were no one in that crowded place, not even the young attendant who went ahead of her, leading her to*

> *the umbrella. She didn't see me and I didn't know whether to call her. she was wearing sunglasses, she carried a purse of bright colored fabric..."*

Sorry, this is Danielle Steele, not "one of the great novelists of our time" (*The New York Times*). There is no discernible reason why Elena (or the reader) would know that "[Lila] was used to having men's gaze on her," nor is the most interesting question raised by Lila's transformation from a cranky bag of bones into a world-class beauty even addressed in the book, namely, how does Lila see herself? She is, after all, the "brilliant friend," but she has no reality for the reader beyond Elena's confusing caricatures (bright student, driven worker, dutiful yet rebellious daughter, diffident friend). And this would be fine if we could parse Elena's perceptions of the world in any sort of interesting way, if we knew where we were to stand as we moved through the streets of Naples with her as our guide, with Elena as the lone voice and judge of the world we have allowed ourselves to be plunged into. But Elena is as much a blank as Lila—smart yet unintellectual, vain but asexual, dutiful but detached, the center of the universe, but maddeningly oblique on most subjects. Elena changes her mind about Lila and about the boys who like Lila and about her parents and teachers and schooling—she's not so much a cipher as a cloud of words; where, I kept wondering, should I rest my attention?

Why is this book so beloved? My cynical view is that books like this one satisfy our urge to read "foreign literature," books in translation—to have multi-cultural experiences without leaving the comfortable precincts of home. Elena Ferrante offers up a nice story about young women who might as well be from Naples, Florida as Naples, Italy. It's a good read, not very long, not at all strenuous, not deep, completely (incredibly) apolitical—didn't the poor of Naples have any political thoughts right after World War II? Pasquale Peluso is a communist, but that appears to hold no interest for anyone. The word "*Bildung*" means "education." A novel of education can be many things, from *The Sorrow of Young Werther* to *Portnoy's Complaint*. But what is wanted in an education above all is great depth and perspicacity, engagement with ideas, insight and revelation. For this, I'm afraid, one will have to look elsewhere than *My Brilliant Friend*.

G.O.

What Happens

What happens to a dream deferred?
Langston Hughes

There was a cold November wind blowing through 116th Street. It rattled the tops of garbage cans, sucked window shades out through the top of opened windows and set them flapping back against the windows; and it drove most of the people off the street in the block between Seventh and Eighth Avenues except for a few hurried pedestrians who bent double in an effort to offer the least possible exposed surface to its violent assault. It found every scrap of paper along the street—theater throwaways, announcements of dances and lodge meetings, the heavy waxed paper that loaves of bread had been wrapped in, the thinner waxed paper that had enclosed sandwiches, old envelopes, newspapers. Fingering its way along the curb, the wind set the bits of paper dancing high in the air, so that a barrage of paper swirled into the faces of the people on the street. It even took time to rush into doorways and areaways and find chicken bones and pork-chop bones and pushed them along the curb.

Cold, gritty, impersonal. Such is the atmosphere created by Ann Petry in the opening pages of her extraordinary novel, The Street. Set and published in the immediate wake of WWII, the story follows Lutie Johnson, a strong and beautiful African-American woman, in her struggle to gain a foothold—a little peace and security—for her and her eight-year-old son, Bub, amidst the poverty, racism, sexism, and violence of 1940's Harlem. By the time the story takes place, the great Harlem Renaissance, with its groundbreaking artists, writers, and musicians, with its headlong devotion to civic participation, political equality, and economic and cultural self-determination, is for many, like Lutie Johnson, but a figment of the past. Her life is defined instead by the Great Depression, which—at the time of this story—still casts its shadow over Harlem. "Last hired, first fired," African-Americans were hit even harder by the Depression than most. At the Depression's height, 25 percent of Americans had no jobs. In Harlem the rate was as high as 50 percent, tapering off only gradually during the war and in the immediate post-war years. Harassed, all but consumed by worry in her daily effort to provide a life for her and her son, Lutie Johnson is haunted daily by reminders of the American Dream and its promise to those who work hard, the prospect of her fulfillment as a woman and mother in Harlem but a cruel and mocking mirage.

Described without a trace of sentimentality or self-pity, in a lucid, hard-edged prose, *The Street* retails the struggles of this African-American woman who battles the odds in her effort to defy the fate that stalks her. "Written with cool anger," writes a critic from *Newsday*: "*The Street* rushes toward its fatalistic climax like a train toward a washed-out bridge."

    P.N.

Eros, Philos, Agape

Seven Years, by Peter Stamm

It was the great scholar and saint, Augustine of Hippo, who first explored with remarkable psychological acuity the nuances of human love and the connection between erotic passion and the love of God. In the *Confessions*, Augustine delineates with exquisite—at times excruciating—self-awareness his journey from *cupidity* to *caritas*, from love of the flesh to love of the spirit:

> *"I was in misery, and misery is the state of every soul overcome by love of mortal things and lacerated when they are lost. Then the soul becomes aware of the misery which is its actual condition even before it loses them."*

In his short, exegetical work, *On Christian Doctrine*, Augustine argues that Scripture, as God's Word, must always be read and interpreted as tending toward the enhancement of divine love—the word alone is merely dross. Its meaning uplifts the devout to knowledge of, and love for, the Divine.

Strange as it may seem, it was Augustine who came to mind as I read through the unusual and unsettling 2009 novel *Seven Years*. Believe me, there is nothing remotely Augustinian or even especially religious about this novel, yet I was compelled to think, as the story of Sonia, Alexander, and Ivona unwound, not of the physical compulsions of human love but of the mysterious psychological or, in this case, spiritual dimensions of attraction and obsession. The force fields of this particular triangle are oddly proportioned—unbalanced and disjointed. Alexander has married Sonia. He is a handsome, charming, and not especially ambitious architect, more deeply engaged by the practical side of design than the aesthetic. He offhandedly woos and eventually marries Sonia. Sonia, we are told (repeatedly) is beautiful, brilliant, dynamic, alluring, etc. Unlike Alex, Sonia is drawn to the aesthetics of architecture, in particular to the murky—authoritarian—utopianism of Le Corbusier. Indeed, the novel's epigram is from the great Swiss-French architect, an often-quoted modernist koan: "Light and shadow reveal form."

If Alexander and Sonia are light and shadow—he all practicality, down-to-earthiness, muddle and she a ravishing mystery, then the nearly mute, devout, lower-class and decidedly unattractive Ivona is "revealed form." For what Stamm has achieved, brilliantly if incredibly, is to make a silent outcast, a mystical washerwoman, the real center of the novel, the source of its energy and cryptic meaning.

How so?

Alexander has a brief tryst with Ivona, not out of attraction, but out of self-loathing. He finds Ivona repulsive but compelling. He strips off her clothes and lies on top of her, fondles her, but does not "possess her." It's a disturbing scene. Not quite rape, but not consensual, and it's not sexual but contractual, a tacit acknowledgment of a connection that persists over years and years, and even though Alex has virtually no contact with Ivona, his life is shaped by her being, and hers by him. It is as if Ivona, the victim of a callous and unfeeling assault, is the seducer. Thereafter, all through his profitable marriage and business partnership with Sonia, Alexander cannot excise Ivona from his consciousness. He cannot be happy with Sonia because the woman he desires is someone he doesn't love. It's a muddle, implausible, but entirely believable. The form of a life is made not by anything real, but by contrasting ideals.

We live in a building that we build ourselves. This "building" is not only our life—that's the least of it—this building is what we *think* about our life. The modernist ethos prescribed functionality, a prescription that grew out of the embrace of positivism and technology that swept through European intellectual life in the late 19th century. The great monuments of modernist writing accept as given the fact that we have built a world and that we are compelled to constantly reconstruct and remodel our view of our place in that world. The tension between a lived and an examined life is the source of what is loosely called "irony." The magisterial work of modernist irony is Thomas Mann's *Magic Mountain*, a novel that excavates the tension between the world we *actually* live in and the world we *think* we live in. Joyce, Woolf, James, Eliot, all wrote from the same ironic perspective, trying or not trying to bring into harmony light and shadow, life and thought, the building and the space it defines.

Augustine, as a believer in an omniscient deity, had no such paradoxes to resolve, and if he thought of irony at all he thought of it in the Greek sense of εἰρωνεία, the rhetorical trope for "dissimulation" or "delusion." Augustinian love is ironic when the lover mistakes his erotic fascination for the real thing, as when Chaucer's Troilus, released at last from the surly bonds of earth, looks down on the world and, at long last, *gets it*.

G.O.

Le Mot Juste *or* To Goad the Ox

> To dissect is a form of revenge.
> George Sand

"From infancy, we are told, [Gustave Flaubert] refused to suffer fools gladly," writes French-born American historian of ideas and culture, Jacques Barzun, in his introduction to his own translation of this remarkable literary curio of Flaubert's, known in French as *Dictionnaire des Idées Reçues* or *The Dictionary of Accepted Ideas*. "[He] would note down the inanities uttered by an old lady who used to visit his parents, and by his twentieth year he already had in mind making a dictionary of such remarks. And of course, like every French artist since the Romantic period, he loathed the bourgeois, whom he once for all defined as 'a being whose mode of feeling is low.' A highly deliberate writer, he detested platitudes and clichés, those borrowed, self-satisfied, expressly unconscious ideas and expressions "with which the 'right thinking' swaddle their minds."

No mere pedant, Flaubert believed that language truly mattered, that the words and phrases with which people interacted with one another, and with which they described and imagined the world, was a faithful reflection of both who they were and *who they might be*. For Flaubert, already wary of the 19th century's mass production of words and ideas, platitudes and clichés were not merely literary faux-pas, to be mocked and derided by those in the know, but "but philosophic clues from which he inferred the transformation of the human being under machine capitalism. This he took as a personal affront. Representing Mind, he fought the encroachment of matter and mechanism into the empty places that should have been minds." Significantly, the word *cliché* has a mechanical origin, referring, as it does, to the sound made by the metal printing plates for moveable type (called *stereotypes*) that click and reproduce the same image mechanically without end.

Yet Flaubert's war against linguistic complacency was also something more: it was a revolt against the tyranny of convention, an attack on mindless dogmatism, an assault upon the smugly stable status quo. Writes Barzun, in describing Flaubert's critique of all such ready-made phrases and expressions: "They all indicate fixity, which on reflection is seen to go beyond forms of speech or lack of ideas or aimless parroting. Social in origin, it is a lust for order through convention."

Here is an illustrative, often humorous sampling of some of the reigning bromides of his day, quite a number of which will certainly be familiar:

Accident. Always "regrettable" or "unlucky"—as if a mishap might sometimes be a cause for rejoicing.

Ambition. Always preceded by "mad," unless it be "noble."

Baldness. Always "premature," caused by youthful excesses—or by the hatching of great thoughts.

Beethoven. Do not pronounce Beathoven. Be sure to gush when one of his works is being played.

Buying and Selling. The goal of life.

Congratulations. Always "hearty," "sincere," etc.

Conversation. Politics and religion must be kept out of it.

Darwin. The fellow who says we're sprung from monkeys.

Descartes. Cogito ergo sum.

Evidence. Is "plain" when not "overwhelming."

Greek. Whatever one cannot understand is Greek.

Heat. Always "unbearable."

Hydra-Headed (Monster). Of anarchy, socialism, and so on of all alarming systems. We must try and conquer it.

Hypothesis. Often "rash," always "bold."

Indolence. Product of warm climates.

Languages (Modern). Our country's ills are due to our ignorance of them.

Locket. Must contain a lock of hair or a photograph.

Machiavelli. Though you have not read him, consider him a scoundrel.

Machiavellian. Word only to be spoken with a shudder.

Mephistophelean. Applies to any bitter laugh.

Nature. How beautiful is Nature! Repeat every time you are in the country.

Nectar. Confuse with ambrosia.

Old. Always "prematurely."

Original. Make fun of everything that is original, hate it, beat it down, annihilate it if you can.

Oysters. Nobody eats them any more: too expensive!

Paganini. Never tuned his violin. Famous for his long fingers.

Philosophy. Always snicker at it.

Photography. Will make painting obsolete.

Principles. Always "eternal." Nobody can tell their nature or number; no matter, they are sacred all the same.

Progress. Always "headlong" and "ill-advised."

Property. One of the foundations of society. More sacred than religion.

Regards. Always the best.

Seashells. You must bring some back from the seashore.

Suicide. Proof of cowardice.

Taste. "What is simple is always in good taste." Always say this to a woman who apologizes for the inadequacy of her dress.

Wagner. Snicker on hearing his name and joke about the music of the future.

Workman. Always honest—unless he is rioting.

If you are anything like me, as you read through these entries you were thinking of the clichés and platitudes, the many howlers, that you yourself would add to this list. Surely first, most pressing, of my own many favorites would be the trusty epithet, *looters*, a term recently resurrected by conservatives and liberals alike, following the rioting in Ferguson, Missouri in their smug, often specious coverage of the related, if more recent rioting in Baltimore. It seems that few if any of them saw the irony in chastising the rioters—mostly restless, disenfranchised African American youth—for their ransacking and burning of a local CVS (not a cozy "mom and pop shop," mind you, but part of a billion dollar corporate empire) in a nation the entire economy of which was recently brought to its knees by the ruthless, still-unpunished, ultimately government-sanctioned, looting of the American middle and working classes by our own hallowed banks and corporations. This even-then-well-known, well-documented bundle of brazen corporate swindles resulted, not in the pilfering of some aspirin, lipstick, hand cream, and diapers, but in an economic earthquake felt round the world, one that crippled the U.S. stock market, shattered the U.S. housing market, triggered a dangerous spike in U.S. unemployment, and has been calculated to have cost the average U.S. household between $50,000 and $125,000 in lost revenue, lost earnings, and additional taxes, taxes which subsequently were used by the federal government to rescue these same corporations and banks. Of course not even the term "looters" is sufficient to describe *them*.

If Flaubert was concerned about this matter then, in the late 1800's, it might behoove us, in this current "global village" of ours, in this dazzling era of high-tech media union and collaboration, to give the matter of our language some thought. Even among my most progressive and skeptical friends, I have long-detected a startling uniformity of ideas, of modes of expression, of political and rhetorical thinking about the world, most if not all of which appears to have been gleaned from the same four "right-thinking" sources: *The New Yorker*, *The Economist*, NPR, and *The New York Times*. It is a phenomenon that Walter Lippmann, in his astonishingly fresh and provocative 1922 book, *Public Opinion*, famously termed "the manufacture of consent"—a phrase, an expression, the great Flaubert would have certainly called *juste*.

P.N.

Is This the End?

Jan Dismas Zelenka, "The Lamentations of Jeremiah the Prophet," ZWV 53
Let Me Be Frank With You, Richard Ford (a Frank Bascombe novel)
The Essential Writings of Christian Mysticism, edited by Bernard McGinn
Crippled America: How to Make America Great Again, Donald J. Trump

The great Czech composer Jan Dismas Zelenka composed his "Lamentations" in the 1720's. They showcase Zelenka's remarkable contrapuntal talents—think Smetana or Dvořák, two musicians influenced by Zelenka's complex harmonic style. The "Lamentations" possess a rich, introspective feeling, slow orchestral cadences, haunting oboe solos, voices that modulate across layered textures of sound—here the brass uplifts, now the viola darkens the mood. The power of the work, as in the prophet's, is in its melancholy, a text and music that meditates on what might have been, distraught, perplexed by the human foibles that have brought us to *this*, to the Kingdom of Babylon.

> *Raise the wail and lamentation for the mountains,*
> *the dirge for the desert pastures,*
> *for they have been burned, no one passes there,*
> *the sound of the flocks is heard no more,*
> *birds of the sky and all animals*
> *all have fled, all are gone.*
> *I mean to make Jerusalem a heap of ruins.*
> *(Jeremiah, 9 "Lamentations to Zion")*

Social catastrophe causes personal catastrophe to be sure, but it is the life of the individual that foretells the future of society, as in the great prophetic books of Jeremiah, Isaiah, Ezekiel, and Amos. In times of chaos, thoughtful and spiritually-inclined individuals, people who are attuned to the subtle connections that bind the world together in counterpoint with the divine, are likely to turn inward, to search for signs that provide a narrative by which they can live. Such is the prophecy of the Old Testament—an indictment of Israel, but also an affirmation of Yahweh's intentions for his chosen people. So too do we find in the rich spiritual literature of the late Middle Ages—another chaotic and unsettled era—a profound engagement with the mystical, rendered first in visions and then in the language of subjectivity, an inwardness that adumbrated the Protestant focus on silent engagement with the Word. Aside from their psychological and pathological implications, the visions of the mystics don't much interest me, but their writings are rich with Blakean symbols. Teresa of Avila is perhaps the most eloquent proponent of unity with the Divine:

> *As far as can be understood, the soul, I mean the spirit of this soul, is made one with God who is himself a spirit, and who has been pleased to show certain persons how far his love for us extends in order that we may praise his greatness. He has thus deigned to unite himself with His creature. He has bound himself to her as firmly as any two human beings are joined in wedlock, and will never separate himself from her." (McGinn, Christian Mysticism)*

We yearn to believe in something—it can't be denied—God works for many, but for others there is art and beauty, politics and power, love and friendship, and for those full of "passionate intensity" there is money and what it buys. Or the glorified Self, the one Frank Bascombe, at sixty-eight, finds not only ephemeral but ludicrous. The baggage of ego permeates all of the four Bascombe novels, but none so much as this most recent. The Self: the roller coaster at Seaside Heights, half-submerged, a wreck, a mockery of amusement.

Richard Ford, among the finest stylists writing in English—his stories rank, in my view, with Alice Munro's for their artistry and deftness at creating character—has, since 1988, followed the career of Frank Bascombe, failed-novelist, sportswriter, divorced person, real estate agent and philosopher of the everyday—the sort of phenomenologist Husserl had in mind when he described the profound ways in which we can come to know the world by simply paying attention. And Frank pays *very* close attention. Ford's Bascombe (the autobiographical elements in his novels and stories are unmistakable), like Updike's Rabbit or Roth's Nathan Zuckerman, travels through the landscape of post-Reagan, post-Bush I and II, post-Clinton America not unlike the way in which Jeremiah wandered through the deserts of Palestine, in search of what thoughtful human beings are in search of— not "truth", that squib of meaning, but coherence, as in, *what is going on here?*

If Frank has a default setting it is bemused confusion. Whether he is meeting with an ex-client whose vacation home on the Jersey Shore has been blown to smithereens by Hurricane Sandy ("I'm Here"), listening to a macabre tale of family homicide ("Everything Could Be Worse"), negotiating the delivery of an orthopedic pillow to his ex-wife ("The New Normal"), or spending a some terrible minutes with a dying acquaintance ("Deaths of Others"), Ford's four interlinked stories evoke a quietly apocalyptic landscape, a suburban world ravaged by climate change, political nihilism (the Republican nay-sayers and Tea Party crack-pots), aging (Frank is recovering from the cancer described in excruciating detail in *The Lay of the Land*), and the daily rub of post-modern, post-meaning, American life. It's the world of Trumpery, where "kicking ass" and "getting rich" and "fixing" a broken American by exiling everyone with dark skin revives, if not our past glory, at least the myth of our past glory. It's a sad fantasy this idea of ours, this lie about a wondrous past of unalloyed glory, but it's the one we want, the one that sells and elects presidents and keeps the machine of greed humming along. Jeremiah would recognize it at once.

Ford writes like an angel. Or like an OT prophet. The cadences of his sentences, the counterpoint of voices—Frank's skeptical inner monologues layered over the voices of those he reluctantly has to deal with in real life—has the quality of lamentation. Frank Bascombe was an ironic wag in the *Sportswriter*, a witty, disillusioned man in *Independence Day*, but in older age Frank is weary, eager to be left in peace, and yet constantly at the beck and call of others. He reads books to the blind, greets returning Iraq War Vets at Newark Airport, visits his Parkinson-afflicted ex-wife, and fields phone calls and visits from his former real-estate clients. In other words, Frank is enmeshed in a social world not of his own choosing, just as we all are, and much of his inner life is a wry commentary on the illusions of civil life, the tedium of others. Saul Bellow would imagine that these interruptions served some higher purpose (as in *Herzog* and *Humbolt's Gift*), but Ford possesses none of Bellow's faith in higher meanings. He's a here and now guy, a what's-this-signify-right-this-second fellow whose only remaining faith is placed in the facts of decay and death. Time is running out for Frank, he feels the "wing'ed chariot" nipping at his heels at every junction of his ordinary days, and he doesn't wish to waste a minute. What he will do with the time he saves is an open question. Mostly, he tells us, he just wants to sit still.

Where are we headed? Back to greatness, lost because of the "stupidity" of our leaders? Should we "trust our guts" as Mr. Trump advises in the most recent of his books, drop a few more bombs, weed out the un-American among us? Frank Bascombe's sensible view of the world precludes such cruelty. A suburban Buddhist, Frank believes in disengagement, in taking a step back, in being agreeable, but without agreeing. His former wife, committed to conspiracies, thinks that Hurricane Sandy (the central trope of the stories) was a *personal* affront, something aimed at her. Frank meditates on this notion:

> *"The Default Self, my answer to all her true thing issues, is an expedient that comes along with nothing more than being sixty-eight—the Default Period of life.*
> *"Being an essentialist, Ann believes we all have selves, characters we can't do anything about (but lie). Old Emerson believed the same. '...A man*

> *should give us a sense of mass...' etc. My mass has simply been deemed deficient. But I believe nothing of the sort. Character, to me, is one more lie of history and the dramatic arts. In my view, we only have what we did yesterday, what we do today, and what we might still do. Plus, whatever we think about all of that. But nothing else—nothing hard or kernel-like. I've never seen evidence of anything resembling it. In fact I've seen the opposite: life as teeming and befuddling, followed by the end."*

Here is a point that clarifies Jeremiah, a cause for lamentation: we find ourselves divided between the Anns of this world and the Franks, those for whom Meaning is built into the nature of the world and those for whom only actions and judgments and muddle are real. The third way, the way of the mystics, lifts us up out of this mess altogether, but isn't a path many of us would choose. The terrible thing isn't that we Americans/humans are divided between these two incommensurate visions of the possibilities of human life, the tragedy is that they are both wrong, or incomplete. Frank wanders back home to Haddam, to his All-Bran and ESPN and liberal ideas—and his dying—without having learned a single thing from the four encounters that lie at the heart of *Let Me Be Frank With You*.

That's the joke: Frank can only be frank with us, and frankness for Frank is a recitation of confusion and doubt. But, to be frank, I am relieved and pleased that there is nothing more, nothing deeper for me to learn. I too am tired of the essentialists, the truth-mongers, the ideologues, the big talkers. We come to this point eventually, to the moment when we only want to pay attention to the here and now, and to make (as Bascombe does) the world just a little bit better around us, in our own neighborhood. We've learned all the lessons there are to learn. Time, simply, to live.

    G.O.

Love and the Abyss

The first Caesare Pavese story I ever read was one called "Wedding Trip," completed on December 6, 1936, a story that opens with the image of a newly married man named George standing with his young wife, Cilia, by the Genoa harbor at night. For all of the ostensible romance of the setting, the scene, he feels the darkness closing in upon them. "We came to the railings of a terrace and caught our breath. The night was calm but dark, and the street lamps floundered in the cold abyss that lay before us." For Pavese this darkness, this abyss, as perceived by the narrator, is not simply hyperbole, a figure of speech designed to intensify the mood, nor is it merely the aggravated projection of a newly married man, pinched with mourning for bygone days, but a stark and telling measure of Pavese's own special dread.

All of the stories included in his collection, *Stories*, the ones for which Pavese is most widely known and admired, were written in the shadow of Italian and German fascism, a period—dating roughly from 1936-1945—that marked a kind of Dark Ages for Italian intellectuals, artists, and writers, like Pavese. Surely this was a part of his dread. Under

Mussolini, the parliamentary system was abolished, all teachers in schools and universities had to swear allegiance to the fascist regime, and freedom of the press was strictly curtailed. Pavese himself was summarily convicted of antifascist activities and sentenced to a year of "preventative detention" in 1935 for a series of articles he'd written as editor of a review called *La Cultura*. After a few months in prison he was sent into "confine" or internal exile in Southern Italy, the common punishment for those guilty of lesser political crimes, the selfsame punishment suffered by fellow writers and Leftists, Leone Ginzburg and Carlo Levi. It was an experience—Pavese's time in prison and exile—that changed him, scarring him psychologically and darkly coloring his work.

That, by the end of his life, Pavese had come to hate (and perhaps fear) women is a fact well-known to readers of his work. This too must be understood as a part of his dread. Plagued by depression, a tortured loner long-enamored of suicide, he suffered one failed relationship after another, first with a mysterious woman he met while at University known only the phrase "la donna dalla voce rauca" (the girl with the husky voice), and finally with the beautiful American actress, model, and former mistress of Elia Kazan, Constance Dowling. So intense was his love for Dowling, so turbulent their affair, that he never recovered from it, finally taking his own life in a hotel room in Turin. "Non scriverò piú ('I will not write anymore')," he concluded his diary that night, swallowing a mouthful of sleeping pills before climbing into bed.

If Pavese felt tortured and betrayed by women, he felt tortured and betrayed by love itself, which he dreaded for the way it exposed him as a man. In his diary he wrote: "One does not kill oneself for love of a woman, but because love—any love—reveals us in our nakedness, our misery, our vulnerability, our nothingness." Indeed his stories and poems are replete with examples of what he came to see as the fundamental treachery of women, of love. Still, Pavese's need of and obsession with women is clear. As Geoffrey Brock puts it in his thoughtful introduction to Pavese's poetry, *Disaffections: Complete Poems 1930-1950*, "Most of the late poems are addressed to a female 'you,' who, while inspired by particular real-life women, tends to blur into an archetypal figure who is by turns, and sometimes simultaneously, attractive and repulsive."

Such is Pavese's complexity—when it comes to women, to his vision of life—that to simply write him off as misogynist is to miss the anguished, hard-won beauty of his work. For while, in his story "Wedding Trip" (to take but one example), his narrator is relentless in his derision of his young wife, Cilia, resentful of her for the inadequacy that her love makes him feel, Pavese's portrayal of her is neither that of succubus nor a shrew. In contrast to him, the narrator, George, Cilia is radiantly human: tender, trusting, romantic. A haunting affirmation of life, she is all he longs for and dreads. Even in his story "Suicides," in which the narrator's callous behavior actually drives his lover, Carlotta, to take her own life, Pavese makes it clear, if only in the way he yields to gentleness and pity in his description of her, that the story's life-force, its humanity, is *hers*.

In this same story, the narrator reflects: "Long ago I realized how essential astuteness is to living, and before being astute with others one must be astute with oneself." Pavese, the man, the writer, was nothing if not astute—with others, and above all with himself. What is plain, what elevates these haunting, often pain-filled stories to the stature of art, is that Pavese himself was well aware of the fact that his much-professed hatred of women had less to do with women themselves than with his own frailty and self-loathing. Cruel as his male characters can be, they remain defiantly human, tortured as they are by remorse, by regret, by longing—by all the "dark angles" of love they are blessed and burdened to know.

As Brock concludes in his aforementioned introduction to Pavese, "Even when his subject is the turning inward, the work itself is a reaching out..." Complex, resounding, often deeply elegiac, his stories have survived him to do just that.

P.N.

Spite

Siamese by Stig Saeterbakken
Beauty and Sadness by Yasunari Kawabata
The Vegetarian by Han Kang

It's been a siege of spiteful characters, plots, and worldviews.

What exactly is spite? Not an easy word to define, *spite* evokes the worst character traits: simmering anger, bitterness, vindictiveness, pettiness, resentment, and vengefulness. I imagine the spiteful would reside in Dante's Fifth Circle, hard on the banks of the River Styx. Filippio Argenti is one of the only souls in hell for whom Dante feels only spite ("I would see him pickled in that swill.") The spiteful imagine great wrongs done to their person. They feel deeply, but only to the end of exacting revenge. Spite presumes a form of justice that doesn't even accounts but obliterates those who have given offense. Perfect spite is nurtured, kept alive as a means of providing the spiteful a reason to live.

A nearly blind Edwin Mortens lives in the bathroom of a flat with his almost deaf wife Erna. They hate each other but depend on one another physically and psychologically. They torment one another, suspect infidelities, are envious and spiteful—a marriage made in hell. Sæterbakken, author of *Journey Through Night* and *Self-Control* specializes in character studies of men and women living *in extremis*, surviving in the face of suffering and loss, spreading the wealth, so to speak, by tormenting those around them. *Siamese* is a novel Beckett might have written or brought to the stage. The sequential interior monologues of Edwin and Erna are perfectly suited to the theater. Edwin seated in the bathroom staring with milky eyes at nothing; Erna seated at the kitchen table in a run-down apartment muttering about her husband's vileness. Nurturing their hatred so as to continue living, after a fashion.

Revenge isn't inherently spiteful: one might get back at someone coolly, just to even the score. But the best sort of revenge is obsessive and therefore steeped in spite, and the payback, ideally, will both duplicate the original offense and quote it. The finest novel of revenge/spite that I know of is Kawabata's *Beauty and Sadness*, a title that suggests the great Japanese writer's penchant for delicate stories of unhappy love, but which actually delivers a bitter tale of terrible revenge enacted long after the precipitating crime. As the novel opens, Oki Toshio is journeying from Tokyo to listen to the New Year's bells in Kyoto. But his real hope is to visit a lover whom he impregnated and abandoned twenty years before—Otoko Ueno. Ueno is now a famous artist who lives with a young lover and protégé, Keiko Sakimi. Keiko is jealous of Ueno's former lover, but her feelings of hatred and her desire for revenge, as is typical in Kawabata, are just as much directed against what to her appear to be the cruel customs and repressive culture of traditional Japan. As Keiko plots exquisite and terrible revenge against Toshio and his family, Kawabata reveals deeper fissures in the social fabric of Japan. The subservient role of women is one of them, but more poignant is the Kabuki-like ritual of love-death. Ueno and Keiko share a destructive passion. Ueno's detachment and world-weariness are well suited to Toshio's deep-seated grief for his treatment of his former lover, but Keiko is nearly driven mad by the passivity and introspection that has allowed Ueno to live her life as a victim. Keiko dispatches her victim callously, methodically, and without a hint of passion. Her spite is reserved for Ueno—this is the genius of the novel—rather than for the man who abandoned his lover.

***

"Before my wife turned vegetarian, I thought of her as completely unremarkable in every way." Thus begins the most disturbing—I suppose I should use the word "transgressive"—of the three novels, the story of an ordinary woman who has a dream of blood and elects to become a vegetarian as a result. Where's the harm? Hardly as serious as the mad hatreds of the Mortens or as obsessive as the revenge described by Kawabata. Vegetarianism, after all, would seem to be a personal and an ethical decision, to be respected and honored. But Yeong-hye's husband and family behave as if she had elected to become a serial killer. They torment her with arguments, they stuff food into her mouth, they treat her as if she were insane. Yeong-hye's response is to become nearly catatonic, to abandon not only meat but her language and, eventually, her life. Her tormentors are ordinary people, but the spiteful ways in which they insinuate that Yeong-hye has no rights over her own body suggest the brutal way in which men assert the proposition that women are not agents and that their bodies belong to husbands and fathers and mothers.

The spite trilogy. Hardly cheering, but each of these three novels was compelling in the way that a traffic accident is compelling—you slow down despite yourself, relieved that it isn't you—this time.

G.O.

Madness Immortal

Christina Stead's extraordinary novel, *The Man Who Loved Children*, is worth buying for the introduction alone. No kidding: you could read it and feel sated; you could read it and feel redeemed, so fine, so telling is the prose. The introduction (some thirty-seven pages short) offers not just a trenchant glimpse of the novel itself, outlining and extolling the story, as it does, in some of the freshest, most surprising language I've read in years, but represents a salient example of the deft, demiurgical criticism for which the poet, Randall Jarrell, was known.

While titled *The Man Who Loved Children*, a facetious reference to the man of the house, the vain, happy, puritanical, self-glorious father, "Mr. Big-Me," Sam Pollit, it is unquestionably around his wife, the neurotic, brilliant, suicidal martyr of a mother, the "Great I Am," Henrietta Pollit *née* Collyer, that this astonishing novel turns. As Jarrell himself remarks in his introduction, "...the book's center of gravity, of tragic weight, is Henny." Indeed, remarkable as Sam and his daughter Louise are as full-blown eccentrics in their own stupendous rights, they pale in comparison to the "dirty cracked plate" of a woman and mother, the deeply, darkly, monstrously empathetic Henny who haunts Tohoga House:

> *She was an old fashioned woman. She had the calm of frequentation; she belonged to this house and it to her. Though she was a prisoner in it, she possessed it. She and it were her marriage. She was indwelling in every board and stone of it: every fold in the curtains had a meaning (perhaps they were so folded to hide a darn or stain); every room was a phial of revelation to be poured out some feverish night in the secret laboratories of her decisions, full of living cancers of insult, leprosies of disillusion, abscesses of grudge, gangrene of nevermore, quintan fevers of divorce, and all the proliferating miseries, the running sores and thick scabs, for which (and not for its heavenly joys) the flesh of marriage is so heavily veiled and conventually interned.*

To read of Henny's life, to follow (with an eye to form and coherence) her useless existential flailing is to feel the fate of women and mothers everywhere, if *in extremis ad infinitum*—the smothered frustrations; the bleak, inchoate rage; the grinding daily theft of autonomy, of self. She is "one of those women who secretly sympathize with all women against all men; life," she knows in her bones, is "a rotten deal, with men holding all the aces." She—clam-and-oyster Baltimore belle, now wretched wife and mother—"shares helplessly 'the natural outlawry of womankind.'" It is through the sieve of her experience, through the fractured lens of her madness, that the entire story is pulled. Yet to feel sorry for her, to reduce her to an object of pity, is simply not possible. "There is something grand and final, indifferent to our pity about Henny," reflects Jarrell, at one point in his introduction, "one of those immortal beings in whom the tragedy of existence is embodied, she looks unseeingly past her mortal readers." Strange feeling, that.

Set in "Tohoga House" in 1940's Georgetown, D.C., an overgrown zoo of a place with its teeming Pollit family and their menagerie of rescued creatures, the ramshackle house and garden is an American Eden run riot and abandoned by God—Sam, with his gluttonous naming (or re-naming of everything and everyone) its exasperating Adam, the heart-scarred Henny its remote and bitter Eve. *The Man Who Loved Children* is one those rare novels that seem to come out of nowhere—starkly original, miraculously, immaculately conceived. You will never read anything like it.

P.N.

Ghost Writers and New Lives

Summary in Baden-Baden, Leonid Tsypkin
Vita Nuova, Dante Alighieri

Like many other readers, I enjoy novels about writers—*Flaubert's Parrot* comes to mind, as well as Philip Roth's *Ghost Writer*—and also non-fiction works that take as their subject not the quotidian lives of those who scribble but the ineffable magic of making art from language: Olivia Laing's *The Trip to Echo Springs: On Writers and Drinking* is one such, as is Geoff Dyer's *Out of Sheer Rage: Wrestling with D. H. Lawrence*. Sarah Bakewell's *How to Live* is not so much a life of Montaigne as an exploration of his ideas; Sebald writes about Stendhal in a similarly oblique way in *Vertigo*, and Jay Parini's *Benjamin's Crossing* is about the last days of Walter Benjamin and is rich in psychological detail (ditto Parini's *The Last Station*). And then there are the books that aren't directly *about* writers but about the authors of the books as they reflect on the lives of authors—a little meta-I admit, but a brilliant form of literary expression if you can pull it off. Alain de Botton's *How Proust Can Change Your Life* and Nicholson Baker's *U and I* are examples, as is Tsypkin's wonderful *Summer in Baden-Baden*, a novel about both Tsypkin and the Dostoevskys (Fyodor and Anna Grigoryevna).

Tsypkin has used the Master's sojourn in Germany—his gambling, his tempestuous relations with his wife, his obsession with and revulsion toward literature—as a mirror reflecting his own life and, in particular, his journey to Petersburg that culminates in a visit to the house in which Dostoevsky died. The novel doesn't move from one story to another, from Baden-Baden to Petersburg, but folds two narratives into one another. Tsypkin's life as a dissident within the USSR overlaps and embraces Dostoyevsky's exile in Germany, an exile that is as much spiritual as physical. The brilliance of the novel lies in its seamless entangling of two literary lives, in Tsypkin's reprising the life of the Master as if it were a facet of his own. Joseph Frank's biography of Dostoevsky (I've read only the one-volume abridgment) makes plain enough the pain out of which Dostoevsky fashioned his art—his time in the house of the dead, his epilepsy, his addictions—to writing and gambling, or perhaps to writing as gambling. His ambivalent passion for Anna Grigoryevna, his self-imposed exile. What Tsypkin does admirably is to reassemble in coherent fashion the fragments of Dostoevsky's outer and inner lives in such a way as to make his genius seem a function of his biography rather than a triumph over it.

It occurred to me a few months ago that I had better get started on my long-postponed project of rereading those books that have meant the most to me, not all of them classics, but each one significant in marking out a period of my life, or, if that's too grandiose, then let's leave it at this, books I've carried with me through a lifetime of being the sort of person who carries around books and throws away everything else. Carried them because I meant to read them again "someday." And, at last, someday has arrived. For no special reason I've started this project with Dante's beautiful *Vita Nuova*—a hymn to his muse Beatrice Portinari and to the making of poems—and C.S. Lewis's *The Discarded Image*, one of the handful of works of literary criticism that isn't a chore to read and which is a perfect companion to Dante. Lewis's book teaches us how to read medieval and Renaissance poets. Dante teaches us how to read Dante—or perhaps how to misread him. I reread my 1973 Mark Musa edition, with its no-nonsense literal versions both of the *canzoni* and the prose excursuses through which Dante not only prepares us with scanty biographical tidbits for his poems, but in which he explains, as a coy philosopher might, the progress of his Platonic-Christian love for the maiden Beatrice, on whom he laid eyes (if at all) exactly three times, and yet 'she seemed to be the daughter not of a mortal but of a god,' as Dante describes her, reworking Homer. It was Boccaccio who identified the married (to one of the banking Bardis, according to my old guidebook to Florence's churches) Beatrice with Dante's sacred muse, his companion from Purgatory to Paradise, and the inspiration for his 'book of memory,' as Dante called the *Vita Nuova*. Thoroughly medieval, that is, rooted in the neo-Platonic and Augustinian epistemology of the fourteenth century, Dante's love poems in the VN remind one of *Symposium*, with its yearning for erotic transcendence, but also of the medieval *romans* of Chretien de Troyes or, more intimately, of the *Lais* of Marie de France. But Dante is an original, and no comparison can do justice to the richness of his imagery, his mastery of the rhetorical tropes that defined late medieval poetry, or the alternating repression/confinement and overflowing of his emotions.

The first time Dante is addressed by Beatrice he nearly swoons. He records the event in detail: "*It was precisely the ninth hour of that day, three o'clock in the afternoon, when her sweet voice came to me. Since this was the first time her words had ever been directed to me, I became so ecstatic that, like a drunken man, I turned away from everyone and sought the loneliness of my room, where I began thinking of this most gracious lady, and, thinking of her, I fell into a sweet sleep, and a marvelous vision appeared to me.*"

This is conventional. Boethius's *Consolation of Philosophy*, allegedly written while its author was in prison, awaiting execution, also falls into a dream, but his "Lady" isn't a teenage beauty but Philosophy/Wisdom herself, summoned to bolster Boethius's justifiably waning faith in God's sense of fair play.

Dante, who has only *just now* "taught himself the art of writing poetry"—as if!—sets out to write a sonnet for his lady, the first of thirty-two sonnets, *canzoni,* and a single ballad that make up the poetic matter of the *Vita Nuova*. The first sonnet has always been one of my favorites, especially the arresting image of stanza two:

> *Joyous, Love seemed to me, holding my heart*
> *within his hand, and in his arms he had*
> *my lady, loosely wrapped in folds, asleep.*
> *He woke her then, and gently fed to her*
> *the burning heart; she ate it, terrified.*
> *And then I saw him disappear in tears.*
>
> [*Poi la svegliava, e d'esto core ardendo*
> *lei paventosa umilmente pascea.*
> *Appresso gir lo ne vedea piangendo.*]

"Ardent," is right, but "burning" is better; and she ate his heart, not in terror, but with humility (*umilmente pascea*) as if, let's face it, she were eating sacramental bread and wine. In his gloss Dante mentions how the meaning of this poem was not clear to anyone at first, but is now clear *even to the unlearned*. The *Vita Nuova* isn't only about a rebirth in love, but about death, including, in the final sections, the death and transfiguration of Beatrice. This Beatrice, real or no, turned out to be a gold mine for Romantic and Pre-Raphaelite painters and poets, swirling clouds of dust and soul-stuff, eternal love, chaste longing. Gustave Dore does a fine job of capturing the overwrought frenzy of pure love, in the same vein as Bernini's St. Theresa.

   "After I wrote this sonnet there came to me a

miraculous vision in which I saw things that made me resolve to say no more about this blessed one until I would be capable of writing about her in a nobler way."

Poems and glosses, prayer and prophecy.

G.O.

Where the Stones Come From

One Afternoon

A professor of History from Bayit Va-Gan took his family for a picnic in a quiet pinewood near Giv'at Shaul, formerly known as Deir Yassin. It was not too cold to be in the shade and not too warm to build a fire, so the professor passed on to his son the camping skills he had acquired in the army. They arranged three square stones in a U, to block the wind, leaving access on the fourth side. They stacked broken branches on top of the twigs on top of dry pine needles. He let his son put a match to it. Listening carefully, they heard a faint low hum from the curves of the winding highway, hidden from view by the trees. The professor did not talk of the village, origin of the stones. He did not talk of the village school, now a psychiatric hospital, on the other side of the hill. He imagined that he and his family were having a picnic, unrelated to the village, enjoying its grounds outside history.

From 1947-1949 the newly minted Israelis, the majority of them just arrived as refugees from Hitler's Europe, conspired, in their ironic and headlong embrace of nationalism, to forcibly remove more than 750,000 Arabs from their homes and villages in what is now the State of Israel, terrorizing the people, burning their houses, and pillaging their goods—their livestock, their utensils, their tools.

For all of the post-war wonder that was the birth of Israel, for all of its phoenix-like glory and potential as a force for good in the Middle East, it cannot be understood today (nor truly, justly appreciated) without also recognizing the violent and systematic expulsion of Arabs from the land, a fact that is now and will always be an essential part of its national-cultural DNA. It is a practice (this ethnic cleansing *avant le mot*), begun as early as the 1930's, that continues to this day in the cynical, nearly relentless government-sanctioned expansion of Jewish settlements in the West Bank, a movement now motivated less by the utopian (if still fundamentally racist) Zionism of the early European settlers than by the hidebound, often hateful, always fiercely anti-democratic fanaticism of the Jewish ultra-Orthodox, the aggressive, politically intractable *Haredim*, who exert (with the help of U.S. taxpayers and such bullying right-wing lobbying groups as AIPAC) what is now a veritable stranglehold over public policy and discourse, both here in the U.S. and in Israel itself, what is still a predominantly secular, cosmopolitan state.

Now here is where it gets tricky. Take all that you have ever read about Israel, and about the Palestinian-Israeli conflict, then spend a few weeks there and see what sifts out in the end. I can almost guarantee you (even those of you who, like me, are intensely critical of Israeli policy and practice toward the Palestinians) that you will leave the country charmed, not only by the general brilliance and sophistication of Israeli Jews, but by their humanity and compassion as a people, not to mention astounded by what they have done, in some sixty short years, to transform that arid, much disputed patch of land. You will leave deeply moved by them (for, such is the climate there that, unless you have connections, you are not likely to get to know any Palestinians) and inspired by the land itself. Which is not to say that your position with regard to Israeli politics will change. If anything, it will be profounder, if perhaps a little blurry at its edges. For, however well-founded your criticism of the Israeli government itself, you will like the people there and suddenly find it hard, if not impossible, to generalize about them, to critique them as a whole. It is exactly what happened to me. It is why the Jews of Israel still fill me with hope.

Which brings me to the point of this essay. In my many years of living and traveling, it has become clear to me that one of the truest ways of experiencing the lives of others, short of meeting them in person, in the homes and neighborhoods where they live, is by reading about them in their own books, by seeing them fleshed out before you—in novels and poems and plays—as living, breathing, struggling human beings. "Literature is by its very nature humanist," writes Jewish-Italian author Alberto Moravia in his cogent, deeply heartening collection of essays on the subject of humanism, *Man As End*, making reading itself a powerful act of faith.

So if you really want some clarity about what is happening in Israel today, if you wish, as author Damon Galgut puts it, to "see through events to the people behind them," then forget the newspapers and cable news programs for a while and read a novel or a volume of poetry instead. As I have insisted before, what the regional novelists, playwrights, and poets have to tell us about the conflict there is exactly what we need most: the reminder that the wages of every political stunt and machination, every embedded news report, every grandstanding politician, political lobbyist, and religious extremist, *are tallied in human lives*—lives like yours, like mine. A good place to start might be this short, easily accessible novel, *Picnic Grounds*, by the Israeli author, Oz Shelach.

When interviewed about this 2003 novel, Shelach, in an effort to describe the often deeply conflicted attitude of Israeli Jews toward their own history, told the following story, plainly echoed in the first short chapter of his novel with which I opened this essay:

> *I think denial is built into the national culture… Let me illustrate with an example: My cousin's husband published a guidebook in Hebrew called Fun Family Tours, which is basically an outdoors tour guide with additional games to play with the kids in the car. He took many of the pictures himself, and they're striking—there's so much rubble, so many structures that used to be people's homes, and traces of their agriculture. Of course these are all*

> *indigenous Palestinian traces, but they're described variously as "an abandoned orchard," "a deserted village," or as "ancient structures." The people who used to live there are sometimes two miles away in a refugee camp, but they're invisible.*

Inspired by Thomas Bernhard's laconic miniatures, *The Voice Imitator*, Shelach's "novel in fragments" reads like a collection of modern parables about the tormented land he loves, stories as remarkable for the things left *unsaid* as for those so beautifully said. Described as "the most relentlessly restrained cartographer of the current Israeli scene," Shelach is also an archeologist, preoccupied with the ever-more-pressing facts and implications of the past, so that if history is in part the record of our complicity as human beings, we have writers like Shelach to show us the stones.

P.N.

Falling Into, and Out of, Love

Alain de Botton, *Essays in Love* (a novel)

You see him (her) in a crowded room, on a plane, at a meeting, in a restaurant—someplace you weren't prepared to see anyone, all of your paltry defenses down, a neutral or even a meaningless encounter, a simple hello, a brushing of hands—nothing weighty, no ulterior motive at all. You went on a plane ride and sat next to (in this case) a woman. It was her.

Alain de Botton has the sort of talent I most admire—he can be brilliant anyplace, with any topic, and not only brilliant, but original—he thinks about things that you and I have thought about but never understood, he explains what we are reading or seeing or feeling. Architecture or Proust or, here, love. Not "explains" exactly but teases, probes, uncovers. You've thought about something one way and then, blissfully, you realize that you weren't wrong, just not paying sufficient attention.

In Chicago this summer, browsing in Powell's (yes, the Portland Powell's began in the City With Big Shoulders), I came upon a strange Picador paperback: *Essays in Love* by Alain de Botton, thick newsprint paper, the cover depicting a woman sitting on the floor in a library, seemingly in the ranges holding tedious government reports, reading a book.

De Botton once wrote this: "Booksellers are the most valuable destination for the lonely, given the numbers of books that were written because authors couldn't find anyone to talk to."

The narrator of *Essays in Love*—a novel that is a work of philosophy, a work of philosophy that is, a fiction—feels to me like a lonely man, someone who falls in love by accident and falls out by design. I didn't understand until the last page the meaning of the cover photograph or the structure of the novel. Everything in the book is simple on the surface, yet studded with mystery. Like love itself.

De Botton has read Proust and written brilliantly about the experience. My feeling is that the inspiration for *Essays in Love* is the story of Swann and Odette in volume one of Proust's masterpiece. De Botton, playing both roles, analyses the coming into love that is always so surprising and uplifting, and meditates in painful detail on the unraveling of feeling, the loss of love and the unbearable aftermath of that loss. But de Botton's book isn't Proustian—it's something else, something entirely new.

"By accident," the narrator sits with Chloe on a flight from Paris to London. "Chloe later told me that she had intended to take the ten-thirty Air France flight, but a bottle of shampoo in her bag had happened to leak as she was checking out of her room, which had meant repacking her bag and wasting a valuable ten minutes." I wondered if she had said "wasted" in narrating the bit of happenstance that put her on a British Airways flight instead of her Air France plane, in the seat next to our (I can't help but think) lonely narrator? She might have. Chloe is an honest woman, and one of the marvels of *Essays on Love* is the truth telling. The strangers, then lovers, speak plainly with one another. Often this hurts. In matters of the heart, truth, I think, might be overrated.

The chapter headings are those of a philosophical work rather than of a novel. "Romantic Fatalism," "Authenticity," "False Notes," "Love or Liberalism," "Intermittences of the Heart" (my special favorite), and so forth. The style is mixed, not unlike Menippian satire, though in this case the satire is directed at all of the conventions of romantic love rather than at politics. De Botton imitates Wittgenstein in the scrupulousness of his dissection of his own and his beloved's feelings. From the courtship ("Subtexts of Seduction"): "We talked abstractly of love, ignoring that lying on the table was not the nature of love per se but the burning question of who we were and would be to one another. Or was there in fact nothing on the table other than a half-eaten carrot cake and two cups of tea? Was Chloe being as abstract as she wished, meaning precisely what she said, the diametrical opposite of the first rule of flirtation, where what is said is never what is meant?" A little shuffle here. The narrator semi-accuses

Chloe of precisely his own inclination which is to cover up his feelings with abstractions and small talk. De Botton gets this perfectly. We ascribe to the beloved exactly the feelings and motives that we have and convince ourselves of our own objectivity. See *Swann's Way*.

This is a funny book, especially if you've ever been in love. Early on our hero, an architect, provokes a fight over the sorts of jam that Chloe has to offer at breakfast. It's their first sleepover, and the idea that one would be put off, angered even, by a lack of strawberry jam ("I hate having breakfast without any decent jam") is farcical. But then this scene appears in the "Marxism" chapter, and the point is clear enough:

> "*...the origins of a certain kind of love lie in an impulse to escape ourselves and our weaknesses by an alliance with the beautiful and the noble. But if the loved one loves us back, we are forced to return to ourselves, and are hence reminded of the things that have driven us into love in the first place. Perhaps it was not love we wanted after all, perhaps it was simply someone in whom to believe, but how can we continue to believe in the beloved now that [she] believes in us.*"?

So, it isn't Karl but Groucho Marx at play here—if she loves me, who am so unworthy, there must be some mistake. How could she?

I won't spoil the ending, but it isn't happy. But a happy

ending would have precluded any philosophical meditation on loss. Our hero is cerebral, an over-thinker. "Few things are as antithetical to sex as thought." It is his brooding propensity to over-think every conversation, every act of his beloved that drives her away. In some things instinct should prevail. The road from intellect to instinct is impossible to traverse—better to start with the heart and inch toward the head then to make the futile attempt to move in the other direction.

I was left not only admiring the deft way in which de Botton had alternately skewered and caressed his love affair (it has to be his story), but I was left wondering what, exactly, love might be. One line of *Essays in Love* travels along the road traversed by Plato's *Symposium*: love is not a single thing but an individual's journey toward self-knowledge and, eventually, transcendence of this world. Physical love and human desire are self-negating and, like Wittgenstein's famous ladder out of the *Tractatus*, lead the lovers to a realm of being in which love no longer has meaning; love leads, in this view, to Love. But this isn't what de Botton was up to. I couldn't quite grasp what he wanted me to see until the final pages.

Love is sadness. In de Botton's account infatuation and desire provide the charm of attraction, but habit and familiarity lead a couple to weariness and even disgust. What must endure isn't "love" but friendship and trust. Our narrator and Chloe tire of one another quickly, not because of a lack of desire or a failure to share themselves with the other, but because their love as we see it (through the narrator's eyes) was never about them, it was only about him: "I did not simply love Chloe and then she left me. I loved Chloe in order that she would leave me." Chloe is "merely" an instrument designed to inflict punishment on the narrator for his naive faith in the existence of love. I chaffed a bit at what seemed to me a cheapened psychoanalytic resolution of the plot—after all, it is more difficult to understand the end of love then its beginning. And who believes, really, in love as self-flagellation? No, what I was reading, I thought, was a rationalization: Chloe fell out of love with the narrator because of his egotism and her capriciousness. Very tidy, and if the author weren't de Botton, a plausible enough plot (despite the philosophical asides) to render the book worthy of the Times best-seller list.

But on second reading it seemed to me that I needed above all to take the philosophical nature of *Essays in Love* seriously—the meditations on love aren't ancillary to the plot, they are the plot. De Botton has written a novel about love that recapitulates the history of philosophy, from Plato to Freud, with chapters that subtly invoke Aristotle, Descartes (on the mind-body problem), Hume, Rousseau (a section on pastoral romance in the spirit of his *Nouvelle Heloise*), Hegel, Schopenhauer, Marx, Nietzsche, and ending with ideas taken right out of *The Ego and the Id*. Yes, this was it, a love story that is actually a work of philosophy, or, perhaps, a work of philosophy imbued with the idea that the truth resides in loving. Loving a person, yes, but also, more so, loving knowledge. Our hero doesn't live happily ever after but—just barely—he lives. Sadder, as they say, but wiser.

    G.O.

China Blues

"1937 was a hellish year for China," writes Jonathan Spence in his deeply informative introduction to Qian Zhongshu's popular and highly acclaimed novel, *Fortress Besieged*. "After years of threats and corrosive expansion into Chinese territory, the Japanese finally moved to all-out war, first in the Peking region, and soon after in Shanghai…by the late fall of 1937, the Chinese troops had crumbled, and the Japanese advanced triumphantly through the largely abandoned defense lines to the Nationalist capital of Nanking. There, in December 1937, the infamous 'Rape of Nanking' brought death or agonizing humiliation to hundreds of thousands of Chinese men, women, and children…. It is into this bleak setting that Qian Zhongshu unceremoniously tosses his hapless hero Fang Hung-chien."

Widely recognized as the greatest Chinese novel of the twentieth century, *Fortress Besieged* is, for all its satire of western-leaning intellectuals, scholars, philosophers, doctors, and professors, a remarkably un-political story, given the chaos and suffering amidst which it is set, focusing almost myopically as it does on the picaresque, often comical bumbling of the wisecracking "moral weakling", Fang Hung-chien. The prodigal son, Fang returns to China, to Shanghai, on the eve of the Sino-Japanese War, aboard the *Vicomte de Bragelonne*, a ship packed to overflowing with Chinese nationals, Indians, Vietnamese, French, and Jews in flight from Hitler. With nothing but a fake diploma, no prospects for work, and the not unpleasant knowledge that his wealthy fiancée is dead, he sets out to find his place in the fraught and rapidly changing nation.

Yet the novel is hardly so serious as that, but asserts itself as a clever, unabashedly erudite comedy of manners in which we are introduced to a dazzling assortment of nationals and foreigners in late 1930's China: "the lowly porters, shopkeepers, innkeepers, bus drivers, country folk, soldiers, prostitutes, and French policemen serving their mother country in her Concessions in China; the middle-class returned students, country squires, journalists; and the rising middle-class bankers, compradors, factory managers, Japanese collaborators, and others", each delightfully, indelibly described.

Subtle, sophisticated, rich with allusions to Chinese and European philosophy, literature, history, culture, and folklore (each meticulously footnoted for those interested), *Fortress Besieged* is a highly readable, highly satisfying novel for expert and novice alike.

P.N.

Destruction

The Silence and the Roar by Nihad Sirees

How easy it is to destroy what has taken so long to build! The ruins of Syria—the impulse toward destruction is irresistible. History is the struggle of a few to build something they are condemned to see blown to bits by the fanatics while the indifferent look on.

> *"The split in America, [and elsewhere] rather than simply economic, is between those who embrace reason, who function in the real world of cause and effect, and those who, numbed by isolation and despair, now seek meaning in a mythical world of intuition, a world that is no longer reality-based, a world of magic."* [Chris Hedges, American Fascists]

> *"O soldiers of the Islamic State, be ready for the final campaign of the crusaders. Yes, by Allah's will, it will be the final one. We will conquer your Rome, break your crosses, and enslave your women, by the permission of Allah, the Exalted. If we do not reach that time, then our children and grandchildren will*

> *reach it, and they will sell your sons as slaves at the slave market."* [Public statement of ISIS, 2014]

"*Mythical world of intuition.*" This is surely the world of, among others, ISIS and its enemy Bashar al-Assad, the optometrist turned Leader of Syria. The Arab Spring came late to Syria.

> "*Bashar al-Assad, helped by the nasty reputation of his security services, looked as though he would survive… What changed everything was an incident which threw into sharp relief the untackled problems of his security state. At the beginning of March 2011, children aged nine to fifteen wrote graffiti on the wall of their school in the depressed southern town of Der'a calling for the fall of the regime…*"
> "*It was this simple act—and the later arrest, detention, and probable torture of these school children that brought the Arab Spring, at long last, to Syria. Assad's mythical world met reality in that year, and the unraveling of Syria began in earnest.*" [John McHugo, Syria]

> "*Where once your eyes met the walls of buildings, a silent plain now extended to infinity. Was it a cemetery? But what beings had buried their dead there and then put chimneys on the graves? Nothing grew there but the chimneys emerging from the ground like monuments, like dolmens or admonitory fingers. Did the dead lying below them breathe the blue ether through those chimneys?*" [W.G. Sebald, "Between History and Natural History," from Campo Santo]

> *"To a survival machine, another survival machine (which is not its own child or another close relative) is a part of environment, like a rock or a river or a lump of food. It is something that gets in the way, or something that can be exploited." [Richard Dawkins, The Selfish Gene; file under 'the treason of the intellectuals']*

> *"Out of the night of history old shadows are appearing which menace their bourgeois complacency. Growing groups of unknown men out of the streets are laughing the unbeliever's hollow laugh at all those things the democrat has taught the people to hold dear. Worst of all, a figure appears that they had thought was gone for ever over the great scaffolds of the Reformation ... The oligarchs and the democrats dread this classic figure more than anarchy – for it is the figure of the Leader ..." [James Drennan, Oswald Mosley and British Fascism]*

The Silence and the Roar by the great Aleppian novelist Nihad Sirees asks the question, what is the cost of defying a corrupt *status quo*? The answer, not surprisingly, has it origins in Kafka, in all the obvious places, but also in one of the parables:

> *"Everything came to his aid during the construction work. Foreign workers brought the marble blocks, trimmed and fitted to one another. The stones rose and placed themselves according to the gauging motions of his fingers. No building ever came into*

> *being as easily as did this temple—or rather, this temple came into being the way a temple should. Except that, to wreak a spite or to desecrate or destroy it completely, instruments obviously of a magnificent sharpness had been used to scratch on every stone—from what quarry had they come?— for an eternity outlasting the temple, the clumsy scribblings of senseless children's hands, or rather the entries of barbaric mountain dwellers." [Kafka, "The Building of the Temple"]*

Fathi Sheen, the protagonist of Sirees's deceptively simple novel, falls unwittingly into the mechanisms of the temple, the Temple of the Leader—and from the moment of Sheen's fall, *The Silence and the Roar* becomes a savage satire of all dictatorial regimes, but of Syria's in particular. The first half of the novel certainly invokes Kafka; the second half Orwell. In any case, as Sirees puts it in the afterword (written in 2012 as Aleppo was destroyed), "We must ask, alongside the characters in this novel: What kind of surrealism is this?"

Or perhaps a better way to approach the civil war in Syria—the formation of ISIS, Assad's deliberate destruction of his own country as a means of denying a dizzying array of rebel groups a nation to aspire toward governing, the exploitation of Syria's misery by cynical forces throughout the Middle East—how did the surreal become the real?

G.O.

The Persistence of Suffering

let all those who want to; one of us will talk, the other will listen; at least we shall be together.

"If there is meaning in life at all," writes neurologist, psychologist, and Holocaust survivor Viktor Frankl in his landmark study, *Man's Search for Meaning*, "then there must be meaning in suffering." By this he is not suggesting that one's suffering serves a higher purpose, that it is part of some divine or even biological plan, only that in its recalcitrance, its sheer ubiquity, it has the potential to teach us things—things about each other, things about ourselves.

The Case Worker—the first of five fine novels by George Konrad to be translated into English—is a strange and strangely moving tale. Set in Soviet-controlled Hungary in the early 1970's, in a Budapest so grim, so beleaguered, it bears little resemblance to the charming, spa city of postcards and films, the story follows the life and musings of an ordinary social worker, "an underpaid, disabused, middle-level official," "a burden bearer without illusions," "a professional child-snatcher," whose charge is to sell indifference and normalcy and to protect the interests of the state, a job he performs diligently, if with a mounting sense of impotence and despair:

> *Go on, I say to my client. Out of habit, because I can guess what he's going to say, and doubt his truthfulness. He complains some more, justifies himself, puts the blame on others. From time to time he bursts into tears. Half of what he says is beside the point; he reels off platitudes, he unburdens himself. He thinks his situation is desperate; seems perfectly normal to me. He swears his cross is too heavy; seems quite bearable to me. He hints at suicide; I let it pass. He thinks I can save him; I can't tell him how wrong he is.*

Like Dante in the *Inferno*, this case worker finds himself falling into a "deep place" (*basso loco*) where the sun itself is silent, a "gray-brown realm of unrelieved weariness," a drab, phantasmagoric world unto itself, and crowded with every variety of misfit and tortured soul whose "anguish [is] massive, tentacular, and incurable". The Budapest of this novel is a special ring of hell in which one suffers daily a state of perpetual siege without even the simple consolation of knowing one's pain matters, that it serves the lot of humankind, that, finally, it is homiletic—the handiwork of some remote if sagacious god.

At one point the eponymous case worker recalls a tale he'd heard about a disenchanted rabbi—a tale sharply reminiscent of the Buddha's enlightenment as a young and naïve prince—who, weary of threatening his congregants with the wrath of "Yahweh Ineffable" deserts his synagogue and ventures out into the world to discover it anew. There he finds an old woman dying in her filthy hovel who implores him, "Why was I born when as long as I can remember nothing but misfortune has been my lot?" To which the helpless rabbi replies, "That you should bear it." Drawing the sheet over her face, he decides from then on to be mute. The next person he encounters is a young beggar girl carrying her dead child on her back. When in reference to her baby, she asks the rabbi, "The poor thing got nothing, neither pleasure nor pain. Do you think it was worth his being born?"—a question to which the helpless rabbi nods his assent. Thereupon he decides to be deaf as well as dumb and hide away from the world in a cave. There he finds a ferret with an injured foot, which he heals with bandages and special herbs. Soon the two grow fond of each other. Then one day a condor swoops out of the sky and carries off the ferret before the rabbi's eyes, so that he decides to close them for good. Yet—since blind, deaf, and dumb—he can do nothing but wait for death, he returns to his congregation, where he "did what he had done before, and waxed strong in his shame."

The protagonist of *The Case Worker*, a man all but overwhelmed by the futility of his work and by the boundlessness of human suffering, is on the verge of following the rabbi's example when he is trapped, shackled to this world and its pain by the life of a hideously misshapen, nearly feral orphan named Feri. At last, again, I turn to Frankl: "A man who becomes conscious of the responsibility he bears toward a human being who affectionately waits for him, or to an unfinished work, will never be able to throw away his life. He knows the 'why' for his existence, and will be able to bear almost any 'how'."

P.N.

That Lost World

Badenheim 1939 by Aharon Appelfeld

Books about endings, written in what Edward Said called "late style"—endings not of romances or of nations, but of epochs, of entire cultures: Joseph Roth, *The Radetzkey March*; Franz Werfel, *The Forty Days of Musa Dagh*; Pat Barker, *Regeneration*; Lampedusa's *The Leopard*; John Galsworthy's *Forsyth Saga; Howard's End* by E.M. Forester; Ford Maddox Ford, *Parade's End*; Andrei Bely's *Petersburg*; and, the the granddaddy of them all, Mann's *Magic Mountain*. Central to each of these novels (and there are many others) is a sense of cultural exhaustion, a mood of nostalgia and reminiscence, and a style that is deeply ironic. Each of these novels was written with retrospective knowledge of the disasters that they recount—the end of the Hapsburgs, the Great War, the Revolution of 1905, the long decline of the Ancient Regime. The novel in late style is a European and, with writers like Oe and Kawabata, also a Japanese phenomenon. I can't think of a single example of an American novel that fits the model unless one counts James as an American writer rather than as an English novelist who happened to have been born in Boston.

Anyway, among the very finest novels of endings, written in a perfect version of late style, is Aharon Appelfeld's remarkable *Badenheim 1939*. On the cusp of the disaster that is about to overtake Europe's Jews, a group of dilettantes gathers in the German resort town of Badenheim for the annual arts festival organized by the impresario Dr. Pappenheim. There's not a word of politics spoken. All talk is of culture, pastries, romance, and, of course, past festivals (always the *past*). At the same time, and with the ominousness of a Biblical portent, a team of "Sanitary Inspectors" gathers in the town, nameless and indistinct representatives of the State, and, little by little, they enclose Badenheim in a cocoon of bureaucratic repression—they build a ghetto. With brilliant strokes whose power is cumulative rather than apparent, Appelfeld intimates the doom that is descending over the resort and its oblivious inhabitants. From a mere "sanitary inspection," to the closing of buildings, to the isolation of the town, Badenheim, like Warsaw or Lodz, is shut off from the outside world:

> *"Since one day ran into the next and the sentries [just now mentioned—they've materialized out of thin air] at the gate informed [the salesman] that there was no intention at present of opening it to free traffic, he came to the conclusion that there was no point in living like a thief in the back quarters of the hotel, and he took himself a proper room, as befitting the representative of a well-known firm. The other guests were as delighted with him as if he were a messenger bringing glad tidings from afar...*

> *[the waiter] never stopped talking about his two sons who had been imprisoned in a barracks by a General. 'They must be exercising now,' he would say. 'They must be running.'"*

Pride in appearances, wishful thinking, a focus on empty gestures, deadened curiosity, days that lack the texture of change and that fold into one another so that time disappears. Mann evokes this sense of timelessness better than any other novelist. Ominous persons, unnamed and unknown, come and go, causing ripples of unease. The volition of the characters is sapped by the weight of boredom. There is only indifference—no happiness, no bliss, only numb acceptance. Appelfeld's gradual evocation of a sense of dread is brilliant, unsparing. No one can choose or judge or even feel:

> *"...their amazement was cut short. An engine, an engine coupled to fifty freight cars, emerged from the hills and stopped at the station. Its appearance was as sudden as if it had risen from a pit in the ground. 'Get in!' yelled invisible voices. and the people were sucked in. Even those who were standing with a bottle of lemonade in their hands, a bar of chocolate, the headwaiter with his dog—they were all sucked in as easily as grains of wheat poured into a funnel."*

The train, naturally, is headed for Poland—for the *Generalgouvernment*, where most the killing would be done. The summer residents of Badenheim, the pleasure-seekers and *connoisseurs,* have been eagerly anticipating the journey to Warsaw. They've been told, not commanded, that Jews must register with the Sanitary Commission. They register eagerly, thanking the registrar for the good order of the process, and that they will be *allowed* to travel to Warsaw. The Polish musician Samitzky insists that *"In Poland everything was beautiful, everything was interesting."*

One of the most powerful stylistic and thematic devices found in novels like *Badenheim 1939* is the evocation of *yearning,* the desire for something that cannot be named or described. This yearning is the psychological recognition that meaning has been emptied from the world—a fact that is the source of all literary irony. *"The people were being driven out of their minds by their desires."* But for what? There's art and love and *Bienenstich* and disjointed conversation, but something is missing. If *it* isn't to be found in Badenheim, then perhaps one will find *it* in Warsaw. Besides, *"In Poland there are lots of Jews. The Jews help one another you know."*

Which brings me to Hannah Arendt. You will perhaps recall her 1963 report on the Holocaust and the Nuremberg trials, *Eichmann in Jerusalem: A Report on the Banality of Evil,* a book whose title and contents inflamed a remarkable debate, a debate intense enough to incite a library of rebuttals. See especially *The Ambiguity of Virtue* by Bernard Wasserstein. Is Appelfeld "blaming the victim," as Arendt was accused of doing?

Is the obtuse acceptance of the creeping repressions of the "Sanitary Commission" more than satire? Is Appelfeld's melancholy novel lamenting, or mocking the naive refusal of European Jews, especially German and Austrian Jews, to see what was coming? Certainly not. Who could know, even in 1939, the extent of the murderous intentions of the Nazis and their allies? Who could believe that the filthy train carrying Dr. Pappenheim to the East was carrying him not to another arts festival, but to his doom? When I read Amos Elon's *The Pity of It All: The History of the Jews in Germany, 1743-1933* I understood how deeply Jews were assimilated into German life, and therefore how natural it would have been for the denizens of Badenheim in 1939 to ignore the signs.

In light of recent events—you fill in the blanks—I have had Yeats's great poem of cultural exhaustion much in mind.

> *Turning and turning in the widening gyre*
> *The falcon cannot hear the falconer;*
> *Things fall apart; the centre cannot hold;*
> *Mere anarchy is loosed upon the world,*
> *The blood-dimmed tide is loosed, and everywhere*
> *The ceremony of innocence is drowned;*
> *The best lack all conviction, while the worst*
> *Are full of passionate intensity.*

Appelfeld warned us. We should pay attention.

G.O.

The Defense of the Human, The Defense of the Mind

In a universe more and more abstract, it is up to us to make sure that the human voice does not cease to be heard.
　　　　　　　　　　　　　　　　　　Witold Gombrowicz

If there has ever been a time in my life that called for a wholesale re-evaluation of humanism as an essential way of being in the world that time is now. Donald Trump is but the witless, leering figurehead of a supranational groundswell of racism, misogyny, xenophobia, homophobia, anti-intellectualism, and corporatism, that is currently laying siege to many of the greatest achievements of the human mind, an embarrassment of riches, ranging from philosophy, politics, rhetoric, education, science, medicine, psychology, and law to art, literature, music, and history to agriculture, journalism, architecture, theatre, and dance. Touted by religious and political zealots, and exploited daily by corporate warlords in their ruthless pursuit of wealth, this vengeful backlash is apparent nearly everywhere one turns: in our politics and laws; in our schools and universities; in our healthcare and hospitals, in our policing and our prisons; and in our homes and civic spaces. It is a backlash that threatens to erode and redefine our hard-won thinking about the natural world itself, and our relationship to it, by attacking science at large, its very authority, now openly (if mostly cynically) impugned.

At least a part of the problem lies in the fracturing and general denigration of the humanities in the U.S. as a whole since WWII, by which in particular I mean the steady corporate-governmental takeover of the sciences (and of the mathematics they employ) for their own mercenary, often violent, often starkly anti-democratic ends. Now largely divorced from the *studia Humanitatis*, the time-honored disciplines of science and mathematics are increasingly but the tools, the handmaidens, of wealth and power, faithful servants to that menacing military industrial complex that sociologist C. Wright Mills warned us about, back in 1956, in his groundbreaking study, *The Power Elite*. More critical to the fate of humanity than ever, these ancient fields of inquiry must be wrested from the grip of this powerful and reckless elite and brought back into the fold, so as once again to serve the interests of peace and justice, so as once again to serve the interests of the many instead of the few.

"Humanism," as defined by the American Humanist Association, "is a rational philosophy informed by science, inspired by art, and motivated by compassion. Affirming the dignity of each human being, it supports the maximization of individual liberty and opportunity consonant with social and planetary responsibility. It advocates the extension of participatory democracy and the expression of the open society, standing for human rights and social justice. Free of supernaturalism, it recognizes human beings as a part of nature and holds that values—be they religious, ethical, social or political—have their source in human experience and culture. Humanism thus derives the goals of life from human need and interest rather than from theological or ideological abstractions, and asserts that humanity must take responsibility for its own destiny."

Adolf Hitler believed that the mind was inherently seditious, and therefore that the body alone should be the focus of education, as only the body could be loyal and true. Of course he was right: it is the very seditiousness of the mind—its capacity to question, to reason, to imagine alternatives—that makes us most truly, defiantly human.

To that end, I strongly recommend Clive James' richly provocative compendium of short essays, *Cultural Amnesia: Necessary Memories from History and the Arts*, a light, a beacon, in these deeply dark times. Praised as "a master of eloquent distemper", James "illuminates, rescues or occasionally demolishes" the careers of many of the greatest figures of the twentieth century—and all with an erudition and a faith in the human spirit that will make you shake your head in awe.

Sweeping back and forth through time in his treatment

of such famous (sometimes infamous) figures as Leon Trotsky, Albert Einstein, Josef Goebbels, Marcel Proust, Sigmund Freud, Louis Armstrong, Jean Cocteau, Albert Camus, and Mao Zedong, James is equally compelling in his portraits of such brilliant, if lesser known lights as Walter Benjamin, Anna Akmatova, Nirad C. Chauduri, Robert Brassilach, Nadezhda Mandelstam, Raymond Aron, Federico Fellini, Zinka Milanov, Isoroku Yamamoto, Witold Gombrowicz, Eugenio Montale, Octavio Paz, Edward Said, Beatrix Potter, Charlie Chaplin, and Coco Chanel.

Cultural Amnesia is a stirring, eclectic, often provocative exploration of "the mental life of modern times" that is plainly reminiscent of the great essays of Montaigne. As James himself reminds us in his introduction: "It has always been a part of the definition of humanism that true learning has no end in view except its own furtherance." Read these essays and marvel; read these essays and grin.

P.N.

Animals

Confessions of a Carnivore, Diane Lefer
The Bleeding Stone, Ibrahim al-Koni

> *"I learned long ago that conservation has no victories, that one must retain connections and remain involved with animals and places that have captured the heart, to prevent their destruction."*
> George Schaller

Our relationship with animals is that of rational master to brute creature. Here's Montesquieu:

> *"Brutes are deprived of the high advantages which we have; but they have some which we have not. They have not our hopes, but they are without our fears; they are subject like us to death, but without knowing it; even most of them are more attentive than we to self-preservation, and do not make so bad a use of their passions."*

This sort of language is uncomfortably like the language used by slave-owners to describe their relationship to their species of property:

> *"[Slaves] enjoy liberty, because they are oppressed neither by care nor labor. The women do little hard work, and are protected from the despotism of their husbands by their masters. The Negro men and stout boys work, on the average, in good weather, not more than nine hours a day. The balance of their time is spent in perfect abandon."*

Perfect abandon.

It has struck me more than once in reading Orientalist texts, white accounts of slaves' lives in the Old South, the literature of animal rights (Peter Singer), and much post-modern literary criticism that the key subliminal message of Anglo-Saxon, male, white, patriarchal, mammal writers is a wistful longing for release from Reason. The burdens of rationality loom large in racist tracts purporting to describe the idle promiscuity of great apes and lesser men...*if only* we were allowed to throw over the responsibilities imposed by our Christian moral conscience. *If only* we could enjoy a freely libidinal existence—copulate at will, idle about in perfect abandon, muck about in fecal matter. Freud thought—more or less—that we might enjoy such an existence, though we would rue its un-Victorian idleness and pleasures and therefore wallow in the guilt that we wallow in anyway so—why not? If you've read the extensive social Darwinian racist literature of the late 19th century you know what I mean (just kidding: don't). All that finger wagging at the irrepressible copulations of the "dusky races," a less wistful version of *Passage to India* dressed up as biological truth. Beware their rapacious sexuality, their child-like delight in life! Our immortal soul is defended only by our reason, which comes from God (see Adam Smith, *Theory of Moral Sentiments*). Is it too reductive to write that the history of the West has been waged not between nations or religious persuasions but over the extent to which we are permitted to enjoy being the irrational animals that we in fact are?

Descartes thought animals were soulless. They were, in his view, automatons. Kant may have ascribed to animals a form of conscious perception—the philosophical jury is still out. In his seminal "What Is It Like to be a Bat," Thomas Nagel admits that he has no idea *what* it is like to echolocate, but makes a persuasive argument to the effect that *it is* like something. There is a bat way-of-being. I couldn't agree more. It's their being mute (in our view) that damns them. But then it wouldn't be sufficient if bats merely spoke; they would have to speak English. And have the ability to divide the world up into neat piles for further sorting. What happens, after all, when you are said to have "knowledge of a field"? You've mastered a vocabulary. Mute is brute.

Animals: we share the planet with them, we slaughter them by the billions for our gustatory pleasure, we domesticate them, become attached to them, even, in some cases, love and worship them. But do we take the trouble to think about them? What is like to be one, to be one of my dogs or one of the primates Diane Lefer's character Rae works with at the Los Angeles Zoo?

"No truth appears to me more evident, than that beasts are endow'd with thought and reason as well as men," wrote David Hume, hardly a soft-headed romantic. And John Searle offered that he *assumed* the existence of consciousness in animals just as he did so in his fellow persons. But these are the views of eccentrics, outliers in a world dominated by *homo sapiens.* It seems almost perverse to ask, as Diane Lefer does in many different ways: what's the difference between us and them? Between *any* us and *any* them?

Jennie, another of Diane Lefer's characters in her picaresque *Confessions of a Carnivore*—Lefer, I'm pleased to report, is a true original, a *wit* in the Boswell/Johnson sense— *"won't eat anything with a face."* A fine rule, especially if you've visited one of the horrifying farms on which chickens or pigs are bred for cellophane and the weird taxonomies of the supermarket's meat section. Rae, the carnivore of Lefer's title, does eat meat, ambivalently. I wonder if it's fair to think of Rae as "picar," as "roguish"? In any case, rather like Tom Jones, she is funny and irreverent, and she appears to have an underdeveloped super-ego, or perhaps her animal love has lowered her threshold for human forms of social shame.

Rae speaks a version of the vernacular that I ascribe to Sterne or Fielding:

> *"The smile was what you had to see. It was not a dazzling smile. It was not a placating smile. It was*

> *not a forced, rehearsed, smile-on-command calculated to guarantee the efficacy of some brand of toothpaste or religion. It was effortless. It matched the mildness in her eyes. She could no more keep her mouth from turning up at the corners than a turtle can. It was a pleasant smile. And this in spite of bad bridgework and a couple of gaps."*

Lefer specializes in wise-guys, in women (mostly) who can finish your sentences, look into your soul, dismantle your pretensions. Rae doesn't *prefer* animals to humans—she levels out the difference, she takes everyone from the mad cat-fancier Weezie to her squeeze David to the gibbons Luke and Lulu with deadly seriousness and dollops of irony. And the plot? I don't do plots, and even if I did, I couldn't begin to summarize this one. I haven't read a novel in ages with so much packed into every sentence. *Confessions* is romp, satire, stand-up schtick, Restoration comedy. All about gorilla/guerrilla theater, sex and love, driving in LA, standing up for those who have no one else to bother, Buddhism, the Church of Neoproctology (colonics and LA seem to go, well, hand in glove), vivisection, life on the Rez, murder in Tijuana...Diane Lefer has stories to tell, and she's clearly lived on the edges of things and thoughts that most people only read about.

And there's deep ecology, the possibility of thinking about Luke and Lulu in the same way one thinks about a boyfriend or a best friend. Not anthropomorphizing but the kind of simple caring that's not simple at all. Being as curious about a cat's inner life as your own, turning Montaigne upside down:

we are the ones who are living without advantage. Prosthetic gods. Pathetic in our belief that we are masters of the universe. Perfectly abandoned.

The same week I read *Confessions of a Carnivore* I read the mysterious novel by Ibrahim Al-Koni (titled in Arabic *Nazif al-Uhajar*), *The Bleeding of the Stone*, published in Beirut in 1992 and apparently out of print in Arabic but now translated by May Jayyusi and Christopher Tingley in the indispensable Emerging Voices series of Interlink Books. I can't imagine a book more removed from the contemporary concerns of Lefer's novel, or a book with less of a sense of humor. Al-Koni (or Kuni) has created a spare, harrowing story of a goat-herder's lonely desire to preserve the *waddan*, a rare mountain goat that inhabits the mountainous regions of the southern provinces of Libya. The book jacket confuses the *waddan* with the *moufflon*, a wild sheep found in Iraq. I parade this recently acquired fact as if I were George Schaller. Asouf has a feral personality—raised in isolation in the desert, he can't bring himself to interact with human beings even to the extent of trading, face-to-face, a goat for a bag of barley. When Asouf is confronted by a pair of sadistic hunters who want to kill a *waddan*, he does his best to mislead them. The animal, after all, is not only endangered but a living symbol of the desert he inhabits, a talisman representing a dying way of life.

The story has a strange timelessness: Al-Koni moves the narrative from past to present in ways that conflate the two.

One feels pulled back into a mythic world (the parts I liked best), but for much of the novel one is living in the brutal present, men with guns and a taste for meat and murder mindlessly eradicating life just because they can do so. As I was reading the novel I thought about the armed militias (if they are that) now roaming the southern portions of Libya and Tunisia. It isn't only mountain goats who are at risk in the violent reaches of Fezzan, but innocent people like Asouf. The ending of the novel confirmed, in its ritualized but senseless slaughter, my feeling that what Al-Koni was aiming for was the depiction of a mythic bond between (some) men and animals, and the fragility of that bond in a world gone mad.

The Bleeding of the Stone introduced me to a writer, a place, and a theme that I had never before encountered. An unsettling book, it complemented Lefer's wry consideration of some of the same questions: what happens when the innocent are confronted by the cruel and indifferent, when the weak face off against the men with guns and clipboards? Who wins and who loses? I think you can guess the answer.

G.O.

Machete

According to the Human Rights Council, Rwanda's population in 1994 was composed of three ethnic groups, the Hutu, which comprised roughly 85% of the population, the Tutsi, roughly 14%, and the Twa, a little more than 1%. In the early 1990's Hutu extremists within the country's political elite began blaming the entire Tutsi minority population for the nation's increasing social, economic, and political pressures. Through the protracted use of propaganda and political maneuvering the resentment and bigotry soon reached a feverish pitch, requiring but a single spark to blow it sky-high.

That spark came on April 6, 1994, out of the sky itself, when a small aircraft carrying President Habyarimana, a Hutu, was shot down. What followed was the swift and nearly wholesale destruction of the Tutsi minority. Tutsis (or suspected Tutsis) were killed on sight, whole families massacred in their sleep, their crops and villages burned to the ground. Most of the killing was done by hand, face-to-face, with machetes, axes, and hoes. Not surprisingly, Tutsi women and girls suffered the worst of it all, often raped repeatedly before being hacked to bits where they lay. Within a matter of weeks following April 6, 1994, 800,000 Tutsi men women and children were dead—nearly three-quarters of the total Tutsi population.

Scholastique Mukasonga's *Our Lady of the Nile* tells the deceptively simple story of the students and their teachers at an elite Catholic boarding school for girls in the cloud-covered mountains of Rwanda, near the legendary source of the Nile. For all its propriety and isolation, the school proves a dramatic microcosm of the state of the country at large in the months immediately preceding the Rwandan Genocide. Attended almost exclusively by the daughters of prominent Hutus with but two Tutsi girls per class, as required by law, the tension between the students, at first subtle, even childish on its face, soon overwhelms the daily routine. Even the Hutu teachers are not above this contempt, a bigotry rooted deeply in the history of the region and cruelly exploited by the German and Belgian colonizers who cynically promoted Tutsi supremacy over the majority Hutus as a means of reinforcing their power. Says one of the teachers, Father Herménégilde, in reference to the famously fictitious tract *The Protocols of Zion*, which he had read with interest when he was a seminary student:

> *The Jews wrote that they wanted to conquer the world, that they had a secret government pulling the strings of every other government, that they had insiders across the board. Well, I'm telling you, the Tutsi are like the Jews. Some missionaries, like old Father Pintard, even say that the Tutsi are really*

> *Jews, that it's in the Bible. They may not want to conquer the whole world, but they do want to seize this whole region. I know they plan a great Hamite empire, and that their leaders meet in secret, like the Jews... They're hatching every plot against our social revolution. Naturally, we've chased them out of Rwanda, and those who've stayed, their accomplices, we're keeping an eye on them, but one day we'll maybe have to get rid of them, too, starting with those who infect our schools...*

It is a hatred, a rivalry, the author herself knows well. A Tutsi, she and her family were made to suffer greatly under Hutu rule during the '60's, '70's and '80's, humiliated daily, dispossessed of their lands and finally forced to resettle in the highly polluted district of Bugesera in southern Rwanda. She and her family were later forced to flee for their lives to neighboring Burundi. In 1992, Mukasonga moved to France where she now lives—just two years before the genocidal rampage that swept through Rwanda, claiming the lives of 27 of her family members. When asked why she writes, she replied: "I know why I write. If I close my eyes, I'm forever walking down that path nobody takes anymore. For there are no more houses, no more coffee shrubs, no more sorghum with pestles, no more men in endless discussions around a jug of banana beer, no more little girls dragging their dolls by a string. They have all fallen to the machete, without proper graves..."

P.N.

Celine and Antunes on Hallucination

In 1916, Louis Ferdinand Auguste Destouches, better known to us as Louis-Ferdinand Céline, set out for what were then known as the Cameroons, in French West Africa. He spent one year in Africa, but wove that year into his debut novel, *Journey to the End of the Night* (1934), a hallucinatory voyage through the First World War, European imperialism in Africa, immigrant life in New York, and despair in Paris. I have chosen this passage more or less at random:

> *"What I [Bardamu, Celine's alter ego and anti-hero] couldn't help hearing under their spoken words and expressions of sympathy was this: Nice little soldier boy, you're going to die...You're going to die...this is war...Everyone has his own life...his role...his death...We seem to share your distress... But no one can share anyone else's death...A person sound in body and soul should take everything that happens as entertainment, neither more nor less, and we are wholesome young women...You'll soon be forgotten, dear little soldier boy..."*

What does *hallucinatory* really mean, in relationship to literature? I read Celine as a writer who is recreating dreams, states of consciousness that are offered without editing, where the extraneous is pushed front and center, where the reader's patience is tried by a lack of causality, coherence, and even, at times, of meaning. But then how else should a serious writer represent the horrors of the twentieth century but as a waking nightmare?

Among the most horrid nightmares of the Cold War occurred not in Latin America (there were plenty there) or Eastern Europe, but in Africa, in Angola in particular, a nation torn in three by the Portuguese—the original colonists—the Russians and the Americans, with the Chinese waiting in the wings for whatever scraps of diamonds and domination were left over. I won't recapitulate this history here, but only mention that the great Portuguese novelist, Antonio Lobo Antunes, served both his medical and literary apprenticeship in the horrifying war that pitted the Marxist government supported by Cuban and Russian men and arms against the U.S.-backed UNITA movement led by the charismatic madman Jonas Savimbi, one of the darling psychopaths of the Reagan administration. Antunes, born in 1942, served a medical apprenticeship in Angola, and witnessed scenes of horror that have pervaded his fiction ever since. His stylistic and tonal affinities with Celine are apparent, but his voice is his own. In the great novel *Os Cus de Judas* (*The Asshole of Judas*) translated by Margaret Jull Costa as *The Land at the End of the World* (1979)—the mad, rambling, hallucinating narrator relates his experiences in the horrifying Angolan Civil War that eventually claimed the lives of half a million Angolans:

> "No, I mean it, dusk falls and my heart starts to pound, I can feel it in my pulse, there's a tightening in my stomach, my bladder hurts, my ears hum, as if some indefinable thing waiting to burst forth were throbbing inside my chest: one of these days, the porter will find me lying naked on the bathroom floor, toothpaste and blood dribbling from one corner of my mouth.....I know it was six years ago, but I still get upset: we were traveling in convoy along sandy roads from Luso down to the Land at the End of the World, Lucusse, Luanguinga, past troops guarding the road construction site, past the ugly, uniform desert, villages surrounded by barbed wire, the prefabricated buildings of the barracks. . . . .my cap pulled low over my eyes, an endless cigarette vibrating in my hand, I began my painful apprenticeship in dying."

The hallucinatory is the dream made real. Antunes has a predecessor in Céline to be sure, but also in Coleridge's Ancient Mariner, in Conrad, and in Faulkner, all of whose narrators share with Antunes's doctor an obsession with the hopelessness of rendering into language that which is unspeakable.

The victims of more recent colonial wars in Vietnam, Iraq, and Afghanistan will recognize at once the madness of

Atunes's doctor-narrator as the inevitable outgrowth of war's horror. We call the syndrome PTSD and apply the term to any sort of trauma, but the victims of war suffer more than trauma—they lose their identity altogether:

> *"I am today whom I deep down reject: a melancholic bachelor whom no one phones and from whom no one expects a call, who coughs occasionally just to feel as if he had company, and whom the cleaning lady will find one day sitting in his rocking chair in his undershirt, mouth agape, his purple fingers trailing on the November-colored hair of the carpet."*

Antunes is the author of over twenty-six novels and is widely considered to be Portugal's greatest living novelist.

G.O.

The Wonder That is India

My obsession with India began in 1985. As a graduate student at NYU, I spent much of the little money I had collecting ragas, watching the films of Satyajit Ray, and gorging myself on curry, dal, and nan in nearby "Little India," a single block of East 6th Street crammed, at the time, with perhaps as many as twenty inexpensive Indian and Bangladeshi restaurants. Not long after that I met Annie, my wife-to-be, who'd developed a passion for Asia while studying at Barnard, and fell in love, when together, after a wonderful summer in Japan, we set our sights on India, travelling first to Delhi, Srinagar, and Ladakh, then, a year later, to Bombay (now Mumbai) and south—to Bangalore, Mysore, Ootacamund, Trivandrum, and Chochin, then to Kovalam where we lived for a month on the beach.

In that time I read everything about India I could get my hands on, a stumbling, slapdash initiation into the country and its peoples that included such well-known and lesser-known works as *The Discovery of India*; *The Great Mutiny*; *India: A Wounded Civilization*; *Sources of Indian Tradition*; *The Bhagavad Gita*; *Thy Hand, Great Anarch!*; *Portrait of*

India; The Essentials of Indian Philosophy; The City of Joy; Ramakrishna and his Disciples; The Speaking Tree; Freedom at Midnight; and *The Wonder That Was India.* As fiction was my passion, I devoured the novels and short stories of R.K. Narayan, Attia Hosain, Nayantara Saghal, Mulk Raj Anund, Ismat Chugtai, Ruth Prawer Jhabvala, Gucharan Das, Anita Desai, Indira Mahindra, Kushwant Singh, Altaf Fatima, Raja Rao, and Rabindranath Tagore (with one of whose most prominent English translators, William Radice, I happened to share a train ride between Oxford and London one day). In Kerala I read Rushdie's *Midnight's Children* in a hotel room flooded to the bedsprings by relentless monsoons rains.

Yet it is likely I would never have read any of these, let alone travelled to India itself, had it not been for a chance encounter with a single book—E.M. Forster's novel, *A Passage To India.*

If colonialism produced anything good (a matter much debated to this day), perhaps this, this novel of Forster's, is one of its bright, if bitter fruits. His treatment of the waning days of the British Raj (a time and experience he knew well) is not only politically nuanced and often commendably frank, but eminently sensitive, humane. While for many Forster stands damned by Katherine Mansfield's eager-to-be-witty contention that he never gets any further in his novels "than warming the teapot," I urge you to consider (or reconsider) this last novel of his, a work, a brew, sampled and extolled by readers and critics as distinguished and varied as Leonard

Woolf, Lionel Trilling, and Rebecca West. Among Forster's more contemporary paracletes is the adroit and savvy British author, Zadie Smith, who remarked in a recent interview in *The Atlantic* that her novel *On Beauty* was an homage to Forster, "to whom all my fiction is indebted." What she praises Forster for in general, what I praise him for in particular, is his unshakable liberal humanism, his unabashed, unapologetic devotion to Love and to the sanctity of human relationships, those dear and daily encounters that, for him (as well as for his more prescient characters like Dr. Aziz, Mrs. Moore, and Mr. Fielding) must finally and always take precedence over race, class, country, and creed.

In his life, as in his fiction, Forster lived a kind of golden mean, charting a path, in an age of fanatics, that distinguished him by what might be called a teleological, Anglo-Aristotelian restraint. I love the way Smith puts it:

> *...there is a sense in which Forster was something of a rare bird. He was free of the many vices commonly found in novelists of his generation—what's unusual about Forster is what he didn't do. He didn't lean rightward with the years, or allow nostalgia to morph into misanthropy; he never knelt for the Pope nor the Queen, nor did he flirt (ideologically speaking) with Hitler, Stalin, Mao; he never believed the novel was dead or the hills alive, continued to read contemporary fiction after the age of fifty, harbored no special hatred for the generation below or above him, did not come to feel that England had gone to hell in a hand-basket, that its*

language was doomed, that lunatics were running the asylum, or foreigners swamping the cities.

At the heart of this affecting novel are the valiant if hapless efforts of a few characters (one Muslim, two English) to surmount the many and cruelly consequential barriers that divided British India—barriers of race, sex, religion, nationality, education, and caste. Indeed, the hierarchical structure of human relationships during the more than three hundred years of British rule in India is clearly established in the novel's first few pages with the description of the fictional town of Chandrapore in which the bulk of the novel is set.

Dedicated to his Indian friend, cicerone, and unrequited love, Syed Ross Masood, Forster's *A Passage to India* is an eloquent, polyphonic, deeply empathetic tale about the insidious ways that colonialism corrupts and retards human relationships—a racist, sometimes violent sectarianism that persists in India to this day.

P.N.

Mystical Work

The Selected Poems of Mario Benedetti

> *"The spirituality of work. Works make us experience in the most exhausting manner the phenomenon of finality rebounding like a ball; to work in order to eat, to eat in order to work. Workers need poetry more than bread. They need that their life should be a poem."*
>
> Simon Weil, *"The Mysticism of Work"*

We may forgive the saintly Weil for exaggerating: workers need bread more than poems, but we do need poems and we need poets. Among the poets whose sensibility includes work—its glories and trials and beauty—is the great Uruguayan, Mario Benedetti who died in 2009, and who was among a handful of the most prolific, popular, and versatile of Latin American writers of the boom period, the "generation of 1945" in Uruguay, that hopeful post-War, liberal moment of Latin American history that was crushed—in Uruguay, Nicaragua, Cuba, Guatemala, El Salvador, and elsewhere—by the bipolar hostilities of the Cold War.

Benedetti, born of Italian immigrant parents in Pasa de los Toros, "Was a man of the left who criticized the United States, championed Cuba's revolution, embraced independence for Puerto Rico and, in 1971, helped organize a left-wing coalition in Uruguay called the Broad Front to challenge the two-party system that had prevailed for nearly 150 years." Like many other Latin American intellectuals and progressives, Benedetti was forced into exile. Banned from the United States, he lived in Argentina, Peru, Cuba, and Spain, before returning to his beloved Montevideo, in 1985.

I first read Benedetti, in Spanish, while living in Nicaragua in the 1980s. A friend gave me one of Benedetti's many books—*Viento del exilio*—that I could barely make out. Benedetti's Spanish is lively and idiomatic and attuned to the speech patterns of ordinary people—it is difficult to translate, but thanks to Louise B. Popkin and the good people at White Pine Press, we now have a generous, lucid, and accurate version of some of Benedetti's poems. He was enormously prolific, publishing eighty books, including poetry, plays, song-lyrics, and many novels (which I hope Ms. Popkin will consider translating as well).

I love poets who are engaged with the world, whose political passion informs their writing. Mario Benedetti's work demonstrates the richness of poetry that derives its life from this world, with us, the poetry of workers and of ordinary people who need bread and poems:

In this everyday poem I miss autumn
  with its permanent radiance
that golden sun encircling the pines
  and highlighting their majestic stillness
a certain aroma of boulevards taken over
  by dead leaves and grapes for sale
and of young girls digging their woolens
  out of mothballs.
[y tambien a muchachas que exhumaban sus prendas/de lana y naftalina], from Everyday Poem 4/20

Benedetti wrote some lovely poems to his wife, Luz, to whom he was married for half a century:

We've arrived at neutral twilight
where day and night melt into sameness.
No one can ever forget this interlude.
The sky glides smoothly over my fallen lids,
emptying the city from my eyes.
Don't think now of time on the clock,
the time of petty sorrows,
Now there's only naked yearning [el anhelo desnudo]
the sun breaking free of its weeping clouds,
your face fading into the night
until it's but a voice and the whisper of a smile.
  [from Taking Hold of You]

My favorite Benedetti poems celebrate ordinary life:

From time to time joy
  tosses pebbles at my window [!]
so I'll know it's out there waiting

> *but since today I'm feeling calm*
> *I'd almost say cool-headed*
> *I plan to stash my cares away*
> *stretch out and look up at the ceiling*
> *which is a fine comfortable position*
> *for sifting out news and letting it sink in*
> *who knows where my next steps will lead me*
> *or when the measure of my life will be taken*
> *who knows what words of caution I'll yet come up with*
> *or what shortcuts I'll take to ignore them....*
>   *[from Pebbles at My Window]*

Like all great poets, Benedetti is not for the day, or the mood, or the cause, or the single idea. His poetry touches on the beauty of a life lived with passion, on politics and marriage, on joy and the great sorrow of exile. He can write poems of grief and rage—as in *"At Dream Level"*—and then shift gears to meditate on hope, however fragile:

> *Hope so gentle*
> *so polished so sad*
> *a vow so lightly taken*
> *is not my way*
> *hope so docile*
> *is not my way*
> *rage so meek*
> *so humble so weak*
> *anger so discreet*
> *is not my way*
> *...my way is your gaze*
> *so giving yet firm*

your silence so guileless
is my way....
　　[My Way]

"We've arrived at that neutral twilight/where day and night melt into sameness./No one can ever forget this interlude...."

G.O.

Soul Swallower

How Götz, or was it Meyer, loved children!
David Albahari

On the internet one can find photographs of the converted buses that the Nazis used in their initial experiments in the large-scale asphyxiation of prisoners—of Ukrainians, Poles, and Russians, mostly of the handicapped and Jews. As carbon monoxide canisters quickly proved too expensive for the job, the developers soon settled upon a simpler, more cost-effective method, requiring only that bus driver get out of the tightly sealed cab and reconnect the exhaust hose to a special outlet in the bottom of the bus. After about 15-20 minutes of idle driving about the countryside all of the prisoners would be dead. Not long thereafter, such jerry-rigged buses were replaced by custom manufactured vans, the compact Diamond and Opelblitz, as well as the 5-ton Saurer, the most efficient of them all.

It is a 5-ton Saurer that looms at the heart of the spare, if devastating novel, *Götz and Meyer*, by the Jewish Serbian writer, David Albahari. Based on an actual Saurer van that operated in and around the city of Belgrade during WWII, a van in which—so the narrator discovers—many of his relatives had perished. Through his research he learns in addition that the drivers of this van were two young men, two actual SS noncommissioned officers, identified plainly in the records as Wilhelm Götz and Erwin Meyer:

> *I never saw them, Götz and Meyer, so I can only imagine them. My interest in the two of them came at a time when I was trying to fill in the empty slots in my family tree. I had just turned fifty, I knew where I was going with my life, so that all that was left was to figure out where I came from. I went round the archives, visited museums, brought books home from the library. That is how Götz and Meyer came into my life.*

What ensues in the novel is the narrator's determined, finally desperate attempt to imagine these two men, to slip into their minds, their skins, to understand—as so many have sought to do—what Hannah Arendt famously called, "the banality of evil," the fact that such cruelty and violence, as was perpetrated by the Nazis, was less the product of a handful of psychotic, diabolical freaks (whom we could safely dismiss as aberrational) than the logical, rational, even *inexorable* outcome of an abiding ideological faith, a cultural, national creed embraced and embodied, not by monsters, but by average, often expressly "normal" men and women. Writes Albahari, the two young officers were altogether indifferent as killers, with no apparent stake in the matter at all:

Once you become a part of the mechanism, you assume the same responsibility as every other part. Götz and Meyer didn't know about that. The truck was theirs to drive, and they drove, always smiling, even when the wind blew dust in their faces, and they couldn't care less what was going on in the back, whether the load was Jews or sugar beets.

Führerprinzip, the foundation of political authority upon which the Third Reich was based, consisted essentially of the simple, incontestable belief that Hitler's word was law. Everything followed from that. It was a principle to which Hitler's chief henchman, *SS-Obergruppenführer*, Adolph Eichmann, made frequent reference during his trial in Jerusalem when defending himself and his comrades again the charges of genocide and mass murder, insisting, as he had, that they had only been "following orders." While by now an argument that has been thoroughly discredited, and while Arendt's assessment of Eichmann himself as "banal" has been shaken, and while some violence and cruelty is indeed aberrational, the central mystery of this novel remains: How does one explain the methodical, bureaucratic murder of six million Jews?

P.N.

Does Great Literature Make Us Better?

> *"The aim of the artist ought to be to bring into the world objects which do not already exist there, and objects which are especially worthy of love . . . Works of art are meant to be lived with and loved, and if we try to understand them, we should try to understand them as we try to understand anyone—in order to know them better, not in order to know something else."*
>
> William Gass

As a lover of fiction, I owe a special debt to William Gass, for it was Gass who was among the first writers to awaken me to the sensuality and moral depth of great writing. In his many books of literary essays and in works of fiction like *Omensetter's Luck* and *In the Heart of the Heart of the Country*, Gass showed us that great books are "objects worthy of love," and that serious readers will have the world opened for them, have their awareness pitched higher, discover what is mysterious in ordinary things, and see more clearly into the lives of those around them if they will pay attention. Gass would have hated the previous sentence for its pretension, but I will let it stand. Gass was a poet in prose, who like his beloved Rilke, had the rare gift of being able to make of language both a bearer of meaning and an object worthy of admiration in itself. *The Tunnel* hypnotizes with its meandering fragments of memory and description. I will read four or five pages and then return to unwind the thread of the narrative (if I can—Gass disdains plots). Gass has his imitators, but in my view there are few writers who can play with language in quite the same way.

> *"In the winter he often slept inside the station. He knew to an inch how far from the stove to sleep. He knew where everybody spat and where we stamped the snow from our boots, shaking the floor, and where the wind came pouring, snowflakes with it, rattling the paper spills we kept in the woodbox. He knew where a live ash from a pipe might land or a whittler's shavings, and he figured the fall and roll, I'm sure, of every check to the corner where the board was spilled, as it often was if Jenkins played.... Kick's cat knew everything about the station. He knew where most of the light fell, and talk, and where the smoke went...."*

Kick's cat under the stove. Out here in the West, where the winters are long and a lot of heat comes from fireplaces, paper spills are common—they probably were up near Cornell where Gass received his Ph.D. in philosophy (linguistics, I think, since there was no one to direct his thesis in aesthetics) and maybe in St. Louis where Gass lived and taught from 1959 to his death in 2017. "Where everybody spat." I like to read Gass aloud when the house is empty—"Furber had come in the late fall following that enormous summer...." I'm leafing through Omensetter's Luck (1966).

Here's *Middle C,* nine cat's lives later (2013)

> *"When the soup was clear broth, as it often impecuniously was, Joey could occasionally see his face floating in a brown dream, and he thought of his mother's real self-submerged in a brown dream too, beyond the reach of life."*

I remember the debate between John Gardner and William Gass concerning the "morality of fiction." Gardner, a realist and a bit straitlaced when it came to literary form, attacked post-modern (if there is really such a thing) writers like Coover, Barth, Hawkes, Barthelme, and Gaddis for their focus on language as opposed to the moral quandaries of their characters. At the time I thought Gardner had a point—I disliked Barth and Hawkes and couldn't understand a word of Gaddis—but Gass's aesthetic represented a bridge, I felt, between literary aestheticism and a not-too-rigorous concern with moral questions. And it was reading Gass's literary essays, especially *Fiction and the Figures of Life* (1970), that allowed me to see the connection between language and meaning in literature. Gass argues, and rightly, that fiction, like philosophy, is constructed from concepts: "*There are no events but words in novels.*" So the love of language comes first, the aesthetic work of the writer, and then, if you're lucky, and if the writer is good, the ideas, the moral problems, the inner life of the characters—they too unfold. *The New York Times* published an opinion by the philosopher Gregory Currie this past week on the question that titles this essay. Currie's argument puzzles me a bit. He seems to be wondering how anyone could prove that fiction makes us better, or rather he believes there is no evidence for such a connection

"There is a puzzling mismatch between the strength of opinion on this topic [the moral effect of literature] and the state of the evidence. In fact, I suspect it is worse than that; advocates of the view that literature educates and civilizes don't overrate the evidence — they don't even think that evidence comes into it. While the value of literature ought not to be a matter of faith, it looks as if, for many of us, that is exactly what it is."

By this measure marriage, religion, opera, National Parks, and philosophy are suspect: how could one ever prove in a way that would satisfy a philosopher that any of these cultural institutions, like literature, make us moral? What would such proof even look like? I don't expect much from editorial opinions, especially from philosophers who write sentences like this one: "Many who enjoy the hard-won pleasures of literature are not content to reap aesthetic rewards from their reading; they want to insist that the effort makes them more morally enlightened as well. And that's just what we don't know yet." Not content? In his desire to make reading serious books seem tainted by elitism, Currie makes an odd argument. Reading (say) William Gass, one isn't wishing or hoping or reaching for moral enlightenment any more than philosophers teaching Kant's *Groundwork* are thinking

"I hope my students don't merely comprehend the idea of the categorical imperative; I hope they adopt it!"

Great literature works on us in all sorts of ways, often not at the conscious level of "mere" aesthetic enjoyment. Reading William Gass over three decades has taught me, for example, to pay attention. But I didn't set out to learn this, or learn it all at once, or even figure out for years that it was something I had learned. The causal relation between reading serious books and becoming a more empathetic and therefore a more moral person is murky. Novels aren't self-help books, and the subtle influence of any serious experience is never felt at once and always intermingled with other experiences. When and where and with whom I read Gass matters as much as who I marry, what sort of religion I subscribe to, which philosophers I read. So there isn't likely to be any proof that will satisfy Mr. Currie that great literature makes us better. Books don't make us moral, force us or trick us into behaviors we might not otherwise adopt. Living makes us moral, and good books change the way we live, if only because while reading books we aren't doing other things whose claims to enhancing our character would be *prima facie* weaker. If, as Gass says, works of art induce love in us, who would argue that this is not a moral good?

G.O.

Lebenslüge or Life-Lies

Aquitaine, often billed as "the other south of France," is a culturally, geographically diverse region in France, stretching from the world-famous vineyards of Bordeaux in the north to the precipitous Pyrenees of the Basque country in the south. It is there, in the south, in the mountainous village of St. Michel du Valcabrère, that Ward Just's poetic, quietly unsettling novel, *Forgetfulness*, is set. Thomas Railles, an American artist and former odd-jobber for the CIA, is living happily there in a self-imposed exile with his beloved French wife, Florette, painting, enjoying good food and wine, wandering the countryside, and listening to his favorite jazz records. One day, while he is busy chatting with some American guests in their home after a long and leisurely lunch, his wife sets out for a walk in the nearby mountains, as she is accustomed to do. She never returns. Night falls, the air grows cold, yet she is nowhere to be found. Set in the wake of 9/11 and the Bush administration's blundering "War on Terror," *Forgetfulness* is an often poignant mediation on the personal, starkly human cost of the violent, evermore fateful intersection of nationalism, religious fanaticism, and unfettered global capitalism.

When later his wife's body is discovered on the mountain, Railles learns that she had broken her ankle while hiking and then been murdered by unknown assailants, probably North African smugglers who regularly plied the region's rugged mountain trails. The story that ensues is that of Railles' struggle, in a country not his own, to come to terms with his grief and loneliness and to reorient himself in an age increasingly rife with both state and terrorist violence. Finally, *Forgetfulness* is the story of his own conflicted relationship with the U.S., with what it means to be an American today. Appalled, bewildered, by the events of 9/11 and eager that justice be served, Railles somehow "lacked anger of the sort that swept all before it and became a cause in itself, a way of life, the anger of the American…" Even when he finds himself face to face with his wife's killers, four recently captured Moroccan terrorists, he finds he cannot indulge even the *urge* to avenge his wife's death, an impulse that—some would say—is both his duty and due. Instead, he simply wants to meet the men, to talk to them, to understand what happened to his wife on the mountain that day, and in this way piece together again at least a little of the world he knew.

On September 11th my brother-in-law, Greg Rodriquez, was killed in the attack on the World Trade Center where he was working that morning in the offices of Cantor Fitzgerald on the 103rd Floor at One World Trade Center. What makes his story remarkable, what makes it especially meaningful to me, as well as relevant to this essay, was the all-but-immediate reaction of his parents, Phyllis and Orlando. Within days of

Greg's death, before they'd even begun to reckon with their grief, their loss, they wrote an open letter to *The New York Times* called "Not in Our Son's Name" in which they spoke out against the use of their son's death as a pretext for the war then already underway. Even in the midst of their suffering, they understood the trap and futility of vengeance. So, too, Just's character, Thomas Railles, refuses to seek vengeance as the solution to his anguish and loss, consoling himself instead with the illusion of forgetfulness, a simple lie that allows him to rise each morning and paint, that allows him to live.

P.N.

Wanna Get Away?

My Year of Rest and Relaxation, Ottessa Moshfegh
The Journal, 1837-1861, Henry David Thoreau
The Intimate Merton: His Life from His Journals, ed. Patrick Hart and Jonathan Montaldo

I've always been intrigued by solitude, by the rich resonance of being alone, and by those who can leave the world behind without a thought. Thomas Merton was such a person, and while his introspection, circling endlessly around his faults and his guilt before God, can become tedious, nonetheless his commitment to living an austere life of reading, writing, and meditation refreshes through its purity of purpose. Not only did Merton flee the life of an aspiring New York writer and intellectual for the austere existence of a Trappist monastery—a strict order requiring vows of poverty, chastity, and obedience—but at Gethsemane Abby, feeling distracted by his emerging fame as a writer, requested and was granted permission to live alone in the Hermitage. His journals, of which *The Intimate Merton* is a selection, remind me of Thoreau's journals. Each sought peace in solitude, each believed that separating himself from "ordinary life" would put him in touch with higher truths, each had a "calling," and both were at times lonely and disappointed that in their solitude they found not fulfillment but a deeper, inchoate yearning. Being alone causes you to doubt yourself. Perhaps that's why so few people are able to bear solitude.

> *"I sometimes seem to myself to owe all my little success, all for which men commend me, to my vices. I am perhaps more willful than others and make enormous sacrifices, even of others' happiness, it may be, to gain my ends. It would seem even as if nothing good could be accomplished without some vice to aid in it." Thoreau, Sept. 21, 1854*

I find refreshing the minutiae of solitude, the little moments of unguarded confession that range from trivia—Thoreau's July 25, 1853 entry on the difficulty he has keeping his shoes tied—to the profound—Merton's tortured description of his physical love for the nurse he refers to as "M".

> *"I feel that somehow my sexuality has been made real and decent again after years of rather frantic suppression (for though I thought I had it all truly controlled, this was an illusion.) I feel less sick. I feel human."*

Merton doesn't go so far as to break "the vow that prevents the last complete surrender," and he remains "suspicious of the tyranny of sex," but, taken together, his journal entries on his love for M show how difficult it is for even the most committed ascetic and solitary to give up life in the world.

***

Which is why, if you aren't a transcendentalist or a Trappist and you want to escape the world you have to go to sleep. Not for eight hours, but for eight months or a year or forever. You have to load up on Ambien and Restoril, Xanax and Ativan. Pay all of your bills automatically, quit your job, say goodbye to your (one) friend, and....go to bed.

It might not be fair to contrast the meditative and spiritual solitude of Thoreau with the seeming (see below) escapism of the narrator of Ottessa Moshfegh's latest novel *My Year of Rest and Relaxation*, but Moshfegh is so smart that the comparison is inescapable. Instead of turning a year of drug-induced rest and relaxation into a soap opera of millennial *angst*, Moshfegh imagines a young, pretty, well-off Upper-East-Sider as a kind of latter-day mendicant, one who seeks rebirth and reawakening with the same earnestness as a transcendentalist or Trappist. The young woman—who remains nameless throughout but tells her own story with an ingenuousness that is at the same time touching and creepy—retires to her couch, takes baskets of drugs prescribed by her lunatic psychiatrist, watches Whoopi Goldberg movies, and seeks not self-destruction but self-renewal, or maybe, in the jargon of today, a reboot. Her father has died of cancer; her mother has recently killed herself with pills and booze; her one and only friend is bulimic and deluded (the married man she loves *will* leave his wife for her someday); her on-and-off boyfriend is a sadist. Who wouldn't want to wake up from this nightmare?

Moshfegh writes scathingly of her own generation. Given the insincerity of so much contemporary writing, I find Moshfegh's deadpan style—bitterness unleavened by irony—refreshing. The narrator's cruel boyfriend Trevor is a dick, but in New York, on the cusp of Y2K, a beautiful young woman could do worse:

> "[Trevor] was clean and fit and confident. I'd choose him a million times over the hipster nerds I'd see around town and at the gallery. In college, the art history department had been rife with that specific brand of young male. An 'alternative' to the mainstream frat boys and premed straight and narrow guys, these scholarly, charmless, intellectual brats dominated the more creative departments.... 'Dudes' reading Nietzsche on the subway, reading Proust, reading David Foster Wallace, jotting down their brilliant thoughts into the black Moleskine pocket notebook. Beer bellies and skinny legs, zip-up hoodies, navy blue peacoats, canvas tote bags, small hands, hairy knuckles, maybe a deer head tattooed across a flabby bicep. They rolled their own cigarettes, didn't brush their teeth enough, spent a hundred dollars a week on coffee."

When you get tired of settling for what is offered and unpalatable, you want nothing more—I feel the same way sometimes—than to sit alone, quietly, with a good book or a dumb movie. But Moshfegh isn't playing for cheap stakes—she never does, not in any of her stories or in her earlier novel *Eileen* (Stephan King meets Thomas Bernhard). Nothing less than a cleansing of her heroine's life, an erasure of memory, a recasting of the too, too solid flesh will do the trick, and so the young pretty woman who looks, we are told, like Kate Moss, sells all that she owns, hires a Japanese conceptual artist as a kind of caretaker, and leaves the world behind on the (fake) drug Infermiterol, concocted in the manner of Don DeLillo's Dylar, a made-up magic bullet that eases one into three-day black outs, mini-deaths that, over the course of six months, succeed in erasing not so much memories as emotions about memories. It's a Trappist retreat. Thoreau's hikes on Cape Cod. May Sarton's winter alone in a Maine cabin. John Muir at Hetch Hechty. A Sand County Almanac for the lonely and neurotic urban dweller of our Brave New World.

Come to think of it, *My Year of Rest and Relaxation*, while wonderfully vulgar, is also, oddly, a religious book. Yes, to be born again we have to die, at least symbolically, we have to take on a new body, a new self. Sleep, after all, is what Lazarus awoke from; death can't be provisional, so he was in a coma, or in REM sleep. He was not only awakened, but, we have to concede, renewed. How could it be otherwise? The great imperative of our age should be: WAKE UP! We're not just watching zombie movies these days, we're zombies ourselves. Not "the blind leading the blind," which at least is touching (think of those images from the trenches of WWI), but the mindless, the sleepwalkers, leading the sleepwalkers.

So Moshfegh's heroine is Everywoman. As I read the book I kept thinking at some level, not sure which one, not how shallow the narrator was, or how cowardly, but how brave. How estimable it was to say, "fuck it," and go to sleep. Not to become like everyone else, but to become someone else. I won't say another word—the ending of the novel is beautiful and astonishing.

Yesterday, watching Stealth bombers and fighter jets zoom over my beloved city—not the Washington of Trump and the rest of the hoodlums, but the city of real people—I wished for some Infermiterol, some Dylar, for a long sleep, a week on the Concord and Merrimack, a retreat to a monastery, time alone to sort things out. To wake up once and for all.

G.O.

To She Who Loves So Sadly

Against Heaven: Selected Poems by Dulce María Loynaz

"The poetry of Dulce María Loynaz is, above all, a poetry of solitude," writes James O'Connor in his introduction to this marvelous collection. Indeed, in reading these poems one comes to treasure her particular solitude like a darkly burnished gem. It is a quality, this reclusion of hers—a relationship to the world, to the word, to herself as a woman, a Cuban, a writer—that gives her poetry (even in English) a grave and lyric beauty, a frankness and aestheticism that is nearly monastic in its clarity and restraint. Yet the object of Loynaz's reverence in these poems is as much Death and Love (and paradoxically the solitude they afford her) as it is some hidebound conception of God. "Loynaz," observes O'Connor, "is a religious poet in the way that Kierkegaard is a religious thinker: melancholy, not ecstasy, is the door to paradise."

As a poet Loynaz thinks often of oblivion, of death, but less as an end to worldly things, to the burdens of this earth-bound life (which she also recognizes), than as a consummation of them, a means of transcendence, a mundane, ultimately temporal rapture that exhilarates, even as it moves one to sadness and dread.

Loynaz's life itself, spent all but entirely in Cuba, was not without its own melancholy hues. Born in Havana in 1902, the daughter of Enrique Loynaz del Castillo, a famous general in Cuba's War of Independence, Maria Dulce lived the privileged, sheltered life of most young women of her class, though she traveled widely, earned a Doctorate of Civil Law, and—thanks to her family's reputation for patronizing the arts—made the early acquaintance of many great writers of the time, such as Gabriela Mistral, Alejo Capentier, Juan Ramón Jiménez, and Frederico García Lorca, each of whom spent time in their home.

After trying her hand at the law, Loynaz directed all of her energy to the challenge of writing poetry. Though she had written and published poetry since she was a teenager, it was not until the 1950's that she really hit her stride as a writer. In a span of eight years, a Madrid publishing house published four works of hers, including three collections of her poetry (*Garden*, *Poems with No Names*, and *Lyric Poems*) as well as a highly successful novel of hers called *A Summer in Tenerife*, which Luis Buñuel tried without success to adapt for the screen.

Around 1959, having refused to join the communist party (for reasons more personal than political), Loynaz gave up writing and publishing altogether to live in seclusion in her family's old house. It was not until the late 1980's, after nearly thirty years of anonymity and solitude, that her work was rediscovered, earning her a flood of national and international distinctions, including the National Order of Carlos Manuel de Cespedes, the Order of Felix Varela of the Culture, the National Culture Distinction Award, the Alejo Carpentier Medal, the Cuban National Prize for Literature, as well as the Nobel Prize equivalent for the Spanish-speaking world, the Miguel de Cervantes y Saavedra Literature Prize, awarded to her in 1993 by King Juan Carlos I of Spain.

Spanish Nobel Laureate Juan Ramón Jiménez had many names by which he knew this modest, elegant, extraordinary woman: "Sister Dragonfly, Saint Lawyer of Lost Jonquils, of Lost Mosquitos, of Lost Rowboats, of Lost Pins, of Lost Toothpicks, Ophelia Loynaz the Subtle, archaic and new..." In his prologue to *Cuban Poetry in 1936* he described her as a cross between "the gothic and the overreal," "a singer desiccated, nailed by her own heart" whose deeply private poetry was alive with a "mystic irony."

While Loynaz was not the first or last of the world's great melancholy writers, she is undoubtedly a singular strain of the breed. Neither misanthrope nor bully, neither narcissist nor suicide nor drunk, she spent a nun's life as a poet, keeping her own grave counsel, admiring her own dark and furtive saints. In his eccentric and magisterial work *The Anatomy of Melancholy*, first published in 1621, the English writer Robert Burton not only defines the condition of melancholy at length (virtually ad infinitum, and with a garrulous digression on human anatomy), as well as its causes, symptoms, and "prognostics," but devotes some 261 pages to describing its remedy. What would he have said, I wonder, to the likes of Dulce María Loynaz, a woman, a poet, with no interest in a cure?

    P.N.

Seeing!

Eye Contact, William Benton (essays on art)
The Museum of Modern Love, Heather Rose (a novel)

During the decade that I spent living in Washington, D.C., I visited the National Gallery several times a month, and Thomas Eakins's "Biglin Brothers Racing" (1872) grew to be the painting that meant most to me. Eakins's composition feels perfect—the postures of John and Barney are balanced as each prepares to dip his oar back into the water, and the care with which Eakins composed the background, visible only upon close inspection of the original, made me feel as if in viewing the picture I had fallen back in time to that day in May 1872 when the Biglins raced Harry Coulter and Lewis Cavitt along the smooth surface of the Schuylkill River. Eakins painted the pair numerous times, and his study of (nearly) nude human figures, a study that gave him the skill to reproduce the musculature in the arms and legs of the straining oarsmen, eventually cost him his teaching position at the Pennsylvania Academy of of the Fine Arts. I love Eakins's work, and, for reasons that are unclear to me, this painting in particular has been one that I have wanted to really and truly *see*.

We often *look* at pictures, but how often do we *see* them? We have to internalize the object, pull it off the wall and into our consciousness in the way that, from time to time, we pull a fictional character, or a poetic image, into ourselves, making it a part of the way we imagine the world. Most of the time I wander through museums reminding myself to pay careful attention. And then, in the Rembrandt room of the National Gallery, or in in front of the Kandinskys at the Guggenheim, or in the astonishing room that holds Monet's "Water Lily Pond" at the Art Institute, I don't have to remind myself at all, I become, as one must, fully attentive, present in my person in the way I always should be but almost never am.

Heather Rose's wonderful novel *The Museum of Modern Love*, which takes as its subject the famous Marina Abramovic piece *The Artist is Present* from 2010, a performance work during which, for seventy-five days, Abramovic sat still and silent, inviting anyone who wished to sit opposite her and to immerse themselves in the commitment to truth that has defined Abramovic's work for decades. *Commitment to truth?* As Rose makes plain in her evocation of the performance as experienced through a cross-section of (fictional and real) individuals, it was indeed the *truth* that Abramovic was seeking, that is, the unmediated experience of looking into the eyes of another human being, without preconceptions, without judgment, outside of language, politics, and even time. Those who sat could sit for as long as they liked. Over 1500 people participated and three-quarters of million visited the gallery space where Abramovic sat. Rose, a Tasmanian novelist, beautifully recreates the effect on the viewer of the raw experience of another's presence. The central character, a musician whose own art has failed him, whose wife is dying, and whose daughter thinks him unfeeling, finds in Abramovic's stoic sitting a restoration of the values that had slipped from his grasp.

Like Rose, the poet and art critic William Benton is attuned to the life-changing power of art. Most everyone enjoys looking at pretty pictures, but thinking about what these pictures mean to us, how they change us, is a rare gift. Among the best essays on art I have ever read is Benton's "Prodigies," a concise recognition of the role played by children's art in the Modernist movement. I thought about these sentences of Benton's as I was thumbing through the images in Sandler's *Art of the Postmodern Era*: "In 'The Dance I,' 1909, the anatomical inaccuracy in Matisse's line has vivid equivalents in the markings of a six-year-old. That no six-year-old could perceive how a departure from precise rendering redistributes energy across the canvas in a way that gives an allover aspect to the composition is what makes art Art. *It bears repeating: perception, not dexterity.*"

True in painting, true also in poetry and fiction—perception, not dexterity or talent. Benton offers us insights into the making and seeing of art in each of the twenty-nine short pieces collected in *Eye Contact*. So much art criticism, taking a cue perhaps from the *ex cathedra* style of Clement

Greenberg, fails to consider how and why art become Art for the average viewer. Greenberg's pronouncement "Value judgments constitute the substance of aesthetic experience" seems wrong-headed to me. Of course value judgments are an important part of our experience of art—what are we to bother looking at?—but the *substance* of aesthetic experience must also include questions about meaning, about our inner transformation in the presence of beauty (however defined), about what in the world art *does* for us, how it unsettles us—"unsettles" in the sense that Heather Rose asks this question in *The Museum of Modern Love*.

Here's Benton on the solitary female figures of Nathan Oliveria, a comment that quickly laid to rest my own inability to make sense of this painter: "Oliveria's women are other. Their native element is mind. They owe their lineage to the formative welter of male imagination. The central position they occupy on the canvas has less to do with existential space than with immanent singularity." This seems exactly right. Not that it matters, but I want to see pictures—not *correctly*—but with the greatest possible insight, and Benton, in his brief essays on Knobelsdorf, Gordon Baldwin, and Oliveria (artists whose work I have seen), and on James McGarrell, Edmund E. Niemann, and Sidney Nolan (artists of whom I knew nothing of before Benton), allowed me to search their work with renewed confidence that I wasn't shortchanging either them or myself.

Not only is Benton a perceptive critic of art, and, in particular, of artists of whom one might know little, he is also a fine poet, as evidenced by his sensitive transformations of images into words:

Tree Trunks Reflected in Water

Standing in a row
at the edge of the river,
those trees are the men.
I'm the water. I mimic the way

they look and what they do
in the sliding wind.
*

I take on the mannerisms, voices,
even the thought processes of others.
I despise my skin and can't escape or fully occupy it.
An empty insufficiency
forces me to act. I pool slowly, all
surface stars and self-doubt.
*

The row of trunks
in a single motion
rakes through my life.

G.O.

Under My Skin

I have now been reading the novels of Spanish writer Javier Marías on and off for about seven years, and it has taken me this long to truly begin to appreciate them, to warm to his cool, aloof, expressly cerebral style. It has taken me nearly seven years to grasp just what an extraordinarily fine writer he is (mind you, most of Europe has known this for decades), nearly seven years of patient reading for his novels to really get under my skin.

Surely a part of my preoccupation with his work (too impatient to wait for the American edition of his latest, I have just this morning ordered it in its English edition) springs from the anxiety, the despair, I often feel, living here in the U.S., at the prospect of not being able to regularly replenish my supply of the dense, unapologetically intellectual novels I love, those artistically uncompromising, often tryingly original tales that have not only defined the novel for me as one of the highest forms of human and aesthetic expression, but have literally made me who I am.

More and more, I crave the work of writers who like

to think, to think hard and in unconventional ways, those writers who refuse to compromise, to apologize for their obsession with character and language and form, whose idea of plot (to paraphrase a popular criticism of Proust) is often just some man or woman turning over in bed.

The great modernist Joseph Conrad once wrote: "We live, as we dream—alone." It is this, this recognition of the fundamental loneliness of human existence that sits at the heart of so much of my favorite fiction. In fact the kind of novels I most admire, those I read and reread, those I study some days like scripture, are often little more than the stories of a man or woman *thinking*, usually in isolation or grief. While I am no misanthrope, in fact every day more grateful for the people in my life, little is plainer (or more significant) to me as a person, than the fact that far and away the majority of my time here on earth is spent in silent communion with myself, with my own joys and sorrows, with my own fictions, plaints, and fears. Think about it: is there anything more quintessentially human than this private daily grinding we do, this Sisyphean sentence *to think*, to live our lives like monks, like nuns, within the confines of our own buzzing heads?

It is this painful, often reluctant solipsism that lies at the heart of so many of the greatest modern novels I've read, from (here comes a list, for those of you who are interested) those of Conrad, Woolf, Proust, Dosotevsky, Melville, Joyce, Kafka, Roth (Joseph), Goncharov, Musil, Forster,

Faulkner, Fitzgerald, Svevo, and Mann to Pessoa, Lowry, Barnes, Cela, Ellison, Castellanos, Bellow, Qian, Saramago, Camus, Carpentier, Oe, Böll, Dorfman, Niwa, Voinovich, Manea, Ishiguro, Rushdie, Gordimer, Saghal, Jin, Brink, Malamud, Cortázar, Gao, McCarthy, Styron, Amado, Pamuk, Vargas Llosa, Jelinek, Klíma, Wright, Grossman, Mistry, Gombrowicz, Lispector, Morrison, Sabato, Silko, Pavese, Coetzee, Nabakov, Kahout, Olesha, Oz, Levi, Okri, Appelfeld, Platanov, Bernhard, Farah, Aksyonov, Fuentes, Bolaño, Ulitskaya, Emecheta, Sebald, Unsworth, Martin, Trevor, Kaniuk, Petry, Naipaul, Szabó, Hong, Chacel, Borges, Bowles, Yehoshua, Sōseki, Tišma, Walser, Ford, Heade Greene, Duffy, Abish, Cohen, Ghalem, Agnon, Baldwin, Handke, Ivo, Rulfo, Benet, Mahfouz, Ali, Megged, Murdoch, Hrabal, Novakovich, Bowen, Houllebecq, Ocampo, Zhang, Rodoreda, Asturias, Sábato, Soyinka, Müller, Fox, White, Adler, Vollmann, Ford, Lenz, Garcia Márquez, Platonov, Toer, Narayan, Schulze, Pekić, Carey, Wallace, Bedford, Ying, Nooteboom, Achebe, Arenas, Desai, Páral, Énard, Robbe-Grillet, Lamming, Kraznahorkai, Machado de Assis, and Gass. It is a condition, a syndrome, that also lies at the heart of Marías's fine novel *The Infatuations*.

Set in contemporary Madrid, *The Infatuations* explores, with elegant intelligence (and with more than a passing nod to the masterworks of Shakespeare, to *Othello* and *Macbeth*), the experience of a single woman, an editor in a local publishing house, named María Dolz who finds herself eavesdropping on the life of a handsome young couple near whom she sits each morning in her favorite café before work. At first just a passing fancy, of which she hardly thinks once she leaves the café, her interest in the couple takes a significant turn when one day they fail to appear, a disruption in the quiet, pensive routine of her life, that is soon exacerbated by the news—detailed in all of the daily papers—that the man, the husband, was brutally murdered in an act of apparently random violence by a demented homeless man armed with a butterfly knife. From there the story traces María's growing, ultimately fateful obsession with the dead man's wife, Luisa. Finely, eloquently told, the novel is at heart a metaphysical inquiry into the timeless issues of love and death, a catechism of betrayal and obsession and truth. It is wonderfully heady stuff.

P.N.

Hiding Out In Lisbon

Like a Fading Shadow Antonio Munoz Molina

Munoz Molina read Hampton Sides's *Hellhound on His Trail*—the history of James Earl Ray's pursuit and murder of Dr. Martin Luther King, Jr. and after conducting a great deal more research he produced a remarkable novel, *Like a Fading Shadow*. Molina uses the fact of Ray's brief stay in Lisbon to create a detailed documentary account of Ray's life from 1967, when he first began to track King across the United States, until his capture in London in June, 1968, two months after the assassination.

James Earl Ray lived in a fantasy world. To say he was paranoid is to understate the case. His daily life both before and after the assassination of Dr. King followed a pattern familiar to us from reading the life stories of his peers—Lee Harvey Oswald, Mark David Chapman, John Hinckley, Jr.—men who belonged to nothing but their fantasies, loners and losers, men who fixated on individuals whose existence either undermined or justified their own. Chapman thought he was Holden Caulfield, Hinckley lived (still does apparently) to impress Jodie Foster, and Oswald developed an obsessive hatred for the racist ex-general Edwin Walker. None of these men, and certainly none of their deeds, were "banal." Hannah Arendt's point in developing the concept of the banality of evil in her book on the Eichmann trial was not to diminish the horror of murder or the evil of murderers but to remind us that evil is committed by men who are, in most respects, not unlike ourselves, ordinary persons whose lives are anonymous, even boring, up until the moment they commit their crimes. I remember how surprised I was when I read about Mark David Chapman—a nobody—and how Hinckley's psychotic fixation on a young movie actress reprised what was normal in American culture—love of celebrity and admiration for fame.

Molina brilliantly captures the banality of James Earl Ray's inner life and the ceaseless turmoil of his outer life. The nondescript man in black glasses and a musty suit wanders the streets of Lisbon, lies in bed in his cheap room, rehearses his lines and tries out new identities, watches his meager cash supplies dwindle, thinks of everything except the murder that propelled his escape from the United State. Molina is utterly convincing as Ray's voice, almost as his *alter ego*.

Molina approaches Ray's story obliquely, through the device of a fictional memoir. The author, Molina himself, travels to Lisbon to reinvent himself as a writer. It was in Lisbon, thirty years before, that the author found inspiration for his first book (*A Winter in Lisbon*). Molina layers his three stories—of himself in the present, of James Early Ray's brief stay in Lisbon, and of his own earlier visit to Portugal—in such a way that eerie parallels emerge. All three strands of the story explore questions of truth telling, of personal identity, and the cost of isolation. Most striking is the way in which Molina uses the idea of disguise, of hidden identities, in exploring both his own and Ray's story. Ray, after all, was a pathological liar, a story-teller and shape-shifter of considerable skills, so much so that he was able, for a time, to convince the King family that he was innocent of the killing at the Lorraine Motel. It takes little imagination to see that what Molina is doing in part is questioning the mechanisms of the novel itself, interrogating the idea of finding truth in falsehood, or perhaps asking if it is possible to create a literary form whose truth can be perceived through its disguises.

G.O.

To Build a Road

The only truly rational means is violence.
                                                Alberto Moravia

Now, more than ever before in my lifetime, it is money that is the nation's Holy Writ, the people who manipulate it—the CEOs and CFOs, the brokers and accountants—our sages and savants. Indeed for many, their reach, their vision, is mystical, oracular. Yet one needn't be a prophet to understand that our adherence to this faith, this *cult*, has proven catastrophic in its impact on the environment, on our civic life, on our very understanding of what it means to be human.

While the base, reductive thinking of Wall Street was once restricted to the financial sector itself, to the hawking of stocks and bonds, to the humdrum vernacular of saving accounts and IRAs, it now has permeated every aspect of life in this country. Not only has this mercenary dogma redefined and subverted democratic governance, healthcare, publishing, sports, news, fashion, entertainment, policing, urban planning, public transportation, food systems, social services, national security, the military, water and land management, social media, the criminal justice system, and international relations, but it has even permeated the arts and education, traditionally the bastions of civil, humanistic discourse.

The result is that now virtually every significant decision in the country is made (or at least highly influenced) by some man or woman with an MBA. Time and again their decisions are sold to us (for now everything is *sold*) as logical, rational (meaning tested, scientific, *objective*), as justly, even supremely, pragmatic. Just ask these "experts", these mystagogues; they will show you the numbers on the page.

Of course to treat something—*anything*—"objectively", is to abstract it, to deform it, to exempt it from the messy realm of human affairs, so as to make it manipulable, so as to make it useful, *profitable*. Look around you: nearly everything these days has been reduced to a "science", a technique, but another method to be mastered and exploited by rational means. A scam, a pyramid scheme, this ubiquitous corporate gospel is the ultimate *Realpolitik*.

If neo-capitalism (or anti-humanism) was a concern to Italian writer Alberto Moravia in 1963, when he compiled this book, it (like the state of the environment today) is now a matter of despair. His warning is plain:

> *So we must have no illusions. We shall have an ever larger number of cheap, well-made consumer goods; our life will become more and more comfortable;*

and out arts, even the most demanding and difficult ones, indeed those especially, will become more and more accessible to the masses; and at the same time we shall feel more and more that at the heart of this prosperity lies nothingness or a fetishism which, like all fetishisms, is an end in itself and cannot be put to the service of man.

In the opening essay of his collection, *Man As An End: A Defense of Humanism*, Moravia writes:

Since then [in Bismarck's Germany] the strides made by Machiavellianism have been triumphant, like a headlong, irresistible river that swells and increases in power thanks to the very obstacles it overcomes on its way. Machiavellianism now seems inevitable, it is taken for granted and seems to have no alternative. In the field of pure thought it appears invincible, and it is the ineluctable center towards which all roads in politics seem to lead… The only result of the universal and indiscriminate practice of Machiavellianism in modern times has been to provoke the two biggest wars in history and to bring infinite suffering and immense destruction on mankind.

Arguably the most powerful part of this book for me appears in his first and aforementioned essay, "Man As An End", an essay and introduction in which Moravia, by way of example, describes two approaches to building a road. The first, a method employed since the beginning of time, involves nothing less than an exhaustive study of the land and peoples through which the new road would pass. As the road is meant to serve them, such an approach makes sense. Central to this approach is the careful consideration of the landscape itself, the hills and mountains, the streams and rivers, the fishes and mammals and plants. What's more, the planners must get to know the people who reside there, their farms and villages, their hunting and fishing grounds, their churches and temples and shrines. They must devote months, even years, to familiarizing themselves with the local customs and traditions, living closely with the locals, as one of their own. Only in this way will the planners know if the construction of the road makes sense, if it will enrich rather than impoverish the locals' lives.

Of course you know the other way. Trump and his kind have made of virtue of it. Writes Moravia:

> *The second way is just the opposite and consists in building the road without bothering about the obstacles. In this case my road will cut across the farm land, span the river at its widest point, flatten the homesteads. I shall hack down mills, oil presses, chapels and workshops, fill in the wells, eliminate the sports ground. Furthermore I shall dynamite hundreds of thousands of cubic rock and dry up hundreds of thousands of square yards of marshland.*
>
> *Nothing binds me to build the road in one way or the other. The law is on my side. There is a decree of my government whose execution is guaranteed by*

force. I can do whatever I want: I can even kill the inhabitants down to the last man and destroy all the farms and farmland... It is enough to say that I want to build a road.

In the first scenario the people and the environment are considered the end itself, the very reason for the road, if the road is to be built at all, while in the second the people and the environment are resources, tools, *things*, but the means to an end that has little or nothing do with them.

P.N.

Life Alone

The Wall Marlen Haushofer

It isn't my intention to put you off this remarkable novel, but it is, hands down, the most depressing book I have ever read. Depressing in a good way. Haushofer set out to write a novel depicting the end of the world, the effects of debilitating solitude, and the hopelessness of the individual in the face of total meaninglessness—and she did. And what's worse (better) is how effectively Haushofer evoked not so much screaming-banshee terror but quiet despair. What has killed off everyone, and why? We have as little idea as the nameless narrator.

There's lots of apocalyptic literature around these days. The little of it that I have read feels either sensationalized or, frankly, disgusting (Cormac McCarthy's *The Road*), or preposterous (N.K. Jemisin's *The Fifth Season*). The problem isn't plausibility—the world *is* ending after all. No, the problem with post-disaster books is that they don't take seriously the existential and psychological cost of living in the end-times. The characters in most of these books are victims whose lives are unimaginable struggles for survival. There's no provision made for reflection. Around every corner is a cannibal, a carnivorous alien, or a another human who is (naturally) one's enemy. In Eden there was scope for cooperation. When the Seventh Seal has been broken it will be every woman for herself.

I won't be forgetting *The Wall* anytime soon. What happens when one wakes up to a world devoid of other human beings, with a transparent glass wall enclosing one in a valley whose outward prospect suggests that you are the only surviving human being?

Haushofer examines with painstaking care the claustrophobic daily life of an ordinary woman who has survived some kind of global disaster. Haushofer never lets on what has happened—where is everyone? Who built the Wall, and why? Like the woman, we operate wholly in the dark, and if we allow ourselves to fall into the conceit of the Wall a nightmare is opened to us: how does one cope with loneliness, with the daily grinding routine of survival? The woman has a few companions—a dog, a cat, a cow—and in her ingenuity and sheer will to survive she reminds one of Robinson Crusoe, but without the human companionship of Friday. There are no voices in the novel but that of the solitary woman, and her voice has the dull cadence and flatness of the dead.

Reading this novel requires one to think about solitude in a way that few other novels do. Hell may be other people, but there surely is a version of hell that is no one, not a human voice anywhere. Our woman survivor is incapable of reading—what's the point of information or art?—or of amusing herself in any way but with Tarot cards (a chilling idea), or of doing anything except sleeping and trying to stay alive. The state of nature so attractive to admirers of Ayn Rand and Rand Paul—well ladies and gentlemen, here it is. Lusty independence, no government regulations, no one else's annoying needs to get in the way of the satisfaction of your own. Madness. I kept thinking of prison, but even in prison someone shoves food in the slot or tries to stab you with a toothbrush, horrible, but better than nothing.

This is a deeply political book, a feminist meditation. For what does our protagonist do but rebuild civilization, remake a tiny world out of remnants of what has been lost. She creates order and routine, does chores, cares for the injured, buries the dead, in just the way that women have always done. She's so depressed she can barely rise up from her bed, and yet she does so because otherwise the whole rickety edifice of her solitary civilization will fall to pieces.

And men? You'll need to read *The Wall* to find out about them.

G.O.

The Eye of Ra

Danger has been a part of my life ever since I picked up a pen and wrote. Nothing is more perilous than truth in a world that lies.
                                             Nawal el-Saadawi

"Nawal el-Saadawi," writes Katherine Roth, in a piece for the on-line journal, *The Best of Habibi*, "is perhaps the best loved, most hated, and best known feminist in the Arab world." Indeed El-Saadawi is like a latter-day Eye of Ra in the might and violence with which she confronts and subdues her enemies—those bloated, hypocritical, essentially male defilers of ordinary people and their homes who continue, Quran in hand, to define the fate of Egyptian girls and women to this day.

An ardent political and social activist, as well as an accomplished physician who has devoted much of her career to serving the rural poor, El-Saadawi is also a writer—an intellectual and artist who has committed much of her power to writing fiction as a means of speaking her mind. For it is through her novels, in their unflinching portrayal of the oppressed and often wretched lives of ordinary Egyptians, that she truly makes her mark, an authority perhaps nowhere more apparent, nowhere more affecting, than in her still-startling 1974 novel, *God Dies by the Nile*.

Set in the fictional Nile village of Kafr El Teen, sometime in the long and unstable period between Egyptian independence from British control (1922) and the 1952 Revolution, led by the Free Officers Movement of Gamal Abdel Nasser (though distinctly the story has the timelessness of allegory, of myth) El-Saadawi's provocatively titled novel tells the simple, if bracing tale of a peasant woman, Zakeya, and her helpless struggle to protect her beautiful young nieces from the ruthless predation of the local mayor. The world of Zakeya is a grim, fatalistic world in which the rich and pious exploit the poor, and the men (be they rich *or* poor) exploit the women and girls—and all in the name of Allah, of God.

In fact the lives of the women in this tale are all but entirely circumscribed by the whims and pleasures of men, whose misogyny thrives in direct proportion to their piety and power. While there is no doubt that the routine tyranny, harassment, mutilation, and rape suffered by the women and girls in this story is an Egyptian, Muslim problem, a religio-cultural oppression decried again and again (and often smugly) in the popular Western press, it would be a shallow reading of this novel indeed if one were to close the book and not think long and hard about the different, if still pernicious effects of patriarchy and poverty here in the U.S..

For the wonder of a novel like *God Dies by the Nile* lies not simply in its ability to show us the lives of others (that alone would be voyeurism, tourism), but also in its power to move us—men and women alike—to consider with fresh eyes the very terms by which we live and relate to each other, to examine daily all we hold to be "right" and "natural" and "true." Grim as it is, this novel is much more than a catalogue of cruelties, for great fiction is always—indeed necessarily—redemptive. For a writer, a feminist, like El-Saadawi, merely *describing* the status quo could never be enough.

P.N.

Rural Beauty

Driftless, a novel by David Rhodes

Horse

In its stall stands the 19th century,
its hide a hot shudder of satin,
an eye brown as a river and watchful:
a sentry a long way ahead
of a hard, dirty army of hooves.

Ted Kooser

For many years I spent my summers driving on the blue highway of rural America, sleeping in my bivy sack on the sides of dirt roads, eating in local diners, drinking Old Style and Hamms in downtown taverns. Each July I'd pick a route that would take me through states I came to love—Wisconsin and Minnesota, Kansas and Nebraska, the Dakotas and Montana. I scrupulously avoided interstates and Holiday Inns. If I slept in a bed it was in the Downtown Motel for nineteen dollars a night. I made a point of driving only a few hundred miles a day, thus leaving many hours to explore every local historical marker, every regional museum, and all of the sights suggested by the locals. If it was America's Biggest, or Oldest, or most remote I would go out of my way to see it: the tallest man-made structure, the last outpost of the pony express, the Kansas Farm Museum, the birthplace of virtually every president. I did this out of restlessness (since passed) and out of an abiding interest in the lives of my fellow Americans, most of whom live nowhere in particular—in small villages and dying towns, in farming communities like Wonewoc, Wisconsin, home of David Rhodes.

I was disheartened, to say the least, when I read Arlie Hochschild's *Strangers in Their Own Land*, a sad book about Louisiana's Tea Party members, men and women filled with hatred for almost everything that feels worthwhile about this country. My own experience of rural America, limited, of course, but compared to everyone but Charles Kuralt I've seen a fair piece of the country, the entire lower forty-eight, and the sad sacks Hochschild interviews, people who prefer cancer-producing toxic spills to government regulations, seem anomalous if not aberrant. I made a point of having morning coffee in rural towns with the local farmers and (once in a while) their wives, and while I found them conservative compared to my urban neighbors, they were reasonable, thoughtful, and welcoming. Of course I am white and male, so there's that to consider.

Anyway, Rhodes, a prodigy who wrote three wonderful novels during the middle 1970s and then was silenced for three decades after a motorcycle accident, is a deeply compassionate chronicler of the lives of invisible people—farmers and small-town ministers and Amish families and housewives whose greatest concern might well be the state of their housekeeping on the eve of Mother's visit. That is to say, Rhodes writes about *us*, for this is who we really are, not gun-slinging heroes or angst-ridden intellectuals or cyborgs; we're ordinary folk, overwhelmed by the cost of living, the loss of love, our kids' future, fear of dying. It amazes me that Rhodes's critics fault him for the quiet dignity of his characters' lives. Quiet dignity is the entire point, and no one I've read, including Kent Haruf, Ivan Doig, and Richard Russo, does a better job of bringing to life the small town, the destitution (economic and spiritual) of rural America imposed on us all by the coastal elites.

Driftless, a novel I read with pleasure and admiration, is a richly imagined collection of short stories, of vignettes, linked by common characters and overlapping themes. July Montgomery, a figure in nearly all of Rhodes's work, settles in Word, Wisconsin and takes up dairy farming after a long life on the road. Over the course of twenty years he takes on a shamanistic character in the tiny farming town. Folks come to him not only to borrow tools but for his good sense and, as July himself puts it, his love for his neighbors. There's a lonely widower, a mystical preacher, a young couple bent on justice, an Amish family and their extended clan, a wheel-chair bound young woman who finds love at a dog fight, a cranky retired farmer whose discovered capacity for fellow feeling is one of Rhodes's finest achievements. Over the course of a year this endlessly interesting cast of characters lives through the kinds of changes that all of us live through. We search for love and truth and justice. Mostly we don't find them, but that doesn't deter us from searching.

Rhodes's style is lyrical, poetic, and generous. I read long passages aloud to my wife, sharing the beauty of language with her but also marveling at the cadences of Rhodes's description, the economy of his character sketches, the visual power of the landscape he describes. Every set piece has a moment of reflection embedded in it, every character possesses a voice that is his or hers alone, an inner world brought to life with great economy. You'll find yourself missing July's wisdom, Olive's impetuousness, Jacob's decency. Not a book to be missed at a time when Americans have been polarized—for nefarious political purposes—into antagonistic tribes. Read Rhodes and discover once again our shared humanity.

G.O.

Him

On April 30th, 1945 Adolph Hitler and his newly married bride, Eva Braun, had a quiet lunch, then met with Hitler's inner circle in the anteroom chamber of his personal bunker in Berlin to say their farewells. Included among the staff members were Martin Bormann and Joseph Goebbels. Earlier, Hitler had given instructions to his personal adjunct, Otto Gunsche, that once he and his wife were dead their bodies were to be burned to ashes. Despite Hitler's claim that the war would "one day go down in history as the most glorious and heroic manifestation of a people's will to live," he'd known by then that the German cause was lost and had ordered two hydrogen cyanide capsules to be prepared for him and his wife. As a typical precaution, he first had the dosage tested on his beloved dog Blondi and her puppies, all of which died. At round 14:30 that day, Hitler and Eva retreated to his sitting room and closed the door. Staff witnesses report hearing a single shot. When they entered the room they found Hitler slumped on the sofa where he sat, blood dripping from his right temple where he had shot himself with his own pistol, a Walther PPK 7.65. On the sofa beside him, his young wife Eva sat slumped away from him, dead from the capsule she had swallowed. In the air was the telltale scent of burnt almonds.

As per Hitler's instructions, their bodies were carried outside, doused with gasoline and burned to ashes. What little remained of them was covered up in a shallow bomb crater just hours before the advancing Soviet Army seized control of Berlin.

Stalin, wary about accepting the news that his nemesis was dead, indeed sensing a trick, was the first to suggest the possibility that Hitler was still alive and in hiding somewhere. In the years to follow, the Soviets helped to spawn a variety of international theories regarding Hitler's fate, most of them ridiculous, some of them simple, cynical Cold War ploys: that he was given refuge by Western allies bent on destroying the Soviet Union, that he and Eva had escaped to Argentina or Brazil, that the Nazis had a secret moon base, that Hitler was an avatar of the Hindu god Vishnu and could never—no matter the weapon—be killed.

Now imagine yourself one of the many Jewish Nazi-hunters who went to work after the war. For there were dozens of them (most notably the relentless and successful Simon Wiesenthal), each of them hell-bent on tracking down such infamous Nazis as Adolf Eichmann, Klaus Barbie, and Josef Mengele. Imagine yourself one of these men, these hunters, at your wit's end deep in the Brazilian jungle where you have been wandering for months with little contact with the outside world. Imagine one morning—hungry, delirious, stung to madness by the midges and gnats—stumbling upon a clearing in the swamp through which you've been slogging for days, a ring of charred stumps, a sudden break of blue sky, and suddenly finding yourself face to face with *him, der Führer* himself.

Such is the engaging premise of George Steiner's 1979 novel, *The Portage To San Cristóbal of A.H.*. Yet Steiner was no conspiracy theorist, to be sure, but uses the idea of Hitler still living as a means of getting at more pressing, more philosophical things. A Jew himself, he was more interested in the larger implications of what it would mean to find Hitler, capture him, and bring him to justice. While not the least bit didactic, the novel raises an array of compelling and provocative questions: What would you feel when you first saw him, this butcher, this monster, this all but mythical man? How would you react to the sight of him just standing before you? Would you kick him, curse him, punch him in the face? What, if anything, would you say? And what about justice, revenge? What—once you'd found him, caught him, and seen him tried—would be the significance of your efforts to Jews, to History, to humanity at large? Would it have any real impact at all? Finally, the novel presses one to wonder how, if ever, a person, a people can comes to terms with such profound and extraordinary grief. Would the killing of Hitler be enough?

As one might imagine, the novel gave rise to instant and bitter controversy, so that for a time its translation into

Hebrew and German was strictly forbidden. Clearly Steiner's aim was to be provocative, to complicate (for Jews especially) what already threatened to become a fixed, hidebound understanding of Hitler and the horror he'd wrought. "*The Portage To San Cristóbal of A.H* is a parable about pain," explains Steiner himself in his 1999 Afterword to the novel, "about the abyss of pain endured by the victims of Nazism." If as a parable it pushed the limits of what was acceptable in thinking about Hitler and the Holocaust, it did so with a wisdom, courage, and conviction we could stand to see more of today.

P.N.

The Five-Mile Wall

Nothing Ever Dies, Viet Thanh Nguyen (essays)
Night Sky With Exit Wounds, Ocean Vuong (poems)

As I write this post, Mr. Trump is meeting in Helsinki with Mr. Putin. Mr. Pompeo, our latest Secretary of State, has met a few times with Kim Jong-un of North Korea. My brother-in-law, a businessman, has made many trips to Vietnam, exploring mutually beneficial economic relations with our former enemy. We briefly forgave Cuba for Fidel, but it didn't stick—too close to home. Iran remains *non grata* going on forty years after that country's Islamic Revolution. We don't care for Venezuela, though this administration doesn't much like Mexico, Canada, or Europe either.

In the peculiar calculus of international relations, friends and foes change places with astonishing rapidity. That our president admires Putin but despises Theresa May is surely wondrous, a fact not even explicable in reference to national interest. The nexus of corporate capitalism and high-end scheming has created strange bedfellows in the 21st century. Like the stock market, volatility and creative destruction (of companies, or workers, or resources) has replaced the once sacrosanct pursuit of stability.

Nothing is more mind boggling to me, a college student in the 1960s, then the about-face on the country we invaded and made war on for twenty years, the domino that wasn't to be allowed to fall, the communist state that would infect all of southeast Asia with the contagion of monolithic communism. But my incredulity stems from my inability to grasp the simple fact that ideology is dead, replaced, worldwide, by the logic, the omnipotence, of capital. There's a franchise here that I hadn't paid enough attention to: destroy a country, then with multinational investments rebuild it. Once rebuilt more or less after a Westernized model use the former enemy as a base of operations for the storage of surplus domestic capital, avoiding taxes at home. Everybody gets rich, except for the people.

Viet Thanh Nguyen, author of the bestselling and remarkable novel *The Sympathizer* attempts in his essays *Nothing Ever Dies: Vietnam and the Memory of War* to catalogue the ways in which for Vietnamese and Americans alike the war in Vietnam, the war of American aggression (as it is known in Southeast Asia) has been memorialized—in graveyards, formal memorials, novels, and films. It's a fine book, but for me at least, unconvincing. As with Drew Gilpin Faust's *The Republic of Suffering*, the award-winning account of the memorization of the Civil War dead, I came away thinking that the construction of memorials, the dedication of grave sites, the commercialization of war in books or films has nothing to do with remembering.

Viet Thanh Nguyen's academic style—he's a professor of English, and writes like one—obscures the fact that for Americans the war in Vietnam isn't a historical fact, but a mythological tale, a story that has taken its place alongside the vast array of myths that define our national consciousness. The Vietnam Memorial in Washington, for example, is a powerful reminder of the human cost of the war for the United States. A similar wall memorializing Vietnam's dead would stretch five miles, from the Lincoln Memorial well up Capitol Hill. But what does this reflective wall have to do with remembering? What does any statue or any field of white crosses have to do with the internalization of a catastrophic historical event? Remembrance depends upon compassion, empathy and imagination far more than it does on the traditional symbols of death and loss. A visit to Gettysburg's famed battlefield, with its plinths and equestrian statues, is like an episode on the History Channel unless one is willing to look inward and feel the mayhem and suffering that took place on those pastoral acres on three summer days in 1863. Americans might be moved by the Wall, but they aren't thinking much about what it really means. If we were, we wouldn't be continuing to behave as we do, creating new memorials to the dead. It's easier to build another Wall than to stop the need for them.

Sorry, I've oversimplified Viet Thanh Nguyen's argument here. He has many subtle and important things to say about the asymmetries of power and the problem (impossibility) of humanizing one's enemies—please do read this book—but I still haven't understood how remembering and memorializing explain America's amnesia or Vietnam's transformation into an "acceptable" communist government. What sleight of hand is at work here? I defer to historians on this question.

If you want to feel things, if you want to know about human beings, it's poetry that is required, not statues.

The young (he's twenty-nine) Vietnamese-American poet Ocean Vuong has produced a remarkable book of poems about war, isolation, foreignness, loss, and memory. Particular impressive is the way in which Ocean moves from formal verse to free verse to idiosyncratic styles in order to blend meaning and feeling with form. There's a violence in the book, a sustained pitch of anger and despair that is inescapable, particularly if one reads straight through in a single sitting. This book is not a sampler but a slap in the face, a call to wake up and share in a stranger's life, and what could be more foreign to us than this young man's life?

There isn't an uninteresting poem in the book. Here's one that shows the range of feeling and mastery of tone:

Prayer for the Newly Damned

Dearest Father, forgive me for I have seen.
Behind the wooden fence, a field lit

*with summer, a man pressing a shank
to another man's throat. Steel turning to light
on sweat-slick neck. Forgive me
for not calling Your name. For thinking:
this must be how every prayer
begins—the word Please cleaving
the wind into fragments, into what
a boy hears in his need to know
how pain blesses the body back
to its sinner. The hour suddenly
stilled. The man genuflected, his lips
pressed to black boot as the words spilled
from his mouth like rosaries
shattering from too much
Father. Am I wrong to love
those eyes, to see something so clear
and blue—beg to remain
clear and blue? Did my cheek twitch
when that darkness bloomed from his crotch
and trickled into ochre dirt? Father,
how quickly the blade becomes
You. But let me begin again: There's a boy
kneeling in a house with every door kicked open
to summer. There's a question corroding
his tongue. There's a knife touching
Your name lodged inside the throat.
Dearest Father, what becomes of the boy
no longer a boy? Please—
what becomes of the shepherd
when the sheep are cannibals?*

 Many of the poems in Ocean's collection are memorials to his father, as here. Some are love poems, and some, among the most moving, are reflections on the poet's own identity as a son, a gay man, an American. See "Someday I'll Love Ocean Vuong". Here's a poem about remembering the war:

Aubade With Burning City

South Vietnam, April 29, 1975: Armed Forces Radio played Irving Berlin's "White Christmas" as a code to begin Operation Frequent Wind, the ultimate evacuation of American civilians and Vietnamese refugees by helicopter during the fall of Saigon.

Milkflower petals in the street
    like pieces of a girl's dress.
May your days be merry and bright...
He fills a teacup with champagne, brings it to her lips.
    Open, he says.
        She opens.
            Outside, a soldier spits out
his cigarette as footsteps fill the square like stones
        fallen from the sky. May
all your Christmases be white
    as the traffic guard unstraps his holster.
    His fingers running the hem
of her white dress. A single candle.
    Their shadows: two wicks.
A military truck speeds through the intersection, children
    shrieking inside. A bicycle hurled
through a store window. When the dust rises, a black dog
    lies panting in the road. Its hind legs
        crushed into the shine
    of a white Christmas.
On the bed stand, a sprig of magnolia expands like a secret heard

for the first time.
The treetops glisten and children listen, the chief of police
facedown in a pool of Coca-Cola.
A palm-sized photo of his father soaking
beside his left ear.
The song moving through the city like a widow.
A white...A white...I'm dreaming of a curtain of snow
falling from her shoulders.
Snow scraping against the window. Snow shredded
with gunfire. Red sky.
Snow on the tanks rolling over the city walls.
A helicopter lifting the living just
out of reach.
The city so white it is ready for ink.
The radio saying run run run.
Milkflower petals on a black dog
like pieces of a girl's dress.
May your days be merry and bright. She is saying
something neither of them can hear. The hotel rocks
beneath them. The bed a field of ice.
Don't worry, he says, as the first shell flashes
their faces, my brothers have won the war
and tomorrow...
The lights go out.
I'm dreaming. I'm dreaming...
to hear sleigh bells in the snow...
In the square below: a nun, on fire,
runs silently toward her god—
Open, he says.
She opens.

G.O.

Dutch Tao

"When the ten thousand things have been seen in their unity, we return to the beginning and remain where we have always been." It is with this epigraph from the great Tang dynasty poet, Ts'en Shen (618–907), that the Java-born Dutch writer, Maria Dermoût, sets the tone for her uncanny, ethereal novel, *The Ten Thousand Things*. Set, near the dawn of the last century, on one of the Spice Islands in the Dutch East Indies (now Indonesia), the story—at points but a gossamer tangle of threads—follows the life of a woman named Felicia who, after a long absence, has returned to the East Indies from Holland with her son, to the house and garden where she was born and raised. There, with affection, with patience, she teaches him about "the ten thousand things".

The Dutch colonization of the East Indies (1800-1949) marks one of the most brutal periods in European colonial history. So rich were the islands in nutmeg, mace, cloves, and cinnamon (and later in tea, tobacco, cacao, rubber, sugar, coffee, and opium), so exceptionally profitable was the trade, that the Dutch exercised a ruthlessness in their greed and exploitation matched only by that of the Belgians in the Congo. Karl Marx, in the first volume of *Capital*, wrote: "The history of Dutch colonial administration—and *Holland was the model capitalist nation of the seventeenth century*—is one of the most extraordinary relations of treachery, bribery, massacre, and meanness. Nothing is more characteristic than their system of stealing men, to get slaves for Java. The men stealers were trained for this purpose. The thief, the interpreter, and the seller, were the chief agents in this trade, native princes the chief sellers. The young people stolen, were thrown into the secret dungeons of Celebes, until they were ready for sending to the slave-ships… Wherever they set foot, devastation and depopulation followed. Banjuwangi, a province of Java, in 1750 numbered over 80,000 inhabitants, in 1811 only 18,000. Sweet commerce!"

It is near the tail-end of this, the darkest chapter of Dutch imperial history, that Dermoût begins this gentle, truly wondrous tale—a paean, a plainsong, to the Spice Islands she loved, to its people, animals, and plants, and to the spirits that haunt that lush and tortured land. Hers is a world steeped in myth and mystery, an experience at once intangible, elusive, and deeply, resoundingly clear. Of the novel, Dutch author Oek de Jonge writes: "It possesses something that wards off hordes of readers, yet still manages to attract a handful, who then embrace it and spread the word of its exquisite nature. The shell seekers among the readers, the slow walkers, those who stop and turn and bend over to pick up that one beautiful shell—they recognize her extraordinary work."

P.N.

A Bad Year for Men

Milkman, Anna Burns
The Testaments, Margaret Atwood
Ducks, Newburyport, Lucy Ellmann

It's been a bad year for men. Although, to be fair, when it comes to men's behavior, every year is pretty much the same.

Just recently, watching what reminded me (from my reading, not direct experience) of the spectacle of devout Bolsheviks falling over themselves to praise the Leader— "The Gardener of Human Happiness," "The Man of Steel," and, perhaps most aptly given that *our* Leader has been likened, without apparent irony, to Jesus Christ, "Dear Father"—I felt deeply embarrassed for my sex, age-group, and ethnicity. The defense of our recently impeached President by the *apparatchiks* of the GOP presented a nearly eight-hour spectacle not only of mendacity, boot-licking, and abject immorality, it also made it perfectly clear to this white male that what we are seeing is the *end*—thank God—of the rule of old white men over women, children, people of color, and our planet.

This can't go on, and the fervid displays of disingenuousness, smugness, and worst of all, the sense of entitlement that have been on display during these past weeks not only here but also in Great Britain—B. Johnson being Trump's twin, bad hair, fascistic tendencies, and a shared aversion to the truth—suggest that what is transpiring is a last desperate attempt by a powerful but increasingly irrelevant class of old men (and young men with old souls) to cling to the prerogatives that they believe must be accorded their sex—power and money it goes without saying, but also unimpeded access to women's bodies, authoritarian control of our political and economic system, dictatorial influence over culture, and, in general, the status of demigods that has been, until now, their presumptive birth-right. That's over, and, believe it or not, it is Trump, the Omega-Male, who is destroying what he hopes to preserve, destroying his half-baked MAGA-fantasy through fecklessness, narcissism, and immorality, and at the same time, for those persons paying attention, undoing all claims of masculine legitimacy—that is, all of the historic nonsense that has turned an ideology of masculine superiority into a farcical circus peopled by preening nobodies whose claims to "natural" domination of the world would be laughable were it not for the tragic consequences these nabobs have visited on human beings and our planet.

A bit of a rant, and poorly punctuated, but it's how we men talk.

My prognosis may appear counter-intuitive given the numerical dominance of white men in business, government, academe, the military, and everywhere else there is power to wield, but bear in mind that the demise of every hegemonic system in history, from feudalism to absolutism to so-called communism, has come at the moment of that system's seemingly greatest power. The right-wing, anti-democratic, misogynistic, racist male egotism embodied by Trump, McConnell, Weinstein, and their devoted followers is unleashing—even as I write these words—a backlash that is global and that will, in time, wash away the so-called principles and self-serving ideas of these men, wipe it away like a great Tsunami sweeping across a landscape laid waste by centuries of greed, stupidity, and arrogance.

This is the central point of Margaret Atwood's continuation of *The Handmaid's Tale*, the (I'm sorry to say) far less engaging novel *The Testaments* whose central premise is that rotten systems of government—in the case of the novel, brutal patriarchy—decay from within. While the sequel to *AHT* was clunky, Atwood's premise is right on the money. Rot begets rot. Corruption engenders corruption. The cult of death—for that is what patriarchy is—kills itself, though, unfortunately, not until it has claimed many innocent victims.

Will the rest of us, women, children, the poor and powerless, and decent fellows like myself, get out alive? That remains to be seen. I don't personally anticipate a long-term residence on earth, but I lament daily the world my daughters, my wife, and the good people I know will inherit, and I resent bitterly the stupidity and callous self-interest that has created what has passed beyond crisis to something more akin to disaster.

Yes, of course, there are wonderful men and awful women, sure, natch.

I generalize to be sure. Congressman Schiff seems a decent sort; Congressman Jordan of the shirt-sleeves, not so much. But this isn't an essay about politicians, but about the trajectory of masculine behavior as it has for too long existed. We're in danger of expiring as a species. Birds and turtles are disappearing, coral reefs are doomed, thousands upon thousands of men, women, and children starve and/or sleep under our freeways while the uber-rich (Rudy Giuliani!) own six homes and belong (Rudy Giuliani!) to eleven country clubs. It's unnatural. The world is being devoured by piggish men who do nothing for anyone—they don't police our streets, fight our fires, teach our children, tend to the sick and the dying, build anything—they spend their wasteful days spinning money into more money, fomenting wars for others to fight, shitting in golden toilets, and spending an inordinate amount of time harassing, degrading, and raping women.

Enough.

***

Meanwhile, women fight back with courage, dignity, and art.

Anna Burns, for example, in a novel of extraordinary originality, plunks us into the odd reality of "middle sister," an eighteen-year-old who "reads while walking," and negotiates the violent world of what is presumably Northern Ireland during the 1970s (Burns was born in Belfast). The unnamed characters who walk the streets of Burns's unnamed city negotiate a masculine world of political and personal grievance that leaves nearly every family mourning a son, a father, a daughter. Burns, with deftness and imaginative scope unusual in contemporary fiction, pushes her story of sectarian violence from realism into the realm of parable. The repetitions of theme and language, the characters identified by their social role rather than by name ("maybe-boyfriend," "Milkman," "renouncers"), the circling back and forth among patterns of action, nearly all of which end in bloodshed—these rhetorical and thematic modes of storytelling add up to a novel that enacts the cycles of violence and degrees of victimization that characterize so many parts of the world in which we live. Most ominous for me are the lurking men, the renouncers, who hate those from "over the ocean" and who inflict vengeance against any of their countrymen who deviate from a strict pattern of permissible behavior. "Informer" takes on the weight of "non-conformist": maybe-boyfriend who is middle sister's maybe love interest is suspect because he likes sunsets and stars. The Milkman (who isn't a milkman) is the chief of the renouncers, perhaps an IRA gunman, and his unrequited love interest in middle-sister isn't offered as courtship but as the threat of sexual violence—he's the most powerful man in the community and is entitled to take whomever he wishes, no questions asked. Middle-sister does her best to negotiate a terrain as replete with fixed rituals and unyielding culture as the Catholic Church. She fights rumors, but truth holds little sway in her world, just as it holds none in ours.

Milkman is narrated throughout by middle-sister; dialogue is reported by her, all descriptions are filtered through her lively consciousness. In this regard, Anna Burns and Lucy Ellmann approach the novel with similar aims. Burns reprises the psychological effect of simmering violence on the consciousness of one sensitive character. Ellmann, over the course of one-thousand pages (and about three sentences) uses a hurtling stream-of-consciousness to survey in (frankly, at times) excruciating detail the anxieties of an Ohio housewife, an Everywoman. In one sense, Burns and Ellmann traverse the same terrain, for both women view a world created by men that is baffling, full of threats, irrational, rapacious, and indifferent to the well-being of the weak, the very people for whom, one presumes, societies were created. Ellmann's housewife isn't faced with the Shadow of the Gunman (see Sean O'Casey) but with the enervating rituals of up-to-the-minute American life. Ellmann, who has resided in Scotland for many years, is utterly hip to what is going on in our local precincts—the slipping away of a sense that we are anything other than a national shopping mall, that we can have a life outside of the internet, that we exist in any meaningful way with other people, that we give a shit about anyone other than ourselves. Ellmann does isolation with the same intelligence that Burns does paranoia; in the end, these feelings amount to the same thing.

With Burns one is, as it were, 10,000 feet above the world, looking down at a grid of unnamed streets and neighborhoods and people, at events uprooted from time and place, at the general pattern of human folly. Ellmann, on the other hand, is like one of the historians of the *annales* school. She unpacks every moment, every impression, every thought of her narrator. Both novels explore the interior life of a woman who possesses the gift of observation but who is put continuously on the defensive by a world that has become unmanageable. Both Belfast and Ohio are sunk in violence, though of different sorts. Middle-sister lives among gunmen; Ohio-housewife lives in the murkiness of a way of life that is disappearing—security, community, child-rearing, marriage, work, patriotism—none of the verities with which Housewife has lived are enduring. Trump makes numerous cameo appearances in *Ducks, Newburyport* as the talisman of this slipping away. Who better to embody the mess we are in?

What, Housewife wonders, has become of us? What, indeed?

G.O.

Orientation

The virtue of maps, they show what can be done with limited space, they foresee that everything can happen therein.
                            José Saramago

It is largely through maps (mostly visual representations of our perceptions, our beliefs, our dreams, our fears) that we as human beings have learned to orient ourselves within the otherwise bewildering phenomena of Time (that is, Death) and Space. From ancient cosmological, religious, and nautical maps to globes, atlases, tarot cards, horoscopes, memory palaces, astrological charts, and Michelin road maps to astronomical, topographical, geological, historical, medical, political, biological, climatological, mathematical, grammatical, and neurological maps, to algorithms, political polling, spread sheets, mind maps, flow charts, the Human Genome Project, and our increasing reliance on Global Positioning Systems to find our way there and back, cartography (in the broadest sense of the term) has helped us to define and enforce our realities with a brilliance and tenacity that is telling.

And what about the book as map? Is literature, too, a kind of essential human mapping? What is certain is that when an author begins to write a novel or short story one of her fundamental concerns is the matter of orientation. She must think: Who is my narrator, my protagonist? What is the psychic distance (to use John Gardner's term) I wish to establish between my reader and my protagonist, that is, the immediate degree of sympathy/empathy one feels for her? Are we watching her from a distance or actually trundling about in her skin? Then there are the matters of subject, time frame, and setting? An author must determine her style, her tone (her particular attitude toward her subject), the mood of the novel, her diction. Finally, significantly, what in the novel is at issue, at stake?

While important in all forms of writing, such basic stocktaking is all the more significant when what is to follow is unusually demanding or unconventional in language, style or form. For the sake of her reader, the author herself must get her sea-legs before the voyage can rightly begin.

Good writing is a kind of witchcraft; before we know it we have fallen under its spell. Indeed what distinguishes the best, most effective openings is the fact that we scarcely notice them at all, so deftly have they been wrought that the imagery, characters, and setting seem less the product of the particular words before us on the page than the fruits of our of own soft-humming brains.

First, there is the more conventional type of orientation—by which I do not mean predictable, prosaic, dull. Here is the inimitable Dickens from his novel, *Nicholas Nickleby*:

> *There once lived in a sequestered part of the county of Devonshire, one Mr. Godfrey Nickleby, a worthy gentleman, who taking it into his head rather late in life that he must get married, and not being young enough or rich enough to aspire to the hand of a lady of fortune, had wedded an old flame out of mere attachment, who in her turn had taken him for the same reason: thus two people who cannot afford to play cards for money, sometimes sit down to a quiet game for love.*

Here now is Israeli writer A. B. Yehoshua from his novel, *Five Seasons*:

> *Molkho's wife died at 4 a.m., and Mokho did his best to mark the moment forever, because he wished to be able to remember it. And indeed, thinking back on it weeks and even months later, he was convinced that he had managed to refine the instant of her passing (her passing? He wasn't sure the word was right) into something clear and vivid containing not only thought and feeling but also sound and light, such as the maroon glow of the small electric cheater, the greenish radiance of the numbers on the digital clock, the yellow shaft of light from the bathroom that cast large shadows in the hallway, and perhaps, too, the color of the sky, a pinkish ivory set off by the deep obscurity around it.*

Note how much is initiated, established, achieved–and how quickly, concisely. Next, consider this opening from Vietnamese author Duong Thu Huong's novel, *Beyond Illusions*:

> *How could I have loved him like that?*
> *She stared at him in the green glow of dawn. Still sleeping soundly, he was both strange and familiar to her, like a waxen effigy. That face. The curve of the nose, those earlobes. He was the same man, the same flesh, that had once been a beacon inside her. Now he no longer radiated life, love.*
> *The man rolled over, his beard grazing her cheek. Repulsed, she sat up.*
> *Odd, how his beard had thinned.*

Simple yet amazing. We feel an instant sympathy for this narrator—and without even knowing her name. We see the light as it creeps into the room, hear the traffic outside, smell her husband's rammish breath. Look now at Heinrich Böll's opening to his novel, *The Clown*, a story about a struggling entertainer trying to find meaning in his life as a German after the war:

> *It was dark by the time I reached Bonn, and I forced myself not to succumb to the series of mechanical actions which had taken hold of me in five years if traveling back and forth: down the station steps, up the station steps, put down my suitcase, take my ticket out of my coat pocket, pick up my suitcase, hand in my ticket, cross over to the newsstand, buy*

the evening papers, go outside, and signal for a taxi. Almost every day for five years I had left for somewhere and arrived somewhere; in the morning I had gone up station steps and down again, in the afternoon down the steps and up again, signaled for a taxi, felt in my pockets for money to pay for my ticket, bought evening papers at kiosks, and savored in a corner of my mind the studied casualness of these mechanical actions.

Here then is Elizabeth Hardwick in her singular novel, *Sleepless Nights*, carefully arranging her props for the performance to come:

It is June. This is what I have decided to do with my life just now. I will do this work of transformed and even distorted memory and lead this life, the one I am leading today. Every morning the blue clock and the crocheted bedspread with its pink and blue and gray squares and diamonds. How nice it is—this production of a broken old woman in a squalid nursing home. The niceness and the squalor and sorrow in an apathetic battle—that is what I see. More beautiful is the table with the telephone, the books and magazines, the Times at the door, the birdsong of rough, grinding trucks in the street.

This, as further illustration of the more conventional opening, is the first paragraph of V.S. Pritchett's comic novel, *Mr. Beluncle*:

Twenty-five minutes from the centre of London the

> *trees lose their towniness, the playing fields, tennis courts and parks are as fresh as lettuce, and the train appears to be squirting through thousands of little gardens. Here was Boystone before its churches and its High street were burned out and before its roofs were stripped off a quarter of a mile at a time. It had its little eighteenth-century face—the parish church, the alms-house, the hotel, the Hall—squeezed by the rolls and folds of pink suburban fat. People came out of the train and said the air was better—Mr Beluncle always did—it was an old town with a dormitory encampment, and a fizz and fuss of small private vegetation.*

Here Pritchett not only establishes the conventional suburban setting for his story with but a few deft strokes, but does so comically, satirically, so that we have a bead on this Mr. Beluncle (and his world) well before we actually meet him. Finally, note here the highly conventional way that the Japanese novelist Kobe Abe begins his highly *unconventional* novel, *The Box Man*—first with the title itself, then with this blunt (if all the more peculiar) statement of the story's central facts:

> *This is the record of a box man.*
> *I am beginning this account in a box. A cardboard box that reaches just to my hips when I put it on over my head.*
> *That is to say, at this juncture the box man is me. A box man, in his box, is recording the chronicle of a box man.*

Yet not all great fiction begins with such apparent clarity, such obvious direction and purpose. There is also another form of orientation—a largely modernist convention—I will call deliberate *dis*orientation. It is a type of orientation that no reader can fail to miss, for it often stops one in one's tracks. Armed with one's ropes and crampons, one goggles at the page as though gazing up at Mount Everest itself. Rest assured: such writers *want* you to climb the mountain—only by different, more daring means. This is what makes modernist novels so remarkable, the fact they actually *teach* you to read them, establishing at once (often by challenging your very confidence as a reader) the terms by which they demand to be known.

Arguably no novelist was more determined to teach (or *re-teach*) his readers to read (that is, to read better—more deeply, more responsively) than the crass and courtly "Sunny Jim". See here how he opens his last novel, *Finnegan's Wake*:

> *riverrrun, past Eve and Adam's, from swerve of shore to bend of bay, brings us by a commodious vicus of recirculation back to Howth Castle and Environs.*
> *Sir Tristram, violer d'amores, fr'over the short sea, had passencore rearrived from North Armorica on this side the scraggy isthmus of Europe Minor to wielderfight his penisolate war; nor had topsawyers' rocks by the stream Oconee exaggerated themselse to Laurens County's Gorgios while they went doubling*

> *their mumper all the time: not avoice from afire bellowsed mishe mishe to tauftauf thuartpeatrick: not yet, though venisoon after, had a kidscad buttended a bland old Isaac: not yet, though all's fair in vanessy, were sosie sesthers wroth with twone nathandjoe. Rot a peck of pa's malt had Jhem or Shen brewed by arclight and rory end to the regginbrow was to be seen ringsome on the aquaface.*

It hardly seems a beginning at all (nor should it, in this case). Just two brief paragraphs and one finds oneself reeling! Fast on Joyce's heels is Brazilian author Clarice Lispector with the opening of her novel, *Near to the Wild Heart* (the title itself taken from Joyce's *Portrait of the Artist as a Young Man*):

> *Her father's typewriter went clack-clack...clack-clack-clack...The clock awoke in dustless tin-dlen. The silence dragged out zzzzzz. What did the wardrobe say? Clothes-clothes-clothes. No, no. amidst the lock, the typewriter and the silence there was an ear listening, large pink, and dead...*

Strange, jarring—one clutches at straws. Here now is Vladimir Nabokov from the opening of his novel, *Lolita*:

> *Lolita, light of my life, fire of my loins. My sin, my soul. Lo-lee-ta: the tip of the tongue taking a trip of three steps down the palate to tap, at three. On the teeth. Lo Lee. Ta.*
>
> *She was Lo, plain Lo, in the morning, standing four feet ten in one sock. She was Lola in slacks. She*

> *was Dolly at school. She was Dolores on the dotted line. But in my arms she was always Lolita.*
>
> *Did she have a precursor? She did, indeed she did. In point of fact, there might have been no Lolita at all had I not loved, one summer, a certain initial girl-child. In princedom by the sea. Oh when? About as many years before Lolita was born as my age was that summer. You can always count on a murderer for a fancy prose style.*
>
> *Ladies and gentlemen of the jury, exhibit one is what the seraphs, the misinformed, simple, noble-winged seraphs, envied. Look at this tangle of thorns.*

Note how little (how much) he gives us, how little (how much) we know! Here, at last, is Shirley Jackson's seemingly conventional, if in fact deftly disorienting first paragraph from her well-known short story, "The Lottery," a contemporary tale—so one gradually discovers—about a ritual stoning in an average American town:

> *The morning of June 27th was clear and sunny, with the fresh warmth of a full-summer day; the flowers were blossoming profusely and the grass was richly green. The people of the village began to gather in the square, between the post office and the bank, around ten o'clock; in some towns there were so many people that the lottery took two days and had to be started on June 2nd, but in this village, where they were only about three hundred people, the whole lottery took less than two hours, so that it could begin at ten o'clock in the morning and still*

be through in time to allow the villagers to get home for noon dinner.

Each of these openings—the conventional and unconventional alike—gives the reader as much as he needs (at least as much as the author *thinks* he needs) to whet his appetite (and expectations), to get his bearings in the particular tale to come. Yet the matter of orientation in great fiction does not end there, but applies equally to individual chapters, paragraphs, sentences, phrases, and words, yes, even—perhaps especially—to words, to one's particular choice of words.

Of course, the importance of orientation far exceeds the technical concerns of the individual writer. In these increasingly irrational, increasingly fanatical times, a blind and blundering age of fake news, Twitter wars, and celebrity gospels, of ideologues, megalomaniacs, and would-be messiahs, there is also the fact of literature itself, of reading widely and deeply and well. I can think of no finer compass that that.

P.N.

Papa!

Adios Hemingway, Leonardo Padura Fuentes
Ernest Hemingway, Mary V. Dearborn

He was a man's man.

The kind of man about whom Richard Slotkin wrote in *Regeneration Through Violence*; the man who won the West, the man with a house full of animal heads, a case full of guns, a rotting liver and a gigantic libido.

A dinosaur. Like God, our culture—dishonest, feckless, preening, consumerist, shallow—has killed off men like Hemingway. Outside of the military, the version of masculinity Hemingway represented has passed into oblivion. He was a bully and a drunk and an artist. He did not suffer fools, he didn't bow down to the gods of money and power. He was, like him or not, his own guy.

In his various biographical guises, Hemingway comes off as brutal and bloodthirsty, buffoonish, drunken, insecure, and, near the end of his life, paranoid. After reading Mary Dearborn's biography it is difficult to disagree with this evaluation But he was also courageous, generous, loyal, and committed to his art.

I am rereading a handful of the novels and trying to recapture some of the excitement they engendered in me when I was a young man. To be honest, I'm ambivalent about all of them except for *The Sun Also Rises* and *The Old Man and The Sea*. The simple cadences of his style—a style learned during Hemingway's brief stint at the *Kansas City Star*—feels more like reportage than literature. In the opening of *To Have and Have Not*, for instance, I can't make out the look of the bar (it's the Floridita in Havana) or the disposition of the characters during the gunfight that initiates the story. The scene is flattened, more like a series of still photos than a narrative describing propulsive action. I understand what Hemingway was aiming for, a laconic detachment implying an unwillingness to judge events, but I can no longer live comfortably without judgments, without a sense of the weightiness of things. This feeling is unshakable during even the best sections of *The Sun Also Rises*, a book that might have been written by Camus or Gide or Beckett.

I want to approach Hemingway in terms of a philosophical problem rather than from the point of view of literary merit. The wonderful Cuban novelist Leonardo Padura Fuentes invites us, in his tiny gem of a novel *Adios Hemingway*, to rethink Hemingway's life and art, and I have tried to do so.

Please bear with this brief sidebar:

David Hume argued that there could be no such thing as a *self*. In our internal life we note a riot of impressions, ideas, memories, sensations, fears, desires, opinions, and so forth. We flit from one thing to another. While we are performing even the most intimate and intensive actions—making love or writing poems—our minds still move to other things: the cool feeling of the air moving through the window, the dog that never ceases barking, the slight pain our knee, the bottle of wine that we will enjoy with dinner. Everyone before Hume simply assumed that the mind was a theater and that the panoply of acts that crossed the stage was objectively observed by the Soul, made note of and rounded up in some fashion in order to create the Self. Kant took Hume's point and ran with it. In the first critique he developed the notion of Transcendental Idealism, of an objective, self-observant critical consciousness.

Kant's understanding of how the mind imposes order on the outside world—in part through the categories of space, time, and causality—was unsatisfactory on a number of levels, and generations of critics wrestled with the fundamental problem that Hume articulated and that Kant believed he had settled. Namely, how does the mind order the world in such a way that it appears to possess continuity and coherence? And what is this self or mind apart from the impressions it receives? The absurdity of Locke's idea of the "blank slate" made Kant's reconstruction of the inner life all the more important.

To get some idea of what Kant was worried about, imagine that you were to forget the past, to sustain a brain injury that eradicated your memory and therefore your personality. Would you still be the person you had been? What is this Self in which we place so much faith, that we give our name, that we trust to be there when we need it? ("Just be yourself" we say, and "Be true to yourself"). This sounds like an argument you might have had in a college dorm room—it probably was—but even this crude formulation of the problem suggests something of the difficulty we face when thinking about our inner life and how it is connected to our sense of self.

What does any of this have to do with Hemingway?

No writer I can think of so carefully (or carelessly) blended his writing and his life. Or, to put it another way, I can think of no other writer whose literary achievements are as inextricably bound to a particular way of life, a way of life that, as Mary Dearborn makes plain, Hemingway deliberately cultivated and consciously pursued. He *lived* his books as few writers have lived theirs, and when he could no longer live a life centered on hunting, fishing, drinking, and pursuing women not only did he cease writing, he ceased living. Beginning in 1958, Hemingway slipped into paranoia, ill health, and senility. He no longer was the man he had been, and therefore the writer he had been.

It is the story of the slipping out of a life that Leonardo Padura Fuentes tells in *Adios Hemingway*. Mario Conde, the hero of Fuentes's wonderful Havana mysteries (try *Havana Blue*), has retired from police work to become a writer. His former partner and now chief of the Havana police asks Conde to investigate the identity of a body that has been unearthed on Hemingway's former Finca, now a museum, or mausoleum, dedicated to the writer's years in Cuba. Conde, who once revered Hemingway and took the novelist as his role model, has come to despise Papa, to see the American ex-pat as loutish and cruel, a man who was, in fact, capable of murder. Conde takes on the job of identifying the corpse and finding the killer, and in doing so he unearths not just the body of an FBI agent and the killer, but also the central mysteries of Hemingway's life.

While Conde sets out to solve a murder, the reader is led back in time to Hemingway's final days in Cuba. I loved these sections for their rich evocation of the writer's life, and for their intelligent exploration of the connection between the self and the artist. In Hemingway's case, this connection was absolute and therefore is a provocation to think about the meaning of literary art.

Fuentes's explores with great economy and delicacy the connection between the self-identity of Hemingway and his sense of himself as an artist. Once he can no longer live as he has lived, once he must renounce the outward roles he has played—as a hunter, a drinker, a lover—his inner world shrivels to nothing. He can't finish *Death in the Afternoon* because he can no longer evoke the drama of a bullfight. And, lacking the ability to write, why go on living?

Have a cigar.

G.O.

The Bewilderers

The condition of native is a nervous condition.
Frantz Fanon

It is no wonder that Zimbabwean author, Tsitsi Dangarembga, chose this line from an introduction to Fanon's landmark study *The Wretched of the Earth* as the epigraph and title for her very fine first novel, *Nervous Conditions*. Arguably no one has written more cogently, more redoubtably, about the cultural and existential catastrophe of colonialism (and the need for violent rebellion against it) than Martinique-born, French-Algerian psychiatrist, philosopher, revolutionary, and writer, Frantz Fanon.

Early on in his book Fanon talks about what he calls "the bewilderers," that multitude of moral teachers and counselors employed by a colonial power to separate the exploited from those in power, to drop upon them daily—in their homes, in their workplaces and schools—what Kenyan novelist Ngũgĩ Wa Thiong'o calls the "cultural bomb." "The effect of a cultural bomb is to annihilate a people's belief in their names, in their languages, in their environment, in their heritage of struggle, in their unity, in their capacities and ultimately in themselves."

Filled with preachers and teachers, Dangarembga's a novel wrestles with exactly that matter. Never dogmatic, never didactic in temperament or style, *Nervous Conditions* is a profoundly human, astutely articulated tale about a young girl's coming-of-age in 1960's Rhodesia* (now Zimbabwe)—one of the last, most stubborn colonial holdouts on the continent, excepting only Namibia (1990) and Eritrea (1993). With great attention to detail, Dangarembga follows the main character, Tambudzai, or Tambu, as she struggles against the odds to negotiate her way through the tangled web of life under colonial rule, that Gordian knot of Christianity, patriarchy, racism, materialism, and cultural self-loathing that defined (perhaps in part still defines) the experience of Black Africans from Morocco and Egypt to Namibia, South Africa, and Mozambique. Fortunately for Tambu, she is a quick study, so that when her spoiled older brother Nhamo, the prince and hope of her all but impoverished family, is swiftly destroyed by the colonial system, his identity shattered, she is finally given a chance to make her way. This not to reveal the story prematurely, as the author herself gives us this and more in the novel's opening paragraph, a provocative sketch of the story as a whole:

> *I was not sorry when my brother died. Nor am I apologizing for my callousness, as you may define it, my lack of feeling. For it is not that at all. I feel many things these days, much more than I was able to fell*

> *in the days when I was young and my brother died, and there are reasons for this more than the mere consequence of age. Therefore I shall not apologize but begin by recalling the facts as I remember them that led up to my brother's death, the events that put me in a potion to write this account. For though the event of my brother's passing and the events of my story cannot be separated, my story is not after all about death, but about my escape and Lucia's; about my mother's and Maiguru's entrapment; and about Nyasha's rebellion—Nyasha, far-minded and isolated, my uncle's daughter, whose rebellion may not in the end have been successful.*

I came across the novel one year, while teaching at a boy's school in Manhattan, when I set out to find a book, preferably by a female author of color, that I could pair with Richard Wright's *Black Boy*. *Nervous Conditions* proved the perfect choice. As I wrote back in 1991, in an article for *The Collegiate Review*:

> *The mere juxtaposition of these books was enough for the students to begin comparing them after only the first reading in Nervous Conditions. Using each as a lens by which to view the other, the students were quick to recognize that in both cases the protagonist was an innocent child opening his or her eyes to a world in which, for reasons largely coded and obscure to them, they were outsiders and outcasts. We were forced to investigate the issues of cultural identity and the crippling, often paradoxical demands of assimilation.*

Seen in retrospect, through Tambu's keen and dauntless eye, *Nervous Conditions* is a sophisticated, highly readable, deeply satisfying tale that you're sure to find persuasive. Recommended by the African Book Club as "a thought-provoking novel that packs a huge number of complicated ideas into a simple and engaging story," *Nervous Conditions* was awarded the Commonwealth Writer's Prize in 1989.

* Rhodesia was named after English-South African mining magnate, founder of De Beers diamond company, politician, and ardent proponent of colonialism, Cecil Rhodes. In 1902 he established the prestigious Rhodes Scholarship, which is funded by his estate.

P.N.

Lawrence

Selected Letters of D. H. Lawrence, James T. Boulton, editor
Mornings in Mexico, D. H. Lawrence
Sons and Lovers, D. H. Lawrence
Women in Love, D. H. Lawrence
Out of Sheer Rage, Geoff Dyer

"The world is as it is. I am as I am. We don't fit very well."
(to Catherine Carswell, May 18, 1924)

He fit not at all, not anywhere. His life was a dizzying procession through temporary lodgings, perennial poverty, ill-health, and flashes of writing, sometimes brilliant, sometimes not so much. The letters—seven volumes of them—are wonderful, better than the novels, none of which moved me when I first read them in college, but all of which have shown me more as I began to reread them in my golden years. Best are the travel books. Lawrence was a keen observer, and his agility in blending objective observation with personal reflection makes his non-fiction more readable than his oftentimes mawkish stories about lust and love.

Here's Lawrence wandering Italy's ancient and sacred hills:

"But gradually, one after another looming shadowily [sic] under their hoods, the crucifixes seem to create a new atmosphere over the whole of the countryside, a darkness, a weight in the air that is so unnaturally bright and rare with the reflection from the snows above, a darkness hovering just over the earth. So rare and unearthly the light is, from the mountains, full of strange radiance. then every now and again recurs the crucifix, at the turning of an open, grassy road, holding a shadow and a mystery under its pointy hood." (from Twilight in Italy, 1916)

There's more eroticism in Lawrence's descriptions of nature than in the stormy couplings of Gudrun and Gerald. And far less melodrama. From *Sons and Lovers* onward, Lawrence was given to precise, microscopic examinations of his inner life. To say he was a romantic or that his passions prevailed over his intellect seems false. The letters and the travel books show Lawrence to have been thoughtful, with a remarkable memory for books and ideas, with an enviable ability to blend feeling and thinking. "I believe that a man is converted when first he hears the low, vast murmur of human life, troubling his hitherto unconscious self. ... Most [men] are born again on entering manhood; then they are born to humanity, to a consciousness of all the laughing, and the never-ceasing murmur of pain and sorrow that comes from the terrible multitudes of brothers." (Letter to Rev. Robert Reid, December 3, 1907). The "laughter" to which men and women are reborn is surely ironic, for while there is pleasure and joy in Lawrence, he is never unaware of life's tragic dimensions. He couldn't be, given his health and the struggle he imposed on himself by declining to live as a comfortable bourgeois. And, frankly, there are some questions to be answered about Lawrence's commitment to "the terrible multitudes of brothers."

It was the provocative Geoff Dyer who forced me to recover from my long disinterest in Lawrence. Reading his unclassifiable, Bernhard-infected rant/meditation on everything *not* about Lawrence and just *sort of* about Lawrence, I knew that I'd lost again. Hard as I try to put away interests—there's only so much time—someone comes along and writes a book that I can't ignore, and that book leads to another, *ad infinitum*. I hope that I am done with Karl Ove, and Founder bios, and Cormac McCarthy, but *Out of Sheer Rage* has made Lawrence, once again, irresistible. Dyer, if you don't know his work, is a fabulist, a Restoration wit, an essayist in a league of his own (Zadie Smith meets W.T. Vollmann)—funny, self-deprecating, vulgar and refined, lyrical and wise. His pursuit of the ghost of Lawrence, from Taos to Sicily to Mexico to Eastwood, is evidence of enviable literary obsession. What's the point of reading books if you don't allow yourself to become obsessed with certain writers? We do it with musicians and hobbies. I know people who followed the Grateful Dead for years, a few who are Miles Davis completists, and others who collect beer glasses from every micro-brewery they visit. So why not chase

Lawrence around the globe, read his letters obsessively, and spend years thinking of all the ways this unpleasant, brilliant, tubercular neurotic changed your life?

I feel especially engaged by Lawrence due to his having lived, thanks to Mable Dodge Luhan and weak lungs, on a small ranch outside of Taos, New Mexico. He's buried near San Cristobal, and the letters suggest that this austere landscape meant more to Lawrence than any other. The Lawrence ranch isn't much to look at. He and Freida lived in a ramshackle cabin that looks about to collapse, but the surrounding desert and mountains invite the contemplative viewpoint one finds in the writing Lawrence did during his sojourns in New Mexico.

I first saw the shrine—for that is what it is—in the early 1990's when I was in the throes of my obsession with visiting writers' homes and grave sites. On a warm summer afternoon, the air still and the sky a blue so deep you sensed, at once, the immensity of the world, there was a holiness conveyed by the plain cross and white-washed memorial that I think Lawrence would have approved. Of course every pilgrimage feels anti-climactic. We ask ourselves if is *this* all that is left of the person whose books have so moved us? But if we carry away a memory of the place it turns out to have surprising resilience, and this memory gives the books a depth of feeling we hadn't experienced before.

***

In preparing for a spring visit to Chihuahua in Old

Mexico, I have been reading Lawrence's *Mornings in Mexico*. It's nearly always summer in Lawrence. As Paul Morel he must have tired of the coal-black skies of Eastwood, of England's grimness, and we know for certain that he tired of his fellow Englishmen:

> *"Curse the blasted, jelly-boned swines, the slimy, the belly-wriggling invertebrates, the miserable sodding rotters, the flaming sods, the snivelling, [sic] dribbling, dithering palsied pulse-less lot that make up England today. . . . God, how I hate them! God curse them, funkers. God blast them, wishwash. Exterminate them, slime."*

Always it was summer, and he bothered to learn the names of the flowers and trees, paid close attention to the birds and to the clarity of the air. Often we find him sitting still, jotting notes or writing letters—what a loss the end of letter writing has been! He doesn't say too much about what he's eating or drinking or wearing, it's the passing impressions on his lively mind that we are privy to, and to what are often stilted conversations with the "natives."

Martin Amis, not jolly himself, has described Lawrence as the most ill-tempered of English writers. We know that Lawrence struck his wife (she was larger and she hit him back). He disliked Jews, wrote cringing sentences about Mexicans (Rosalino, Lawrence's faithful Indian servant in *Mornings in Mexico* is "a dumb-bell, as the Americans would say"), and was as often unkind and gossipy as not. He had a Freudian dossier of sexual hang-ups—his is the finest example of an Oedipus complex since *Hamlet*, and that he loved men more than women is a reasonable inference from the letters and fiction.

His writing can be overwrought, sentimental, incoherent:

> "[Miriam] knew she felt in a sort of bondage to him, which she hated because she could not control it. She hated her love for him from the moment it grew too strong for her. And, deep down, she had hated him because she loved him and he dominated her. She had resisted his denomination. She had fought to keep herself free of him in the last issue. And she was free of him, even more than he of her." Sons and Lovers, Part 2, Chapter 11.

I find most objectionable the way in which his narrators project themselves into the minds of everyone around them, creating a world that existed solely to mirror Lawrence. A lot of writers do this, but *Sons and Lovers* and *Women in Love* feel emotionally claustrophobic, as if there were one voice speaking and everyone else was just moving her lips. This habit imparts sameness to the novels, a predictability in terms of character and plot. And Lawrence's women are sexualized in the way a man might imagine or wish them to be, and they are also, like Lawrence, tormented by sex. His men are austere and predatory, not admirable. Nothing wrong with sex, but what seemed tantalizing when I was in the my twenties—this was long before ubiquitous porn or even the tedium of sex-obsessed sit coms—is now boring, even juvenile. There are times when I imagine

Lawrence sniggering over his foolscap, shocking the Puritans, working himself up for Freida. Joyce's letters to Nora are a nice cure for the flowery pudenda and penises of Lawrence.

Henry Miller mirrors Lawrence's preoccupations, his fear of women, his narcissism. There might be a scholarly book comparing the two, something richer than *Sexual Politics,* but if there is, I don't know about it. Miller grew beyond the *Tropics* and the *Rosy Crucifixion* trilogy, but he remained a dirty old man right to the end of his long life. Both writers were strange, isolated men who appeared to yearn for companionship and yet disdained those who provided it. (See Miller's letters to Anais Nin). Both broke the rules and challenged taboos that now seem incomprehensible. Both had to go to Paris to get their books published, as if that were a hardship.

***

John Middleton Murry, second husband of Katherine

Mansfield, flogged Lawrence in his book *D. H. Lawrence* (1930). Lawrence called Murray "an obscene bug sucking my life away," and Murry repaid the complaint, finding Lawrence domineering and self-centered. Murry and Mansfield both showed up in Lawrence's novels, and the Frieda/DH/Murry/Mansfield quartet is the subject of a group biography by Sydney Janet Kaplan, *Circulating Genius*. Since Murry's book, Lawrence's reputation both as a man and as a writer has undergone several transformations. I find much to admire in the writing, but, with some reservations, I have to agree with Amis—Lawrence is a difficult person to warm up to.

Sheer rage. Dyer's title is from Lawrence's *Letters*, and it is a phrase that turns up often in the correspondence. From rage comes art, of a kind. Would that his sheer rage been leavened with some of Frieda's exuberance, or Geoff Dyer's playfulness. Lawrence wrote in order to be saved. I believe he was religious, despite his protestations to the contrary. And he found his version of the divine in nature, though not of the romantic's sort. He appears never to have made his peace with other people. He was a stranger wherever he went, an émigré Englishmen looking askance at the "wogs," an uptight libertine, dry and judgmental. But, for now—he's fascinating.

G.O.

Mughal Dreams

Ever since I first visited Delhi, I have been fascinated by the Mughals and their influence in India, an influence—though faded—that still can be felt today. "The Mughal House of Timur ruled most of South Asia for more than two hundred years and became arguably the greatest dynasty in Indian history," writes William Dalrymple in his engaging history *The Last Mughal: The Fall of a Dynasty: Delhi, 1857*. "For many, the Mughals symbolize Islamic civilization at its most refined and aesthetically pleasing—think of the great white dome of the Taj Mahal that Akbar's grandson, Shah Jahan, raised in Agra in memory of his favorite Queen..." At the heart of that civilization—an eclectic, richly cosmopolitan culture which reveled in the arts: in painting, architecture, horticulture, and music—was a devotion to poetry the like of which is all but inconceivable today. In Delhi and Agra, poets were cultivated by the wealthy and powerful; Mughal statesman and warriors themselves devoted time to savoring the works of Mir, Ghalib, and Iqbal, as well as to writing and reciting their own *qasidas, rubayis, and ghazals*.

> *The gathering of poets was a popular occasion in the Mughal world. As described by Asad ur Rahman, "A gathering of poets is called a mushaira and it is a small, intimate social function. Traditionally, the poets and members of the audience sit on a carpet-covered floor in horse-shoe formation. The leader is usually the most distinguished poet or the most respected scholar. The reading of the poems starts with the youngest or the least known poet. An oil lamp or lighted candle is placed before the poet to indicate that it is his or her turn to read and to provide better lighting for his reading. In ascending order, the poets read their poems until the candle [comes] to the leader. If the leader is a poet, he will read his poem. If not, he will comment on the poems read that day. Then, he will announce the misra-e-tarha or the half line of poetry on the metrical pattern by which the poets will have to write their poems for the next meeting..."*

It is no doubt this sort of scene that is imagined by the hapless protagonist of Anita Desai's wonderful novel *In Custody* (1984) when he is given the chance, the chance of a lifetime, to interview his hero, the Urdu poet, Nur Shahjahanabadi, one of the last living masters of a long and noble line. The novel tells the story of Deven, a poor widow's son and frustrated Urdu poet and intellectual who earns his living by teaching Hindi literature to bored college students in a dusty town outside of Delhi where he lives with his wife, Sarla. One day he is surprised at work by his wealthy and feckless friend, Murad, who charges him, for the next edition of his magazine, to secure an interview with the illustrious poet. Devon is thrilled by the prospect of meeting the man, of basking in his greatness and in this way quickening the past, and journeys to Delhi, to the largely Muslim neighborhood of Chandi Chowk where the poet lives, his heart full to bursting with nervous expectation.

Not surprisingly, things do not go as planned. Surrounded, if not guarded, by jealous wives, greedy relatives, and lazy devotees, the dissolute, senile, and grossly overweight, Nur himself proves a surprise and a challenge for the tender young protagonist bent on preserving the poet's name and works for posterity. What follows is a wryly-told, often heartbreaking tale of one man's longing for a charmed and bygone world.

P.N.

Coming of Age

Euphoria, Lily King
Intertwined Lives: Margaret Mead, Ruth Benedict, and Their Circle, Lois W. Banner

Steven Pinker's new book, *Enlightenment Now*, argues that the world would be a better place if everyone followed the dictates of reason—defined, I suppose, as linear/empirical/analytical/Western thought. If, in Pinker's view, everyone abandoned magical thinking, religion, superstition, and metaphysics, then the excesses of religious fundamentalism, irrationality, and cruelty would give way to material progress for all. Pinker, high atop Harvard Hill, reminds us that science and technology, leavened by the arts and humanities, have led to progress ever since the Enlightenment. E.O. Wilson, also at Harvard, has made the same point in a number of books, and corporate types like Steve Jobs and Bill Gates have found much to like in this rationalist view of progress. I remain unpersuaded. For one thing, reason, with or without the scare quotes, is a form of problem solving. By itself, our rational (critical, analytical, scientific) mode of thinking has no material or moral content, as Kant famously understood.

At best, reason functions as lines on a blank page, a rubric, an outline. Living a life, building a just society, includes not only analytical thinking but also willing, desiring, believing, and—let's face it—lots of luck.

***

It is impossible, post-Freud, not to see the "primitive" peoples of Samoa as occupying a landscape of desire and will, of cultural expressions innocent of the Puritanical and patriarchal denial of the (female) body. No analytical reasoning was discovered by Mead and Benedict and Bateson and Boas in Samoa or the Amazon basin. The peoples of the Sepik River of New Guinea possess botanical knowledge one associates with hunter-gatherers, simple technologies (these are stone-age cultures), and an intimacy with nature that Rousseau would have admired. In her dual biography, *Intertwined Lives*, Lois Banner does an admirable job of sketching the sexual repressions of American society in the early twentieth century and the effects of these repressions on the two most famous women anthropologists of the twentieth century. Havelock Ellis and other sexologists, bohemians, and free spirits defied the strictures on sexuality, but the psychic price paid by unmarried heterosexuals and all homosexuals (in the language of the age) was debilitating. In Samoa, where, in the 1930s, Christian missionaries were just beginning to spread the gospel of celibacy, a woman or a man could find a culture where sexual taboos were mild, where women had a measure of control over their reproductive lives, and where no one was watching.

***

Of the many discouraging words I hear from young people, the most discouraging have to do with something that those of us brought up in the positivist tradition refer to as "human nature." Thus one can select any assumptions about human beings and ascribe them to a presumably eternal human nature. As in, "People are greedy; it's just human nature," or "People are violent; it's human nature." No amount of questioning can dislodge the conviction that all of us come hard-wired with precisely the set of innate characteristics that define twenty-first century American society: greed, materialism, indifference to other people, a fascination with violence (done to others), hedonism, and a vague understanding of the goods that comes from science and technology. I used to argue with people about human nature, suggesting that even in purely Darwinian terms the struggle for life might as easily include altruism and self-sacrifice as greed and violence. But such arguments get nowhere. After all, the evidence appears overwhelming. Nobody reports the countless daily acts of kindness and selflessness that make our families, communities, and our society workable. Those who are inclined to see the world as something other than a Hobbesian struggle are far less likely to boast about their beliefs. Ordinary men and decent women seldom go into public life, appear on television, or find themselves in the limelight. Adults and young alike know of Gordon Gecko but have never heard of Dorothy Day.

***

I now respond to "everyone is greedy" with the simple admonition "read some anthropology."

***

Do you remember how moved you felt when you read Marjorie Shostak's *Nisa: The Life and Words of a !Kung San Woman?* The book was a revelation, and while I have only taken one anthropology course in my life, Shostak, who died too young, got me to read more books like hers, first-person accounts of people whose world-view is wholly different from my own.

***

Rereading parts of Ruth Benedict's *Patters of Culture* in the light of Lily King's extraordinary novel *Euphoria*, I am reminded again of the indelible fact that human nature, like human culture, is as varied and rich as the heavenly constellations. I am fortunate enough to live in the same region as people for whom selflessness, community, collective identity, spirituality, and life mean more than greed, individualism, materialism, and death. If there is a single culture that practices selflessness and altruism than the human nature argument is fallacious. Marshall Sahlins's view of hunter-gatherers as the "original affluent society"and Marjorie Shostak's work on the !Kung open the door to our understanding of how so-called primitive societies give the lie to the notion that the apogee of human existence is found in the industrial West and in Enlightenment reason.

***

Lily King has taken the rudiments of the story of Margaret Mead, Gregory Bateson, and Reo Fortune in Samoa and turned it into a philosophical novel of the highest order. Nellie, Fen, and Bankson bring to their field work among the Tam three entirely different views of the purposes of anthropology, and, by extension, three different views of life. Nell is generous, open-minded, fearless, empathetic, warm, and humane. Fen is harsh and judgmental, engaged with other cultures to the extent that they allow him to ignore his own demons. He is married to Nell but treats her as if she were a foreign culture, someone whose habits of mind are unworthy of his attention. The effect that Fen has on Nell is predictable. She feels alone, a stranger in a strange land, and while her isolation helps deepen her skills as a passive observer of other cultures, it diminishes her spirit. Bankson, who narrates most of the novel, is diffident, uncertain of his skills as a scientist, but, like Nell, he possesses patience and compassion. How ironic that in this novel it is the least "rational" among the scientists who understands most deeply what it means to live in a world defined by custom and not laws. Bankson's shy approach to his anthropological subjects takes him far more deeply into the world of the Tam than Fen's ultimately tragic attempt to *become* his subjects. Lily King subtly brings Nell and Bankson together; that they will come to love one another is foreordained, but what's really beautiful is how the study of the Tam and the cautious circling of this trio of anthropologists reflect each other. Just as Nell and Bankson use their good hearts to uncover the mysteries of a stone-age culture, so too do they gradually begin to understand one another. Fen is the odd man out. He doesn't wish to study anything—he wants to dominate those around him, he wishes to exert his will over others, and in this he serves both as the perfect model of the Westerner among "savages" and the perfect foil to Nell and Bankson. The old dichotomy between head and heart is played out in *Euphoria* with delicacy and brilliance.

***

The practice of field anthropology is an odd one. That a Westerner could live among people as foreign as the Tam (a fictional tribe, but there are plenty of real-life examples) and somehow come to understand them seems like folly. If the observation of a physical state changes that state and makes objectivity impossible, how much more so does the physical presence of a stranger among an isolated tribal group undo any possibility of understanding? And, worse, as *Euphoria* makes plain, how much damage do well-meaning scientists do when they intrude upon the intimate lives of strangers? *Euphoria* does many things well—it's a love story, an adventure novel, a philosophical investigation—but above all it is a book that raises fundamental questions about the pretensions of Western reason and science. Our brash conviction that we can understand, and by understanding control, the world feel especially hollow when that understanding and control is directed at a group of people who might prefer to be left in peace. The notion of picking a tribe and, uninvited, going to live among them, studying them as one might study an exotic species of bird, feels at times more like imperialism than science.

    G.O.

Minha Terra: Ivo's Brazil

But sometimes, it was as if the sea did not exist,
and he lived among stones, in a nest of snakes.
                                    Lêdo Ivo

"During a dictatorship, all narratives are poorly told…" writes Lêdo Ivo in reference to the rambling, unreliable narration of this brilliant short novel, *Snakes' Nest or A Tale Badly Told.* Indeed, as University of New Mexico professor Jon Tolman explains in his helpful introduction, *Snakes' Nest* is a set in Brazil in the 1940's, during what was known as the "New State," a semi-fascist experiment in *caudillismo*, a cult of personality around the charismatic leader, Getúlio Vargas, that lasted from 1930-1945. At heart an allegory of good and evil, this "sunny nightmare" rises like a miasma from the streets of Maceió—from the bars and brothels and sugar depots that distinguish this seedy port city in northeastern Brazil that even today is renowned for its rampant corruption and violence. As described in a 2011 article in *The Economist*, "The road from Maceió, the capital of Alagoas state, to its airport passes luxury-car showrooms and shops selling outsize Jacuzzis. In the central reservation, indigent families live under plastic sheeting. Even by the standards of Brazil's north-east, Alagoas is scarred by poverty and extreme inequality. With 107 murders per 100,000 people, Maceió is also the most violent state capital in Brazil, just as, with 60 murders per 100,000, Alagoas is the country's most violent state. It is a place of sugar and cattle, where the sugarcane cutters settle scores with fists and knives and the well-connected escape punishment by using contract killers instead."

It is this latter world that serves as the setting for this collection of powerfully rendered vignettes about the workaday men and women of Maceió—the lawyers, gangsters, sailors, poets, prostitutes, and nuns—a story, a novel (though Ivo denied it the name) in which the narration flits like a hummingbird from character to character, from place to place, sipping here, drinking there, darting back and forth in time as if drunk on the nectar it finds. In an age when more and more American writers are forced by the market to answer to the same dull master, that is, plot over character, murder and mystery over language and symbol and theme, this novel comes as a positive relief.

Ivo's heterodox approach to storytelling, to fiction, should come as no surprise to anyone who knows of him, for he was a poet, first and foremost, a writer who flirted with modernism before turning his back on it to embrace more classical, more traditional forms. One feels the poetry in his language and rhythms, in the weight and balance of his words, yet there is nothing fussy or self-conscious about his style. Even in English his phrasing has the blunt simplicity, the force and gravitas, of prophesy or scripture, as in this passage describing the moments—the minutes, the seconds—before one of his characters, a manager of a local airline agency, blows out his brains:

> *It was raining—it was a rain of words. The wind blew—it was a wind of words. The world wasn't made of skies, clouds, cities, sugarcane mills, ports, dams, yards, old cars, streets, power plants, houses, men. It was made only and exclusively of words— and the people spoke in words. Even the paving stones of Maceió were made of words. Alexandre Viana ate words, slept words, worked words. And he felt more alone than ever, as if the very weapon that sketched itself before his eyes would turn into a word.*

While *Snakes' Nest* is set in the Maceió of Ivo's childhood, what he calls "minha terra" or "my land," it is important to note that the period in which the novel was written, that is, the early 1970's, was actually a more politically repressive time for Brazilian artists and writers than that of the quasi-fascist *caudillismo* of Getúlio Vargas, evidence enough that such authoritarianism is perfectly at home in the rich Brazilian soil. What makes this significant, what makes it especially poignant to me, is that I have only just now finished reading the Austrian writer Stefan Zweig's book, *Brazil: A Land of the Future*, a gushing, 250 page hymn to the nation that had given him home and sanctuary as a Jew in flight from Hitler's

Europe. The picture he paints of early 1940's Brazil and its future in the world is just short of utopian, an incredible feat, given Vargas' staunchly corporatist, right-wing, anti-Marxist politics, a tyranny over thought and expression that included censorship and the harassment, torture, and execution of Leftists. Somehow, for all of Zweig's perspicacity as a writer and exile, he had failed to see the forest for the trees. Blinded to the rise of fascism there, in Brazil (the selfsame period described by Ivo's novel) by his desperate need to keep faith with the human race, to believe in the possibility of a paradise on earth, Zweig ends his introduction to this Panglossian tribute by writing: "For that reason, one of our best hopes for a future civilizing and pacification of a world that has been desolated by hate and madness is based upon the existence of Brazil." That Brazil was indeed a sort of Garden of Eden to Zweig is clear; what is also clear—a fact perhaps only acknowledged by Zweig himself on the eve of his suicide there in 1942—is that, by the time he'd finished writing *Brazil: A Land of the Future*, the Serpent was already in.

P.N.

Balkan Ghosts

Girl at War, Sara Nović
The Road to Unfreedom, Timothy Snyder

Though we could not have known it at the time, the war and ethnic cleansing—that is, genocide—in Yugoslavia foreshadowed all that was to come following the breakup of the Soviet Union. The patched-together, multi-ethnic, multi-religious, polyglot Yugoslavia was itself the creature of another empire's implosion—the Austro-Hungarian, which was, in turn, the mid-nineteenth century remnant of the great Hapsburg Empire founded in 1279. Large, ungainly conglomerations of people never endure. Tribalism trumps cosmopolitanism. Hopeful chatter about how people of different "races and religions" can put away their differences and live together in peace have proven time and again to be illusion. The horror that erupted in the Balkans in 1991was mostly ignored in the West until the Srebrenica massacre in 1995.

Timothy Snyder demonstrates with his usual clarity and enormous erudition—he reads not only the usual European languages but also Polish and Russian—that the Russia of

Putin was founded, with sclerotic assistance from Boris Yeltin and the ever-naive West, as an embodiment of eternal principles, of ideas related to the fascist disbelief in historical change, in liberal progress, in the dialectic processes that underpin republicanism and democracy. Putin is of course the new Tsar but, more than that, he embodies Ivan Ilyin's view that history isn't about people at all, it is about the recovery of Divine Will as personified by an absolute ruler—a fascist prince not unlike Mussolini, Hitler, or Putin himself. A ruler who brooks no opposition, no compromise, no critics.

Ilyin, as Snyder shows, is the hero of the New Russia, the court philosopher and, though dead, its guiding light. Of course unquestioning obedience suits a kleptocracy perfectly, and those who worry that any democratic compromises will undercut their power are naturally drawn to the rabid thinkers like Ilyin who loathed any form of popular governance.

Girl at War, Sara Nović's strong debut novel, answers, with great empathy, the question: What happens to the victims of war? We might read about unspeakable crimes—as with the Balkan war, massacres, mass graves, torture centers, rape—but don't have a clue as to how those who survive carry on with their lives. Nović's "girl," the resolute and courageous thirteen-year-old Ana Juric, watches Zagreb, her home, succumb to the Serbian Cetniks (or Chetniks), an ultra-rightest, Serbian nationalist group committed to the ethnic cleansing of what they considered greater Serbia. Her own family falls victim to a Serbian militia, and she finds herself living, and fighting, with the Croatian resistance. A remarkable, yet credible set of circumstances sees Ana rescued from the fighting and sent to live in the United States with the family that has already adopted her younger sister.

The central section of this triptych of a novel is set ten years after Ana's rescue and describes her difficulty—one can well imagine it—adjusting to a the normal life of an American college student. We understand that overcoming memory is impossible, and that returning to Zagreb offers Ana the only hope she has of finding—what? People like to say "closure," but what does that mean? Healing isn't an option. I think of Ana's return to the scenes of the crimes committed against her and her family as a validation of her identify. She is no longer Croatian, nor is she American, rather she is one of the millions—a number that grows daily—of the victims of war, of forced migration and displacement, of ethnic and tribal hatreds that give the lie to the fantasy of globalism and cosmopolitanism.

Girl at War powerfully evokes recent history in retelling Ana Juric's story, but the novel is important because its theme is universal. Victors have short memories; it is the victims who are obliged to keep the past alive for the rest of us.

"Now I'm retired, but I'm still in a good mood to kill people," asserts Vojislav Carkic, an actual person, in fact an Orthodox priest who served with the Chetniks during the

Yugoslav war. God's work, in this priest's view, remains unfinished so long as there are non-Serbs in God's Serbia. This was what Ilyin had in mind back in the 1930s, a righteous Holy War of the Orthodox, a war to cleanse God's earth of sinners and unbelievers. That war continues.

    G.O.

The Art of Nostalgia: Di Lampedusa and Tanazaki

Oh call back yesterday... bid time return.
William Shakespeare, *Richard II*

It has been said that nostalgia is memory with the pain removed. If that is true, it is only true in part, for real nostalgia is nothing if not painful, involving as it does the haunting, sometimes exquisite disjunction between the world one knew and the world beating daily at one's door. In fact nostalgia—a catch-all term coined by medical student Johannes Hofer in 1668 to describe the anxiety disorders displayed by Swiss mercenaries far from home—is a Greek compound comprised of two parts, the first meaning "return home", the second simply "pain". While it is clear that nostalgia can be abused, manipulated for profit or nurtured jealously as a hedge against change, what seems less clear, what is perhaps more difficult to grasp, is that we—as people, cultures, religions, and nations—would be helpless without it.

At its best, and for all its obvious conceit, nostalgia is one of the essential means by which we, as individuals, reckon with our own mortality—with the weakening of our eyes and limbs, with the growth of our children, with the fading of hope and love. It is how we shore up and safeguard our position in a world now promiscuous with change, a sort of homing instinct for the heart and mind, so that in the end nostalgia is less about persuading others that life was better in the past (even if it was)—that children had manners, that everyone pulled his own weight—than about consoling oneself in times of struggle and pain. For nostalgia, like death itself, is an expressly lonely, deeply personal thing, best savored in private or in the dusty, shuttered worlds of novels, poems, and plays. I myself have always had a weakness for works of loss and remembrance; deeply sentimental, I have always had "eyes in the back of my head."

"This is one of the great *lonely* books," wrote E.M. Forster in an early review of Guiseppe di Lampedusa's novel *The Leopard*. I think I know what he meant, for I have returned to this novel again and again over the past twenty years, often when I'm feeling out of sorts with the world, its particular sadness as fine, as affecting as any sadness I know. First published by Giangiacomo Feltrinelli Editore in 1958, one year after the author's death in Rome from lung cancer, the novel centers upon Don Fabrizio Corbera, Prince of Salina, one of the last scions of a decadent Sicilian aristocracy threatened by the forces of democracy and revolution known as the Risorgimento (Italian: "Rising Again"). Beginning in the year 1860, as Garibaldi and his Red Shirts (known as the "Piedmontese" or, more derisively, as the "Garibaldeschi"), are laying siege to Palermo, the story of Prince Fabrizio—an elegy at heart—describes, in elegant, sometimes sumptuous detail, the passing of a corrupt, if exquisitely cultured man and his age.

With the unification of Italy in 1861, under King Victor Emmanuel II, the eight autonomous states by which the peninsula was then divided (including the Bourbon states of Naples and Sicily called the Kingdom of the Two Sicilies) were united as one, much to the outrage and consternation of the Pope and his conservative allies. Often lauded as a triumph of liberalism, as propagated by the writings of philosopher Benedetto Croce, the Risorgimento is understood by others today—the unification of Italy notwithstanding—as an aristocratic and bourgeois revolution that failed.

Even to Don Fabrizio, whose own future and that of the illustrious House of Salinas is gravely imperiled by the democratic militancy of Garibaldi and Mazzini, it is plain that, for all of the revolution's smoke and fire, for all its egalitarian rhetoric, nothing for the peasants of Sicily will change. "Much would happen," he reflects, near the start of the novel, in thinking about his beloved if wayward nephew, Tancredi, and about the rebels gathering force in the hills around Palermo, "but all would be playacting; a noisy, romantic play with a few spots of blood on the comic costumes…" Indeed, while predictably reactionary in his politics and values, the Prince is as deeply scored by the fatalism of that parched and subject land as any goatherd, nursemaid, or priest. "Between the pride and intellectuality of his mother and the sensuality and irresponsibility of his father, poor Prince Fabrizio lived in perpetual discontent under his Jovelike frown, watching the ruin of his own class and his own inheritance without ever making, still less wanting to make, any move toward saving it."

It is partly this, the Prince's quiet resignation to the change then sweeping the peninsula—his fine and melancholy wisdom, his love of the cosmos, his long and philosophical view of life—that makes him such an appealing character. Effete, surely, the occasional tyrant and womanizer, no doubt, he, like a priest, like a poet, redeems himself as a man and character by the gentle grandeur of his vision, his eyes (with the aid of his precious telescopes) searching the heavens for solace each night, patiently charting the movements of the stars.

"Anyone with a taste for traditional architecture must agree that the Japanese toilet is perfect," writes novelist Junichiro Tanizaki in his lovely, sometimes surprising 1933 meditation on traditional Japanese arts and architecture. On the matter of toilets he waxes poetic: "...the Japanese toilet truly is a place of spiritual repose. It always stands apart from the main building, at the end of a corridor, in a grove fragrant with leaves and moss... there one can listen with such a sense of intimacy to the raindrops falling from the eaves and trees, seeping into the earth as they wash over the base of a stone lantern and freshen the moss and the stepping stones... the toilet is the perfect place to listen to the chirping of insects or the songs of the birds, to view the moon, or to enjoy any of those poignant moments that mark the change of the seasons." This—to those familiar with the author—is classic Tanizaki, embracing as it does a somber affection for traditions past, an aesthetic—according to translator, Thomas J. Harper—not of a celebrant but a mourner. For Tanizaki, much of what he describes in this short book, and in his many novels that followed, "had either perished or was preserved, fossil-like, in surroundings that betrayed its true beauty."

The Makioka Sisters, Tanizaki's longest novel, begun in serial form in 1943 and not completed until 1948, tells the poignant, exquisitely detailed story of the aristocratic Makioka sisters and their struggle to preserve their dignity and traditions in the face of rampant modernization and war.

Set in the mercantile city of Osaka in the years just prior to World War II, a period of intense militarism and international aggression under Shōwa emperor, Hirohito, the novel traces, with nearly seismographic precision, the quakes and tremors of this new Japan. It is a cultural transformation writ small within the once-great Makioka family itself, with the eldest sisters, Tsuruko and Sachiko, representing the subtle forms and aesthetic of old Japan and the youngest, Taeko, with her doll-making business, her boyfriends, and her smart Western clothes, the foreign and flagrant and new. Focused primarily upon securing a suitable marriage for the third sister, the humble Yukiko, this fine and patient novel retails the daily lives of these four women and the painful compromises they are forced to make. Originally entitled *Sasameyuki*, meaning "lightly falling snow," it is a story of great beauty that explores the timeless Japanese obsession with the transience and fragility of life.

As is the case with most great fiction, the illusion of eavesdropping on the action of these kindred novels is, for readers, the key to their success, indeed instrumental to the triumph of these wistful, nostalgic tales. For in both cases, and for all of their more public scenes, what we as readers are ultimately made witness to is the private grief of the authors themselves, through the characters, the proxies, they've made.

P.N.

Obscure for Sure

Thomas the Obscure, Maurice Blanchot

Reading *Thomas the Obscure* reminded me of my college days, spent, in part, reading writers like Hermann Hesse, Par Lagerkvist (*Barabbas*), Knut Hamsun, and Max Frisch—but especially Hesse, and, in particular, Hesse's *Siddhartha*. At the time, as an aspiring literary *poseur*, I found these writers inspirational, and books like *Demian, Steppenwolf, The Glass Bead Game*, and *Journey to the East* struck me as profound, beautifully written, and indisputably great. Now, I'm afraid, I find Hesse mostly unreadable, dated, and labored. Though I didn't see it then, the impact of Freud on Hesse's thinking was pernicious. But this judgment merely shifts the blame away from me. The honest thing would be to admit that I had no clue what made a literary work worth my time, and often confused seriousness with profundity. There's a quality in all of these writers, in Hesse especially, that struck me as I was reading Blanchot. At first I couldn't put my finger on what this quality was, or why I felt unable to engage with the *text* (as Blanchot himself would have put it), but it has come to me that the great weakness of the kind of philosophical literature represented by

Hesse and Blanchot is the substitution of murkiness for clarity, a narrative misdirection that is intended to invoke metaphysical truths but which ends up seeming inscrutable.

Is it too obvious to mention that Thomas is, of course, doubting Thomas? (John 20:24) "Happy are those who have not seen and yet believe."

> *"What [Ann] said to [Thomas] took the form of indirect speech. It was a cry full of pride which resounded in the sleepless night with the very character of dream. 'Yes,' she said, 'I would like to see you when you are alone. If ever I could be before you and completely absent from you, I would have a chance to meet you. Or rather I know that I would not meet you. The only possibility I would have to diminish the distance between us would be to remove myself to an infinite distance. But I am infinitely far away now, and can go no further. As soon as I touch you Thomas....'*
> *Hardly out of her mouth, these words carried her away: she saw him, he was radiant."*

Blanchot, among the founders of post-modern French literary theory, is recreating a myth—some say of Orpheus and Eurydice, but I'm not sure that's right. In any case, the fragmented, dreamy, semi-erotic, thanatopsic, disjointed story of a man who is obscure to himself and others, a sort of ghost, and a woman who yearns for oblivion. A story that has all of the qualities of myth—the suggestiveness, the yearning for universality, the reduction of all things to the personal:

"On the retina of the absolute eye, I am the tiny inverted image of all things," Thomas tells us, and then "With me, the laws gravitate outside the laws, the possible outside the possible." Madness, of course, lurks behind the plots of many of these semi-surrealist writers. Siddhartha, who may or may not be the historical Buddha, always struck me as a bit daft for his insistence that staring at a river all day long could teach one the truths of life. Thomas also spends his time floating in the sea, wandering in forests, and reading without noticing the words—in a bubble of self-regard that tries to pass itself off as cosmic and universal. I am sure that in a room full of undergraduates, well stocked with that which alters consciousness, these Thomistic pronouncements would evoke ejaculatory cries of pleasure among the readers or auditors. For me, an older gent with lots of postwar French literary shenanigans under his belt, the effect was quite different.

Blanchot was an important philosopher. Serious students read *The Infinite Conversation* (available only in French) in the heady 60's. I came at Blanchot's theoretical work mostly at second hand—especially through my reading of Georges Bataille. I heard that Blanchot had taken principled stances against fascist collaborators during the war, although it appears now that his writing before the Occupation might not have been as anti-fascist as his supporters have maintained. This time around I was inclined to enjoy *Thomas the Obscure*, but was disappointed, and thought again about how often philosophers fail to write novels that live. Sartre, for example, has never tempted me, and while I can enjoy scattered pages of some of her vast output of fiction, Iris Murdoch engages me more for her writings on ethics than for her fiction. Ditto Camus, whose essays seem far better than his novels or plays. To what extent, I wonder, can fiction bear up under the weight of ideas? Thomas Mann, the finest of philosophical novelists, excelled at blending in-depth character studies with lengthy ruminations on obscure topics (scholastic theology!), but who else can pull this off? *Thomas the Obscure* felt a bit like an undergraduate seminar in metaphysics—a little too solipsistic ("It seemed that, through a phenomenon awaited for centuries, the earth now saw him"), a bit too sophomoric ("I think, it said, I am subject and object of an all-powerful radiation..."), and a little too full of yearning for my tastes. Anne's "death" reminds me of Werther's—pointless, freighted with meaning that it cannot sustain and that it doesn't deserve. Blanchot is celebrated as the first post-modern novelist. This seems right to me. He was a precursor to Alain Robbe-Grillet and for this reason his novels and his critical writing have great interest for the scholar of French thought in the pre- and post-war years. But as a novelist he leaves me yearning for a bit of Germanic refreshment—a few pages of Bernhard, for example, or a bowl of Böll.

G.O.

After Babel: Foreigners and the English Language

The need for translation is self-evident.
George Steiner

It is to a Frenchman that I am most indebted for my love of the English language. Though he wrote exclusively in French, Marcel Proust (with the aid of his greatest champion and translator, C.K. Scott Moncrieff) transformed my understanding of the richness and potential of English. This is not hyperbole. Until I read Moncrieff's rendition of *Swann's Way* (a copy of which my stepmother had given me as a gift when I started college, convinced without reason that I would find my way round to it), this language I'd been born to was something—like my eyes, my eardrums, my teeth—that I'd taken for granted, speaking it without hearing it, reading it without seeing it, and writing it without curiosity, affection or joy. Testing the water with just the first few pages of Proust one day was like suddenly discovering I could read Sanskrit or Greek. I knew the words (it was English after all), yet the world they described (both the fin-de-siècle world of Paris *and* that uniquely Proustian world of words themselves) was distinctly exotic to me. So heady was the novel's English, so complex its sentences, so dogged, so solipsistic, so all-consuming its dream, that at points I remember gasping for air. Above all the writing was beautiful, sonorous—like the plays of Shakespeare, a song of songs, a protracted incantation to the kingdom and glory of words.

Translation—its usefulness, its sheer practicability—has long been a matter of debate. Paul Celan, a Romanian poet and translator who read widely in translation, remarked, "Only in the mother tongue can one speak his own truth, in a foreign tongue the poet lies." It is a position remarkably widespread. For years I taught at an independent school in Manhattan where my department chair forbade us to teach literature in translation (though he himself taught *The Odyssey* each year) arguing, as he had, that the act of translation was inherently flawed, if not fraudulent, that it could never do justice to art. The argument is not without merit: a good translation is not and can never be a duplicate of the original. What it is instead is a brilliant re-creation, something both derivative *and* new, an attempt—according to Valéry—to produce similar effects by different means.

Yet in truth *any* attempt at communication, even in one's own language (as in speaking, reading or writing) involves translation of a kind, our every gesture to connect with one another a transmutation of forms. While surely there are good and bad translations, the necessity itself is clear. Translation is not just fundamentally human; it is all we have. Think of the story of the Tower of Babel. God, in his anger at humans for attempting to build a tower to heaven, shatters their once-unified language into a thousand mutually unintelligible tongues. For avid readers and writers, it is a story rife with implications. With the destruction of the tower and the confounding of human language, "The people ceased to be one," writes Octavio Paz. "The beginning of plurality was also the beginning of history: empires, wars, and the great piles of rubble that civilizations have left." For Paz, as for readers and writers everywhere, our hope as humans is plain: "...the Spirit is One, languages are Many, and the bridge between the two is Translation."

A good translation is as miraculous as alchemy—and vastly more fruitful. For the translation of world literature not only enriches us—morally, culturally, aesthetically, politically—but enriches our language, coloring the words and phrases we know, pressing hard upon our conventions, and generally expanding the "the compass of observed and rendered life."* I can hardly imagine how small and impoverished my world would be were it not for the work of such fine translators as C.K. Scott Moncrieff, Robert Hollander, Robert Fagles, Edith Grossman, Gregory Rabassa, George Szirtes, Joachim Neugroschel, Hillel Halkin, Sophie Wilkins, David Magarshack, David McLintock, Arthur Waley, Donald Keene, Lydia Davis, John E. Woods, Celia Hawkesworth, Jorge Luis Borges, William Maynard Hutchins, Constance Garnett, George Henson, Edward Fitzgerald, Sophie Wilkins, Francis Price, Nicholas de Lange, Susan Bernofsky, Michael Hulse,

Charlotte Mandell, Giovanni Pontiero, William Weaver, Maureen Freely, Anthea Bell, Sergio Pitol, Richard Pevear, Larrisa Volokhonsky, J.M. Cohen, Frances Steegmuller, Margaret Jull Costa, Edward G. Seidensticker, Rabindrinath Tagore, Ann McLean, Rosemary Edmonds, Harry Morales, H.T. Lowe-Porter, Damion Searles and Michael Hofmann. After the writers themselves, it is to their translators—those all but invisible agents of poetry and prose—that I owe the greatest debt.

* From "The Retreat from the Word" by George Steiner

P.N.

The Workshop of Potential Literature

Why I Have Not Written Any of My Books
(Pourquoi je n'ai écrit aucun de mes livres)
by Marcel Bénabou

Together with Marcel Duchamp, Italo Calvino, Jacques Roubaud, and Harry Matthews, Perec and Bénabou were member of the playful and inventive Workshop of Potential Literature founded by Raymond Queneau and Francois Le Lionnais in 1960, a group of writers interested in what might best be called the playful or ludic forms of literary expression. I have written elsewhere about Perec's novel *A Void,* a full-length and complex book that dispenses with all words that include the letter "e." Bénabou, a historian of ancient Rome and author of a dozen scholarly works in this field, also wrote numerous fictions and meta-fictions in the Oulipoian mode—think of Borges's *Other Inquisitions* pushed further over the brink of self-reference, literary-mindedness, and surrealism. Or, as Warren Mote suggests in his own witty introduction to *Why I Have Not Written Any of My Books,* look to Raymond Roussel's truly eccentric *How I Wrote Certain of My Books* (which is about everything but) to get a sense of what a writer who loves puzzles can do with fictional form. This little-known circle of mostly Francophone writers not only eschewed the conventions of the realist novel, they also negated the conventions of modernist and post-modernist fiction as well by doing away with characters, plots, themes, and even the anxiety of influence. Perec's masterpiece, *Life: A User's Manual*, takes the reader on a guided tour of an apartment building, room by room, fragmented story by fragmented story. And Bénabou's *WIHNWAOMB* not only renounces authorship, it also plays with the notion of the book as an actually existing entity—as if Heidegger were asking the question "What is called writing?"

> *"Don't you go believing, reader, that the books I haven't written are pure nothingness. Quite the contrary (let it be said once and for all), they are as if suspended in the literary universe. They exist in libraries by word, by groups of words, by entire sentences in certain cases. But they are surrounded by so much empty filler and trapped in such an overabundance of printed matter that I myself, truth be told, have not yet succeeded, despite my best efforts, in isolating them and putting them together. Indeed, the world seems to me full of plagiarists, which makes of my work a lengthy tracking down, an obstinate search for all those little fragments inexplicably snatched away from my future books."*

Northrup Frye, in *The Anatomy of Criticism*, suggested that all existing literature belongs to a universe of words and sentences, thus unifying the efforts of all writers from all places and times. When I first encountered this idea it seemed to vindicate my own sense that literature had the mystical power of Kabbalah—the word, the Word, was indeed the creator of a universe, and that it was this world of words that made sense, if any sense was to be made, of the real world. That language creates reality is hardly a new idea. George Steiner, for one, wrote brilliantly about the implications of this view in *After Babel*, and the fictions of Borges interrogate the world that is language, rather than the world of language. The writers of Ouilpo have created fictions whose oddity comes from their self-conscious examination of the conventions of writing, authorship, and of language-use itself. It seems for Bénabou, and in some sense for Frye, Steiner, and Borges, that the act of writing is more akin to collecting words and sentences than of creating *ex nihilo*. The God/gods (Gen. 3:22) of Genesis create first with the Word, and then with earth and breath (Gen. 1:3; 2:7). The writer, in Bénabou's view, moves among fragments of language and pieces together works he "has not written" but dreamed into being.

The question Bénabou asks in *Why I Have Not* is this: what is the point of writing (or reading)? Why not feast on reality instead? Why shouldn't we give up stories—poems too, while we're at it. After all, we nearly have done so already, in the name of what we are told is more compelling, or practical, or profitable. Any writer worth his or her salt knows the answer to this question: *"I accepted a book's function as being not a useless redoubling of reality but its continuation by other means."* The form of the book is endlessly plastic. Instead of the mirror or the lamp, we discover in literature the earthiness that Yahweh shaped into human beings, a reality unlimited by human imagination. A book can be anything, even a book that is not a book. When Bénabou claims not to have written his books he means it. Authorship implies creating, but books are already written into the world and need only be discovered. This is a Platonic notion of authorship, but appealing for where it leads—which is, like everything else, to a form of love:

> *"Well, let's say that in the final analysis, this text could claim to be a very classic novel. Is it not the story of an ever deferred meeting, of a frustrated love strewn with obstacles and crosspieces which is the victim of illusions and regrets? Of an unhappy and perhaps ultimately impossible love, that of its author for a certain idea of literature."*

I've been reading Bénabou's colleague Georges Perec this week as well, his *Thoughts of Sorts*, and came upon this passage last evening in "On the Art and Craft of Sorting Books." I read it because I've been sorting mine. If you think Perec will be any help with your own literary taxonomies, forget it:

> *"Like the librarians in Borges's Babel looking for the book that contains the key to all others, we waver between the illusion of completion and the abyss of the ungraspable. In the name of completion we*

would like to believe that a single order exists which would allow us immediate access to knowledge; in the name of the ungraspable we wish to believe that order and disorder are two identical terms signifying chance."

G.O.

A Lack Somewhere

In his 1899 short story "The Wife of His Youth," Charles Chesnutt tells the story of the pretentious and conservative Mr. Ryder, a Southerner and man of mixed ancestry who runs a club known colloquially as "The Blue Vein Society," a relatively exclusive association patronized by up-and-coming members of the fictional town of Groveland who are "more white than black," that is, "white enough to show blue veins." "I have no race prejudice," he is proud to declare, "but we people of mixed blood are the ground between the upper and the nether millstone. Our fate lies between absorption by the white race and extinction in the black." They are words that might very well have been spoken by the fearless, brilliant, if now sadly little-read author, Nella Larsen. Indeed there is perhaps no American writer who was more haunted by and preoccupied with the punishing, existential stigma of mixed-race ancestry than Larsen.

Born to a white Danish mother and a black Danish West-Indian father who, as a couple, chose to cross the color line, Nella, "a visibly brown child," writes Thadious M. Davis in his introduction to Larsen's novel, *Passing*, "was raised as the lone 'colored' person in a family that had refashioned itself, consciously changed its name, erased its racial past, and, with the disappearance of that past, obscured familial ties to the dark child in its midst." For this Larsen suffered all her life, inspiring in her (just as in her protagonist, Helga Crane) a desperate, often angry iconoclasm that kept her shuttling restlessly between one people and another, always searching, never satisfied, rarely if ever happy in her skin:

> *Helga Crane couldn't, she told herself and others, live in America. In spite of its glamour, existence in America, even in Harlem, was for Negroes too cramped, too uncertain, too cruel; something not to be endured for a lifetime if one could escape; something demanding a courage greater than was in her. No. She couldn't stay. Nor, she saw now, could she remain away. Leaving, she would have to come back.*

Such, in broad strokes, is the story of Helga Crane in Larsen's grim, uncompromising, if highly readable and deeply worthwhile first novel, *Quicksand*. The title alone is nearly sufficient to describe the painful daily crisis of so many African Americans in the 1920's who suffered the triple curse of miscegenation (whether forced or consensual)—alienation from both the greater black and white communities, as well as from themselves. The ubiquitous and insidious racism that Larsen describes in the story of Helga Crane, in her life in the South, in Harlem, and in Copenhagen, to where, briefly, she flees, must eventually penetrate even the toughest of skins, as it does in time with hers, manifesting itself first as chronic dissatisfaction, self-censorship, insecurity, denial, and self-reproach, coupled at points with a bitter arrogance, then finally—if not inevitably—as bitterness itself, as apathy, submission, and self-loathing. Tragically, and for all of the evidence to the contrary, Helga's problem seems to her, by the end of the novel, to stem less from the cruel and inhuman strictures of America at large as from a personal failing or flaw in her nature, from a lack within. To say, as a host of critics once did, that such an ending is overly pessimistic, is almost obscenely ridiculous—as if the pain Larsen describes was contrived for narrative effect alone, as if the novel itself has no greater function than to *please* its readers. Writers like Larsen didn't write to be clever, to exercise their imaginations, to be creative; she wrote to tell the truth and, by telling it, to dignify her own life in all its pain and complexity. One has only to think of the recent events in Ferguson, Missouri, of the virulent, widespread, and blatantly systematic racism that still thrives in the U.S. today, to appreciate just how astute and courageous she was.

Quicksand, while available in a number of different editions, has recently been republished as part of a collection of short novels called *Harlem Renaissance: Five Novels of the 1920's*. Edited by Rafia Zafar, the collection includes work by such African American greats Jean Toomer, Claude McKay, Jessie Redmon Fauset, and Wallace Thurman. There is also a companion volume called *Harlem Renaissance: Five Novels of the 1930's*. Do yourself a favor and buy them both. They are beautiful books.

P.N.

Neither Fish nor Fowl

Moderato Cantabile, Marguerite Duras
Frenzy, David Grossman

It's neither fish nor fowl. The novella, defined as a "short novel" or "a literary work less developed in plotting and characterization than a full-scale novel" in many literary reference works—a fine lot of good that does us!—isn't a novelette or a short story or, obviously, a novel. Oddly, works like *The Secret Sharer*, *The Old Man and the Sea*, and *Billy Budd* are counted by some as novellas, but they seem more like short novels. Each has the kinds of thematic complexity, character development, and intricate plotting one associates with the longer form. And why would anyone think that *Heart of Darkness* was a novella while Paul Harding's *Tinkers*, easily readable in one sitting, is a novel? Both books have the characteristics of novels, though Conrad, as one would expect, packs more philosophy and psychology into his short classic. Or what must one do with the slender final novels of Philip Roth (*Indignation*) or the trilogy of short autobiographical (but fictional!) works of Coetzee, or the many tiny mad monologues of Bernhard (*Wittgenstein's Nephew*)? It's a baffling distinction, and word count alone seems to me to have nothing to do with the matter. I always marvel at how Alice Munro can unfold in twenty-five pages all of the richness of novels that are ten times as long.

Genre aside, I thought it would be fun to read novellas by two writers who are as diametrically opposed in style and theme as any two writers I can think of, but who nonetheless share two interesting qualities: both are often found writing about what I think of as the pathologies of love, and both substitute interior monologue, indirect discourse, telling instead of showing, and loads of opaque description detached from place and time and character for the traditional engines of plot.

Marguerite Duras's *Moderato Cantabile* is representative of her other novellas (collected in a handy Grove Press edition). The theme of her work is the difficulty of living a reasonable life in a world that is wholly unreasonable. Duras hasn't a romantic bone in her body (Grossman has many). Anne Desbaresdes, whose son has no interest in the piano lessons he is forced to take, witnesses a man shooting his girlfriend. Anne becomes obsessed with this act of, presumably, passion. It's difficult to know the facts—are there facts? In any case the shooting leads to an obsessive series of conversations with a mysterious but attractive barfly named Chauvin, in which Anne peppers him with questions about the murder, inciting him to concoct a fable about the shooting and the lives of the murdered woman and her male assassin. What does Chauvin know? Nothing much, but his myth making has about it the same seductive qualities of the myth making that Duras used to such powerful effect in the screenplay of *Hiroshima, Mon Amour*. Anne isn't interested in having an affair, or rather she isn't primarily interested in Chauvin as a potential lover; what interests her is death, the death of the unknowable woman and her own death as well. It appeared to me partway through the novella that she was tempting Chauvin to kill her, but at the end it seemed that this wasn't her intention at all. Duras isn't one to tidy up loose ends, but it occurred to me that moderately and melodiously we are led toward the recognition that neither the murder, nor Anne's questions, nor Chauvin's fabulated responses have any meaning at all. "I'm already dead" Anne declares, and we believe her.

David Grossman is an Israeli, the author of the remarkable epistolary novel *Be My Knife* as well as several books on the Arab-Israeli limbo. (What to call it? Tragedy? Crisis? Standoff? As it appears hellish and unending I'll use the word "limbo," optimistically). Where Duras writes lovely elliptical sentences that flit around unspeakable truths—Anne's indifference toward her child—Grossman writes long, meandering, poetic paragraphs, dense with indirect quotation, unattributed dialogue, brisk physical description, and deep psychological probing that leaves this reader both stimulated and perplexed. The story is simple: Shul's much beloved—adored, neurotically obsessed over—wife Elisheva has apparently been carrying on an affair with a Russian émigré named Paul for ten years—ten years at precisely fifty minutes per day. Since the entire book, though narrated in the third person, presents only Shul's speculations about the affair, and these speculations are rife with self-lacerating but, one presumes, purely imagined details, we can't say for certain if this illicit relationship is taking place in the way that he says, or, indeed, if it is taking place at all. It seemed at several points in the short (130 pages) whatever-you-call-it that Shul, like Chauvin, was fabulating to win the sympathy, or perhaps the affections, of his sister-in-law Esther. But this relationship is impossible to parse. The long dialogue/monologue that occupies most of the book involves fragmented conversations between Esther and Shul as they drive toward an anti-climactic rendezvous with Elisheva. The story's ending leaves many questions unanswered, but, I think, properly so. It is impossible to describe the dynamics of any relationship, and Grossman skillfully examines the meaning of what is unspoken. At one point I wrote in my notebook: "This isn't a novel about what is known but about what is wished for, *yearned for* in some perverse way." In this regard Grossman and Duras are working common ground. Though Duras maintains a magisterial distance and deeply ironic detachment from her story, and Grossman imbues his with deep feeling, both writers wish to understand the drives that push us toward, or repel us from, one another. They don't write about love, but about the impossibility of love, its inherent misunderstandings and the stories we must tell ourselves to persist in believing in love's possibility.

Whatever a novella might be, these compact books, each

of which can be read in a summer afternoon on the front porch, casts a strange spell over our hours—so foreign are these stories, so removed from (at least my) ordinary existence, and yet, in their understated styles, utterly compelling.

G.O.

Critics Be Damned: Aharon Megged and the Golden Hump

Pour ce que rire est le propre de l'homme.
Rabelais

"Asking a working writer how he feels about critics," declared English playwright, John Osborne, "is like asking a lamppost how it feels about dogs." So might have gone the epigraph to this witty, erudite, ever-surprising exploration of the age-old relationship between writer and critic.

My first taste of Aharon Megged's work was the novel *Foiglman*, and I'd been so impressed by that strange and melancholy tale of an Israeli historian named Zvi Arbel and his anguished, ultimately tragic relationship with a man named Foiglman, a Yiddish poet and Holocaust survivor, that I'd bought up every book in his name. Among them (and the subject of this post) was the curiously titled novel, *The Flying Camel and the Golden Hump*. Set in an apartment building in 1980's Tel Aviv, it tells the story of a writer named Kalman Keren who makes the horrific discovery one day that his arch-enemy, the literary critic, Naphtali Schatz, has not only moved into his apartment building but into the apartment directly overhead!

Keren, having just started work on what is to be his masterpiece (the book to end all books, the *ultimus liber*), in short, the translation into modern Hebrew of François Rebelais' five interconnected scatological novels, *La vie de Gargantua et de Pantagruel*, suddenly finds himself paralyzed by the presence of this literary specter, this "Mr. Bookflayer," this "degenerate descendent of Zoilus the Scourge." It is too much for the hapless writer to believe: "Impossible!—I repeated to myself—the devil has tricks no mortal can imagine, but in the field of literature?! It's inconceivable that he would think up an allegory like this, a literary critic living right above a writer, walking on his head, as it were. Especially a critic whose first book was a polemic against allegory!"

Brilliantly, the antipathy Keren feels for the critic is rooted, not in some harsh or captious review he'd received from the man, but from the intolerable fact that the widely esteemed Schatz never even acknowledged his last, most successful book, *The Flying Camel of the Golden Hump*, let alone reviewed it. "Twenty-eight articles written about this book of mine in six months after it was published. But Schatz—not a word!" It is a slight, a damnation, further compounded by the fact that the critic—now his neighbor—refuses even to greet him on the stairs.

Stymied each day in his effort to make headway on his

magnum opus by the machine-gun clatter of Schatz's typewriter upstairs, and humiliated by the thought of the critic's daily sewage gurgling past him through the pipes in the wall, Keren decides to exact his revenge upon the cocksure man, both by means of his disarmingly kind and sensuous wife, Naomi, who has made no secret of her interest in Keren and his work, and by viciously satirizing the man and every critic in Israel like him—the very tale this novel tells. Yet *The Flying Camel and the Golden Hump* is also the story of Keren himself—of his emigration from Romania, of his brief marriage and divorce, and of his life as a writer in Israel. Clever, allusive, punditic, it is remarkably delightful to read, a story, finally, about the wonder of wonders, that of literature itself.

P.N.

The Second Circle

Quando leggemmo il disiato riso
esser basciato da cotanto amante,
questi, che mai da me non fia diviso,
la bocca ma bascio tutta tremante.
galeotto fu l'libro e chi lo scrisse:
quel giorno piu non vi leggemmo avante.

Inferno, V, 133-138

"That day we read no more." Never will I forget my Dante professor in graduate school reading these lines, and those that follow. Dante, upon hearing the tale of the eternal torment of Paolo and Francesca, swoons (*"con corpo morto"*) at Virgil's feet, so deeply does he feel the story of the young lovers. This Canto also contains one of Dante's most unforgettable images: "As winter starlings riding on their wings/form crowded flocks, so spirits dip and veer/Foundering in the wind's rough buffetings/ Upward of downward, driven here and there/With never ease from pain nor hope of rest." (V, 36ff. trans. Robert Pinsky). Thus are the lustful souls of the Second Circle driven hither and yon by the winds of passion. William Blake placed the spirits in a kind of diaphanous digestive tube, generic flesh whirling eternally; Dante lies at the Leader's feet, and, in the background, a nimbus shining with, perhaps, "those two who move along together, so lightly."

I was eager to read Clare Messud's new novel, *The Woman Upstairs*, since I enjoyed *The Emperor's Children*, her story of New York just before September 11, 2001. *The Woman Upstairs*, multilayered with literary references (the madwoman in the attic), also merges two fairy tale themes: Cinderella and Sleeping Beauty. Nora Eldridge is an unhappy teacher of third graders in Cambridge, Massachusetts—a frustrated artist who creates Joseph Cornell-style boxes, dioramas, or who once did, but who has surrendered her dreams for a more mundane life. She mourns her beloved mother, yearns some of the time for love—she is single, childless, empty, and a part-time or perhaps incoherent feminist—and seems resigned to sadness. Then she meets the extraordinary (too-good-to-be-true if you don't live on Brattle Street in Cambridge) family of Reza Shahid. Reza is Nora's eight-year-old pupil, his mother Sirena is an Italian artist, and his father, Skandar, is a Lebanese-born, French-educated philosopher of history (vaguely looking for morality in the past, rather like looking for wisdom in Congress) who is teaching for a year at Harvard. Nora falls in love, one by one, with each member of the family. First with the precocious little boy with the beautiful eyes and the soul of the Buddha, then with the eccentric but brilliant Sirena who is deeply engaged in a Judy Chicago-like installation called "Wonderland". Yes, the metaphors are piled on thickly, and Ms. Messud, so deft at subtle characterizations, escalates the emotional pitch—Nora's anger, Nora's yearning—by creating a kind of whirlwind of escalating emotion, a series of set encounters (Nora with Skandar, Nora with Sirena, Nora with her gay friend Didi) without a moment of calm reflection and with no sense that Nora's self-awareness increases as she is buffeted about by the winds of her passion.

"Wonderland" will be installed in Paris, and will be a kind of feminist "We are the world," and since Nora is smitten to her mousey core by the scarf-wearing, frizzy-haired, chain-smoking Sirena (with her charming accent; this business of accents was rather embarrassing), she becomes the older woman's confidant. And, of course, eventually, reluctantly, that and more to the husband, who comes across as an out-of-focus Edward Said, cosmopolitan, charming, a sort-of intellectual, but utterly incredible as the lover of Nora. And Nora herself? Her back-story is hastily assembled, as if her life was lived in one of tiny boxes she makes to satisfy some dark yearning of her soul. Messud invokes Emily Dickinson and Andy Warhol's Edie Sedgwick in Nora's portrait, and that seems about right. Nora is both cloistered madwoman and modern wild woman, Emily and Edie, prim schoolteacher, overworked Cinderella, but, around the Shahid's her inhibitions vanish, and her deep yearning for meaning, for love, blows her about like a starling in the wind. I pictured Nora as Edie—with a look of perpetual surprise, or perhaps of ingenuousness, on her face as she slipped into and out of the lives of Reza, Sirena, and Skandar. That Nora will be betrayed is a foregone conclusion. How could she not be? Everything about the Shahid's feels shallow. But it's worse than that. They're evil in the way of all narcissists and self-seekers. Reza's affection for his teacher is genuine, but what is it exactly that the parents want from this attractive, vivacious, but self-pitying woman? Messud puts the reader in a difficult position. She needs Nora to be vulnerable and therefore open to the overtures from this glamorous academic family, but in making Nora vulnerable, she also makes her weak, a victim awaiting attractive predators. I happened to be reading an essay of Karen Horney's as I was reading *The Woman Upstairs*. Horney's remarks on "Inhibited Femininity" seemed almost a gloss on Nora Eldridge's character, so willing was she to surrender to "stronger" types, so eager to find fault with herself and to childishly place her faith in those who appear to have life figured out.

Or perhaps she is Francesca da Rimini, blown about by desire, not sexual desire, but a desire for life. As Nora says of herself, she is "ravenous" for living, she "wants it all," and in her eagerness to live fully and deeply, she places her life in the hands of those who cannot value it. *The Woman Upstairs* seemed to me above all a novel about social class, a Jamesian meditation on the innocence of Americans when confronted by the decadence of Europeans (the French!). Harvard elites and elementary school teachers, lions and lambs, upstairs and downstairs. Poor Nora! Like Ibsen's Nora Helmer, she's crushed by her family, even if it isn't hers.

G.O.

The Natural Prayer of the Soul

The Australian novelist and Nobel Laureate Patrick White is one of those literary giants whose work few people seem to read any more. His voice, his style, while in many ways expressly, distinctly modern, are of another rhythm, another age.

In his illuminating short essay on the experience of translating the poetry of Paul Celan, John Felstiner quotes Celan as having remarked, as if as his credo, "Attentiveness is the natural prayer of the soul…" It is a statement that naturally makes one think of poetry itself, and of the poets who write it, those who live by what they notice, what they *see*. Yet such is the purpose, finally, the achievement, of all great writing, that of lifting the blinders from our eyes. It is this devotion to patient, hard-won observation, to turning the world around him inside-out, that distinguishes the novels of Patrick White, the very pages of which seem to twitch and shudder with life. What he notices few of us have ever seen, at least with such intensity, such affection, such detail; still, *we know that he is right*, that he has seen us (and his characters) clearly, seen us well; we know it because he taps something ancient in us, something latent in our brains, perhaps reminding us of how we once used to see.

I have now spent the better part of three days making my way through his extraordinarily fine novel, *The Eye of the Storm*, while sitting by the fountain in the small cool garden at the side of my house. I read and read until something—a phrase, a hummingbird—makes me look up and the effect is nearly always the same. The fine focus of White's prose, that densely woven world in which I was just engrossed, has been superimposed upon the world about me, here in New Mexico, in the garden where I sit—upon the fountain, upon the lavender and rosemary, upon the clatter of dishes inside. For a shimmering instant it is as though I am sensing this too through the lens of White's eye. And for a time—brief as that may be—I feel I actually do see better, see more, and more truly, as if the world itself is suddenly anxious to be seen.

As in so much great literature, this novel is born of a reunion, of the fateful gathering of a mother and a daughter and a son. Set in the Sydney suburb of Centennial Park, it focuses on the once-beautiful, now blind and embittered widow and matriarch, Elizabeth Hunter, who spends her days in bed, attended—like a diva or Fury or queen—by her trusty lawyer, and by an eccentric collection of nurses, each of whom (this too is White's genius) we come to know quite well.

When the novel opens Elizabeth is awaiting the arrival

from France of her recently divorced daughter, Dorothy, an adoptive aristocrat by the name of Princesse de Lascabane, and of her son, Basil, a celebrated, if increasingly superannuated stage actor in London. What follows is a finely textured family drama of cruelty, impotence, and longing that is worthy of the stage itself, an antipodean *King Lear* (as one critic put it) in which the stakes for each of the players are as tragic, as fateful, as they are petty, ruthless, and vain.

Well-known for his novel *The Vivisector*, White himself was a master of that same trade, peeling back the skin of his characters to consider the mysteries within. Here, to give you a taste of his language, his prose, is the chastened daughter, Dorothy, just returned from France, as she considers her mother holding court from her bed:

> *At her most loving, Mother had never been able to resist the cruel thrust. To have loved her in the prime of her beauty, as many had, was like loving, or 'admiring' rather, a jeweled scabbard in which a sword was hidden: which would clatter out under the influence of some peculiar frenzy, to slash off your ears, the fingers, the tongues, or worse, impale the hearts, of those who worshipped. And yet we continued to offer ourselves, if reluctantly. As they still do, it appears: to this ancient scabbard, from which the jewels have loosened and scattered, the blind sockets filled instead with verdigris, itself a vengeful semi-jewelry, the sword still sharp in spite of age and use.*

"One seeks among debased superlatives for words that would convey the grandeur of *The Eye of the Storm*," writes Shirley Hazzard, in her review of the novel for *The New York Times*, "not in destitute slogans but in tribute to its high intellect, its fidelity to our victories and confusions, its beauty and heroic maturity… every passage merits attention and gives satisfaction." I could never have said it so well.

P.N.

Apathetic and Not

Katie Kitamura, *A Separation*
Laurent Binet, *The Seventh Function of Language*
Ta-Nehisi Coates, *We Were Eight Years in Power*

Those indelible lines from Yeats's "The Second Coming" have been bouncing around my brain all week, in particular the line about the best lacking all conviction (and the worst, well, you know how it goes). Not an original thought, but the great insight that flows through much of the poetry of Yeats is that more often than not courage isn't equal to desire, and that the age in which we live (the one in which he lived), prefers conformity to conviction. What was once thought of as honesty and plain speaking is now the worse form of gaucherie; what was known (long ago) as having convictions or being passionate is now seen as stridency. My circle of the world is diminutive, and I have no doubt these generalizations are faulty, but the evidence suggests that something has given way, that a consensus has been achieved among liberal persons that moral neutrality spares one the sorts of collisions that we now prefer to avoid. Many of the brightest people I know are cynical or apathetic. Even irony feels like a commitment to a point of view. And, the truth is, with the current regime in power, we've moved past satire and irony into a darker realm.

Perhaps the Second Coming is at hand—not the Gnostic ascent into higher wisdom of which Yeats dreamed, but an epiphany more akin to Dante's—to the Circles of Fraud, Duplicity, and Violence. Or perhaps we must go about numbed, our feelings shot through with Novocaine.

Katie Kitamura's strange, disaffecting little tale of a marriage on the rocks, while domestic to the point of claustrophobia, embodies this ἀπάθεια—in Greek literally "without passion," a Stoic notion, and a positive characteristic for those yearning to rise above the tribulations of this world. Apathy has come to describe slackers, burn-outs, compulsive gamers, the apolitical and the narcissistic. But Ms. Kitamura does something far more interesting in her novel than merely describe (yet another) thirty-something, educated white woman who has been burned in love and is in danger of self-immolation. (To be fair, there are plenty of educated white males in the same boat).

The unnamed narrator receives a phone call from her mother-in-law, a preemptive demand that the (presumed) wife travel to Greece, to the tiny fishing village of Gerolimenas, to find her husband who has been uncharacteristically out of touch. What Isabella, the mother-in-law, doesn't know is that the narrator and her son have been separated for six months. There's no reason for the wife to seek out her philanderer of a husband, and yet she agrees, travels to Greece, and begins a half-hearted search for clues as to her husband's whereabouts.

There are plenty of echoes of Paul Bowles's *The Sheltering Sky* in *A Separation*—cynics abroad, the anti-Jamesian view of no-longer-innocent Americans mucking about the poorer precincts of the globe. The Greek landscape has been decimated by fires, everything is covered in gray-black ash, and the Greeks themselves, though formally hospitable, appear to the narrator to radiate a kind of menace, as if they knew something about Christopher's disappearance that they aren't disclosing. In fact, one of the female members of the hotel staff has had a fling with Christopher, at least she claims that she has done so, though in this and in much else we are left in the dark. So much ambiguity surrounds the story that one isn't certain if there is any truth to be found, or if the narrator's mission isn't merely to confirm her own ambivalence. All we know for certain is that days pass in a desultory pursuit of a missing husband about whom we know practically nothing (*Spoiler alert*: he is found, but I will withhold the details).

Kitamura's flat, uninflected style reminded me of an essay I read recently by James Wood on Cormac McCarthy's *The Road*. McCarthy's novel is, of course, much, much darker than Kitamura's, but I think *The Road* and *A Separation* share certain stylistic traits. Wood writes: "Minimalism can be very good for the life of fiction: description, thrown back onto its essentials, flourishes as it justifies its own existence. Worlds are returned to their original function as names." Like

McCarthy, Kitamura's prose is stripped to the bone. She runs her narrator's ruminative sentences together, but the descriptive language is anything but lyrical—clinical is more like it, strangely precise yet resolutely ambiguous.

The narrator of Kitamura's strange tale—a novel without a hero, a story without a plot—observes the world as if through the lens of a camera, with both sincerity and detachment. Here's Kitamura's narrator as voyeur, telling us her impressions of the (presumed) meaning of an interaction between a Greek cab driver and the hotel concierge who may or may not have been Christopher's lover:

> *"The contempt [the concierge] felt for the [Stefano, the cab driver] man who held her in his arms! And yet there were plenty of women who would have been only too delighted to love the driver, he was handsome and not without charm, and evidently he was capable of loyalty. There was of course the problem of his temper, but women could be surprisingly accommodating, as well as optimistic, one could live in the hope that his anger would subside, especially once he was loved in return, it was not impossible. Yes, it would have been better if she let him go—if she told him that she would never loved him, that they had no future together."*

Such a strange passage! The galloping parataxis, the presumptions ("evidently," "there were plenty of women," "it would have been better"). Naturally one assumes that the narrator wants the cab driver for herself, but there's little more than innuendo to support this supposition. What is striking is that Kitamura maintains this curious judgmental detachment throughout the novel. That her husband has cheated on her, that her mother-in-law demands that she travel to Greece to search for Christopher, that the concierge boasts of sleeping with her husband, that there is something both attractive and frightening about the cab driver—none of these facts do more than pique the narrator's curiosity and her penchant for what can only be called philosophical analysis:

> *"She spoke with enthusiasm, nonetheless I was aware that her words did not make much sense, these things that were not true and about which I did not know (how could I have known about them, if they were not true, what there have been to know about? Or did she only mean that I did not have the same false suspicions, had not heard the false rumors?)"*

Such a remarkable passage. Direct discourse punctuated with parenthetical clarifications, the aside, worthy of J. L. Austin, that one can't know anything about something that isn't true, the wistful "or did she only mean," regretful of a lost chance for clarity now that Maria is no longer available for questioning? I image that if Wittgenstein had read novels he'd have enjoyed *A Separation*.

Most of all, I was left with the impression that what Kitamura had achieved was the perfect novel of apathy—not of indifference or disengagement, but of detached and philosophical observation. Perhaps the Greek setting evokes such stoicism. Many sentences begin with conditionals— "I suppose," "perhaps," "and yet," "on the other hand," "at the same time." Most of the direct discourse is offered as a preliminary to understanding, propositions that may later be falsified, tentative conclusions awaiting further evidence: "... Perhaps all deaths were unjust, but some were more so...." and then "No, it was almost certainly as it had appeared," and the ending which drops a dark curtain of ambiguity over the entire novel: "I could only say that I was sorry, and that I agreed—although what we were waiting for, what exactly it was, neither of us could say."

***

The feud between Cornel West and Ta-Nehisi Coates has caught me up short since I am an admirer of both men, and, in ordinary times, I would have thought them to be natural allies. I must admit that I was disappointed when I read *We Were Eight Years in Power* for Coates has overlooked all of the less savory aspects of the Obama presidency—the drone wars, the unfulfilled promises (to close Guantanamo for example), the alliance with Wall Street that has allowed the perpetration of the conditions that brought down the world economy under Bush/Cheney. There is no doubt that Obama's election was a significant event, a moment that should have made all Americans proud. But an honest accounting of Obama's achievements must move beyond symbolism to governing. Cornel West, never one to tread lightly, savaged Coates in an article published in the *Guardian*, accusing Coates of being a neoliberal (not a good thing to be these days), of betraying the struggle for social justice, and other crimes. While Coates leaves out too much, West probably goes too far—there's no clear middle ground in their debate. Perhaps this reflects the overall erosion of constructive political discourse. Still, it pains me to see these two men so at odds when what is needed now are strong agreements and a way forward.

***

On a lighter note, I've just finished Laurent Binet's *The Seventh Function of Language*, an engaging quasi-detective novel set in the hothouse of French intellectual history circa 1980. The plot revolves around the investigation of the infamous laundry truck accident that eventually killed Roland Barthes. A hapless assistant professor, Simon Herzog, and a humorless French police investigator, Jacques Bayard, interview such intellectual luminaries as Michel Foucault (in a bathhouse), Julia Kristeva, Bernard-Henri Levy, Gilles Deleuze, and a dozen other famous and notorious figures. Binet's heady mix of intellectual history, detective-mystery tropes (parsing obscure clues, Bayard can't refrain from mocking the pointlessness of academic culture). I kept thinking of Jim Rockford and Columbo. Yes, there are games galore, word play and oodles of literary references—from Saul Bellow to William Empson. Binet's is the best kind of literary entertainment—witty and provocative.

G.O.

Unicuique suum

I have never been fond of thrillers, which tend to make me feel like a puppet on strings. The artifice, the manipulation, is too much for me, too conspicuous, too plain; it is often all (what little) I see. What makes reading such popular fiction so difficult for me, so unsatisfactory, so discouraging, is that, not unlike most video, it is generally constructed in such a way as to merely tell you—rather than show you—a tale. By its nature, it asks very little of you, the reader, but that you be passive and receive. It *imposes* rather than *supposes*.

A literary agent who specializes in "literary fiction" once replied to a query of mine (I'd sent her the opening chapters of a novel I'd written) by chiding me, "I hope you're not one of those writers who thinks that plot is secondary." It was everything I could do not to respond, "No, I am not one of those writers. To me, plot isn't even a *tertiary* concern." It would not have been an exaggeration. F. Scott Fitzgerald famously wrote, "Character is plot, plot is character." I too believe this, that literature is first and foremost the study of character, of what it means to be human, of what it is (may it never be discovered) that makes us tick. Reading literary fiction is nothing if not the expression of a deep-seeded desire to know others, to be less lonely, to see ourselves more truly. It is about confronting—again and again—what Neruda calls "the confused impurity of the human condition."

Yet there is more to great fiction that that. Now more than ever, it is also, and essentially, about empowerment and agency in an increasingly corporate, increasingly anti-democratic world, one that thrives more on servility and conformity and consumption than on freedom and dignity, on courage and struggle and change. The sort of fiction I love to read is that which not only invites me to participate in it, in the active construction of its meaning, but actually *requires* it, indeed is incomplete, impossible, without me, without my intelligence, my engagement, however uncertain and imperfect they may be. Reading literary fiction is a time-tested way of training the heart and mind to participate, to question and resist, to engage meaningfully with the world at large.

As a reader I revel in ideas, in meditations, in irony, ambiguity, ambivalence, and doubt, those very qualities that, to me, most truly define our daily human toil. Great literature doesn't simplify life but *complicates* it. It must—or it deceives.

All of which is to say how pleasant it was to read Sicilian author Leonardo Sciascia's perhaps best known detective thriller, *To Each His Own*. It surprised me at every turn—its lack of gimmickry, its depth of character, and its language itself, not to mention its brooding, finally fatalistic critique of the codes and culture of Sicily, the author's own home and hell. Philip Hensher puts it best: "Some of [Sciascia's] books, like the brilliant *To Each His Own*, look like bleak, inclusive thrillers, and slowly turn into grand indictments of the abuse of power. They are all very different books, united by a ruthless, unsparing gaze, and common subject in power and its abuses."

Unicuique suum. *To each his own.* Yes, to each (and everyone) her own.

P.N.

Death in the Afternoon

A. L. Kennedy, *On Bullfighting*

Can there be beauty in cruelty? When a man stands alone in an arena before a thousand pounds of bloodied brute force, an animal blind with pain, when the matador flashes the *muleta* before the bull and raises the *estocada* or killing sword for the final thrust—the *faena*—is there something sublime in this dance of death, something ugly yet touching in ritualized violence?

My father was a fan of the "sweet science"—as a kid he'd boxed flyweight—and he and I took in many bouts at local venues, and once, memorably, saw Sugar Ray Robinson box at the Garden. But these were fair fights. Aside from the palooka who took on Sugar Ray, all the fights I ever witnessed were evenly matched. Not so in the bullring, where the victim comes to the matador already pierced by the *banderillas*, weakened by loss of blood, crazed with fear. Boxing is fighting. The *corrida* is killing, pure and simple.

First the lance, then the barbed pikes (twenty-seven of

them), the cape passes (*tanda*) that exhaust the bull, and finally the thrust of the sword into the *rubio*, the point where the razor-sharp blade enters the bull's heart, and the beast, gloated over by the matador in his baroque attire, topples into the dust.

Hemingway found beauty in death—in the deaths of bulls and wild animals and, perhaps too, in the deaths of men. He was, it seems, in love with it, with the sharp edge of danger, the way all things tip toward dying. I never finished *Death in the Afternoon*, not for dislike of Hemingway's flirtation with self-destruction, but out of disgust at the pleasure he took in the slaughter of a wounded animal. Perhaps if it were a fair fight....I know, the *corrida* is culture, sacred ritual, an expression of *machismo* or Catholic piety or something else incomprehensible to the outsider. Bulls, as A. L. Kennedy demonstrates, have a long history in European societies. I remember viewing frescoes of frolicking bulls in the Palace of Knossos, the *auroch*, a symbol of fertility and (male) power. Was it the Catholic Church that needed the bulls to be killed, for their blood to be offered to propitiate the millennia of pagan animal worship? The earth was given to man to dominate, and animals to use—to slay a bull at the tail end of a hot afternoon in Seville, to prance about in the costume of a courtier wielding a sword, processing through a catechism of almost sensual *rebolera* (cape passes), to flirt with goring (like the death of St. Sebastian, impaled)—isn't this a kind of sacrament? Someone, or something, has to die so that we can go on living. Better the bull than the man.

But A.L. Kennedy, whom I have been reading obsessively for the past week, isn't interested, or isn't only interested in the deaths of bulls. Her little book is about her own dying, or near dying, and about how she hoisted herself up from the grave on the blood of what is, to any but an *aficionado*, a macabre spectator sport:

> *"And if it does so happen that a human being finds death in the corrida's rarefied afternoon, if a torero, or perhaps one of his cuadrilla, is fatally wounded, then the corrida is intended to redefine the moment of death, to act as our translator. Even the almost always inevitable death of the bull is meant to be controlled within the corrida's physical language, the structure and the sad necessities of its world. The corrida can be seen as an extraordinary effort to elevate the familiar, mysterious slapstick, the irrevocable, indecipherable logic of damage and death, into something almost accessible. The corrida can be seen as both a ritualised escape from destruction and a bloody search for meaning in the end of a life, both an exorcism and an act of faith."*

If I were to encounter this paragraph in the work of a literary theorist I'd blanch—what would be coming would be a dense "reading" of the *corrida* with much deployment of jargon and a lot of references to Nietzsche. But Kennedy is an artist, a novelist and short story writer who just happened to be unable to write, who was in several kinds of pain, close to suicide, when she set off for Spain to write an account of bullfighting. While *On Bullfighting* is erudite, its preoccupations are personal in the way that the investigation of the universal always feels personal. The book is a quiet, and beautiful, meditation on death. Not on its sublimity, but its inevitability.

When Kennedy describes the *faena*, the stylized and almost religious posture of the matador as he drives the sword home, her tone flattens, as if she too felt the anti-climax. One imagines that at the end, were the bull to be granted speech, he would say, "Let's get it over with. All this fuss. And what have you proved?" For in the end, as Kennedy's vivid account of the *corrida* shows, the bull's dying isn't the point, and neither is the sad spectacle of the "fight." In the end the *corrida* has the pointlessness of a Mass or an exorcism. When it's over, and if you've survived, you must go on. And the beauty of Kennedy's book, and of her stories and novels, is that everyone finds a way to go on, whatever the cost.

The last words of the book? "I don't know what to do."

G.O.

Hope and Humility

Reserving judgments is a matter of infinite hope.
F. Scott Fitzgerald

If great literature does anything it humbles us. We are humbled by its artistry, by the force of its vision, by its insistence upon the messiness and complexity of life. At its best literature checks our need and proclivity to judge.

This seemingly reflexive human practice of rating and ranking, of calculating, simplifying, typecasting, and generalizing, of pronouncing upon, of *presuming* to know, seems all but ubiquitous these days, aided and abetted as it is (to a degree I fear we are no longer capable of tracking) by the crass, essentially consumerist nature of the internet, that is, by the corporate, self-centered, civically inimical logic by which each day we are training ourselves to live.

While founded surely in a natural, even evolutionary, need to organize and classify the world around us, this restless propensity to judge, and judge quickly, with impunity, to compare value, to make ever finer distinctions between celebrities and products and brands, seems more and more to me, and for all the apparent abundance of this age, to signify the opposite, the reverse—that in fact we are happy and satisfied *with less*.

When I was a student in college I had somehow been convinced (or had convinced myself) that being opinionated and judgmental was synonymous with being intelligent, even intellectual. If someone asked me about an issue, about a particular politician or writer or painter, or about some moral or philosophical conundrum, I didn't even pause to consider the matter but told them exactly, succinctly, what I thought. Yet what I told them wasn't actually *what I thought*, for most of the time I wasn't *thinking* at all. What I was doing was judging—swiftly, prematurely. For all my purported love of books and ideas, I had little patience for analysis, for the taxing, deeply humbling discipline of thought. What mattered was that I had an answer, an opinion. What mattered was that I *knew*.

I've changed a bit since then—thanks to my wife, to the fact and complexity of my sons, and to the many good friends and colleagues I've known. Of course I am also deeply indebted to literature itself, to the countless poems and novels and plays I've read. And I must thank my students as well. Over the years they too have helped to shape and temper who I am. Directly and indirectly, they have helped me to refine the way I think about literature and language, the way I think about life.

Often now I advise them, my students, that before they can rightly judge a work of literature (as they are nearly always eager to do), they first need to know what it is. What exactly (to use the term broadly) is the argument it makes? Each time we read a story or poem or essay, each time we read a novel or play, I insist that, before they render their verdict on it, they must turn it inside-out, describing it as clearly and objectively as possible. I ask them to tell me everything they notice about it, everything they see. Not surprisingly, this radically changes the dynamic of the class. Instead of judging (with all its inherent pressures, its stakes) they find themselves merely looking, observing, *seeing*. Without knowing it, they have made themselves susceptible.

Even less surprising to me, now that I've done it for years, is the fact that once my students have invested the time required to get to know a piece of literature on its own terms, in its own right, they often find that the need, the impulse, to judge it has faded, if not vanished altogether. This is not to say that they always come to love what we read—certainly not. In fact they often end our study of a given text with clear reservations about it. That of course is their due. They have earned it; it is theirs.

Which brings me to the matter of literature in general, and why the act of reading widely, deeply, *patiently*, is more important today than ever. "The poet judges not as a judge, but as the sun falling around a helpless thing," writes Walt Whitman, an insight, an assertion, that applies equally to writers of fiction and plays. Simple on the face of it, what he proposes is astounding—that literature is something different, special, that literature is *something else*. Milan Kundera, in his defense of the novel, of its power to render the world more justly, more truly, insists that "Suspending moral judgment is not the immorality of the novel [or poem or play]; it is its *morality*. The morality that stands against the ineradicable human habit of judging instantly, ceaselessly, and everyone; of judging before, and in the absence of, understanding. From the viewpoint of the novel's wisdom, that fervid readiness to judge is the most detestable stupidity, the most pernicious evil."

Literature then is that rare, imaginary terrain wherein *moral judgment is suspended*, a realm in which characters move and interact "not as a function of some preexistent truth, as examples of good or evil, or as representations of objective laws in conflict, but as autonomous beings grounded in their own morality, in their own laws." As readers we are pressed to see them not as they could be or should be, but *as they are*. That—of all its merits—is literature's greatest gift.

P.N.

Acknowledgments

Many thanks to the following friends and colleagues for encouragement: Michael Keith, David Gutierrez, Marnie Bethel, Diane Lefer (may we one day sit down and talk), Mark Dunn, Cynde Moore, and Steve Allen. My father-in-law, Fred Hart, with whom I have shared rich discussions for two decades, has been especially kind about my writing. And Joan Hart, my late mother-in-law, not only raised eight wonderful children, she read serious books and was generous in her thinking about why art and literature matter. My share of this book is for her.

Marc Estrin and Donna Bister have been remarkably open to my writing, have encouraged me to work harder, and have treated me with a professionalism and respect that is all too rare in the book business these days.

Peter Nash and I have taken, by my rough calculation, 3,234 walks over the past two decades, on each of which we have conversed about our shared passion for literature. Without these leisurely perambulations I'd be bumbling about, chatting nonsense to myself. Thanks Peter for the miles we've traveled.

Brigid supports everything I do, listens to my ideas (most of them deadends), and reads everything with cool precision. Thank God she doesn't have to type and re-type my manuscripts as did wives of yesteryear.

My three daughters, Alexis, Dorothy, and Ada leaven my days with joy.

G.O.

Acknowledgments

First and foremost, I'd like to thank Marc Estrin and Donna Bister for their initial enthusiasm for these essays, as well as for their insight and encouragement along the way.

I wish also to thank my friends and fellow readers David Gutierrez, Hugh Himwich, Diane Lefer, Cynde Moore, Marnie Bethel, my sister, Maggie Nash, and my mother, Linda Rennie Forcey.

George, to you I can only say that my world is vastly richer for knowing you. Thank you.

Finally to my wife, Annie, and my sons, Ezra and Isaiah, I wish to express my special gratitude for the love and understanding you have given me. I have only to think of you and I smile.

P.N.

About the Authors

Peter Nash is the author of the biography, *The Life and Times of Moses Jacob Ezekiel: American Sculptor, Arcadian Knight*, the novels, *Parsimony* and *The Perfection of Things*, and the forthcoming novella, *The Least of It*. He lives in New Mexico with his wife and two sons.

George Ovitt's most recent books are the novels *Stillpoint* and *Tribunal*, both published by Fomite. He lives in New Mexico with his wife and children, three dogs, and the unfulfilled aspiration to someday play blues guitar like Robert Johnson.

More essays from Fomite...

Robert Sommer — *Losing Francis: Essays on the Wars at Home*
William Benton — *Eye Contact: Writing on Art*

For more information or to order any of our books, visit:
http://www.fomitepress.com/our-books.html

Writing a review on Amazon, Good Reads, Shelfari, Library Thing or other social media sites for readers will help the progress of independent publishing. To submit a review, go to the book page on any of the sites and follow the links for reviews. Books from independent presses rely on reader-to-reader communications.

www.ingramcontent.com/pod-product-compliance
Lightning Source LLC
Chambersburg PA
CBHW030144100526
44592CB00009B/112